QUIVIRA SOCIETY PUBLICATIONS

VOLUME VI

ARNO PRESS
NEW YORK
1967

"THE ALAMO," SAN ANTONIO DE VALERO

HISTORY OF TEXAS

1673-1779

BY

FRAY JUAN AGUSTÍN MORFI

MISSIONARY, TEACHER, HISTORIAN

TRANSLATED, WITH BIOGRAPHICAL INTRODUCTION

AND ANNOTATIONS, BY

CARLOS EDUARDO CASTAÑEDA

LATIN AMERICAN LIBRARIAN

UNIVERSITY OF TEXAS

In two parts: Part I

THE QUIVIRA SOCIETY

ALBUQUERQUE

1935

First Published by
THE QUIVIRA SOCIETY
1935

•

Republished by
Arno Press
1967

•

Library of Congress Catalog Card
Number: 67-24718

•

Manufactured in the U.S.A.
Arno Press Inc.
New York

CONTENTS

LIST OF PLATES

PREFACE

BY a fortunate coincidence the writer discovered the manuscript of Fray Juan Agustín Morfi's *History of Texas* in the National Library of Mexico early in January, 1931. For a long time this work of the celebrated Franciscan missionary was known by name only and its existence had come to be doubted. It is, nevertheless, the most complete and detailed account known, as it presents a connected narrative of the principal events in the history of Texas from 1673 to 1779. It is wider in scope than any work now available in Spanish or English. Convinced of its importance in the study of the history of Spanish Texas, the writer is pleased to present a critical edition of this invaluable record with a biographical sketch of the author based on all available data.

It should be kept in mind that Morfi, tireless missionary, teacher, historian, and champion of his order, was equally industrious in making a systematic collection of data for the activities of the Franciscans on the northern border. He had been aroused by the *Breve Compendio* of Antonio Bonilla who, in his summary of events to 1772, placed on the missionaries the responsibility for the failure of the various attempts to colonize Texas. This imputation Morfi resented, and he took up the cudgels in behalf of his brother laborers. Having compiled his sources, he arranged them in a preliminary manner in what is commonly known as his *Memorias para la Historia de Texas*. This work, well known to students for many years and of which there are several copies, has been erroneously confused with the *Historia,* a confusion which is now definitely ended with the present publication in full of Morfi's masterpiece in the annals of Texas. Through the courtesy and interest of the Quivira Society, this significant book is now made available for the first time to students of Southwestern history. Its publication this year is particularly appropriate, in view of the celebration of the first centennial of Texan independence in March and April, 1936.

The writer wishes to express his sincere appreciation to Doctors Eugene C. Barker and Charles W. Hackett, of the University of Texas, for their encouragement, helpful suggestions, and patient reading of the original translation. Further acknowledgments are due to Mr. E. W. Winkler and Miss Maurine T. Wilson, of the University of Texas Library, for valuable aid and suggestions in preparing the bibliography; to Señor Vito Alessio Robles, of Mexico, for his generous help in securing biographical data; to the National Library of Mexico for permitting the original manuscript to be photostated; and to Miss Wynnie Allen, archivist of the University of Texas, for aid in making the index. Special thanks are due to Doctor George P. Hammond, of the Quivira Society, for his interest, invaluable suggestions, and the painstaking care with which he has supervised the edition of Morfi's *Historia*.

C. E. CASTAÑEDA.

University of Texas,
Austin, October, 1935.

BIOGRAPHICAL INTRODUCTION

REFERENCES to Father Fray Juan Agustín Morfi and his *Memorias para la Historia de Texas* are numerous,[1] * but few facts are known about his life. As great, if not greater, is the confusion concerning his writings about Texas. His *Memorias* and his *Historia de Texas* have, up to the present, been indiscriminately referred to as one and the same work. That they are two distinct works, that the first was a collection of data for the second, and that the *Historia* was left unfinished because of his death, are all facts that have been ignored. Basing their judgment on the *Memorias,* some have declared that Morfi's work "as regards Texas is, in the main, nothing more than a transcript [of other documents on the subject] . . . and in addition has the disadvantage of having been copied with many errors";[2] while others have affirmed that his *Memorias* were "the standard authority for Texas history" down to the date of his death in 1783.[3]

Before discussing the relation between Morfi's two works, of which only the first has been used so far by historians, and before examining their relative merits, a word should be said about the life of this indefatigable Franciscan who, during his lifetime, gathered, with amazing industry, thousands of documents relative to the missionary endeavors and the heroic achievements of the sons of Saint Francis of Assisi not only in Texas, but in New Mexico, Nuevo León, Coahuila, California, and even the faraway Philippine islands.[4] Many of these he painstakingly copied while arranging the others preparatory to writing.

It has been asserted erroneously that Morfi was a na-

* See the notes at the close of the Biographical Introduction.

tive of the Spanish province of Galicia,[5] whereas he was born in the province of Asturias. The date of his birth, the names of his parents, and the name of the town in which he first saw the light are not known. Unfortunately, in the various references to his death his age at that time is not given. Nor is this noted, as was customary, in the official records of the Franciscans which Father Fray Francisco de la Rosa y Figueroa so carefully prepared between the years 1765 and 1771.[6] He must have come to America in 1755 or 1756, for in his *Historia,* which he was writing in 1782–1783, he declares that he had been in Mexico for twenty-seven years.[7]

Though it has been asserted that Morfi came as a friar from Spain, the records prove that he came as a layman, for he made his profession in the province of the Santo Evangelio in Mexico city on May 3, 1761, where he is designated as *hijo de provincia.*[8] It appears, therefore, that he came, like many other young men, in search of fame and fortune. He must have found, after a short stay in Mexico, that gold was not to be swept up with a broom and that there were no new kingdoms to conquer. This may have induced him to join a religious order, a natural course in those days for a young man who felt despondent and disillusioned with the world. He doubtless entered the order as a novitiate, and after two or three years of study was duly ordained. This would explain why, even though he arrived, according to his own statement, some time in 1755 or 1756, he did not make his profession until 1761.[9]

There is nothing known about Morfi's early years in Mexico or his first years in the Franciscan order. It seems that he soon became noted for his learning, however, and for his ability as a sacred orator. For several years he taught theology in the old college of Santa Cruz de Tlaltelolco,[10] which was under the direction of the Franciscans. While engaged in this work he wrote, in 1766, a treatise on theology entitled *Tractatus de Fide, Spe et Charitate,* which he used in his classes and which remained in manuscript.[11] Thus we see Morfi teaching during his first years in the order, and writing at the same time his first known work, five years after he had made his profession. That his reputation as an orator was attracting public attention is shown by his having been invited, in 1772, to preach the principal sermon in a public festival in honor of the Virgin of Guadalupe. On May 17 of that year he delivered a sermon at the annual celebration of the farmers on the generous and loving protection of the Virgin of Guadalupe, which was ordered printed. He was at this time lecturer on sacred theology at the principal monastery of the Franciscans in Mexico, having been promoted from his work at the college of Tlaltelolco.[12] Three years later, on the fourteenth anniversary of his profession, he was again the leading orator at the first celebration held in the principal monastery of the Franciscans in honor of the Holy Christ of Burgos. This time he chose for his subject, "The Nobility and the Piety of the Mountaineers," in honor of the noble sons of La Montaña, his own native province. He must have been unusually eloquent on this occasion, for the sermon was ordered printed at the expense of the noble sons of La Montaña, who dedicated it to all those "who live there or come from there." [13]

Morfi's fame and his reputation as an orator and writer were soon to take him from his beloved Mexico to the wild frontiers of the kingdom of New Spain. As a result of the recommendations of Visitor Joseph de Gálvez, the king of Spain decided to reorganize the government of New Spain. The royal order of August 22, 1776, erected a new jurisdiction to be known as the *Comandancia general de las Provincias Internas* and which included the provinces of Nueva Viscaya, Coahuila, Texas, New Mexico, Sinaloa, Sonora, and the Californias, which, under the new arrangement, were made practically independent of the viceroy of Mexico. They were placed under the immediate supervision of a military official to be known as *Comandante general de las Provincias Internas,* who was to be directly responsible to the king.[14] The appointment for this important post fell to Theodore de Croix, the young nephew of the former viceroy of that name who had proved his ability in the trying days of the expulsion of the Jesuits.[15] Croix arrived in Mexico on December 22, 1776,[16] and immediately began his preparations for a tour of inspection of his vast jurisdiction. According to instructions he was to ask the father provincial of the Franciscans to appoint a friar to accompany him as chaplain, who was to assist also in making a report on the conditions of the frontier missions.[17] Croix wrote to Fray Isidro Murillo, provincial of the order, on July 25, 1777, that, there being no objections on the part of the viceroy or of his reverence, as expressed in the note of the previous day, he again begged and requested his reverence to order Father Fray Juan Agustín Morfi, "under oath of obedience," to accompany him on the expedition he was about to undertake in the service of God and the king. He asked that an immediate reply be given him as he was on the point of leaving.[18] It seems that he had asked for Morfi to accompany him before and that Morfi had expressed a desire to be excused from this duty. Though not inclined to accept the appointment, this second notice in which Croix underscored the words, "under oath of obedience," must have decided the father provincial and the unwilling Morfi to accept the inevitable. In less than a week after this note was written, Morfi was ready to set out on the expedition with the new commandant general of the Interior Provinces. On August 4, 1777, Theodore de Croix, accompanied by his secretary, his chaplain Morfi, two companies of dragoons, and three companies of *tiradores*, started on his tour of inspection, after having stopped to invoke divine guidance at the shrine of Guadalupe.[19]

During the course of the next six months Morfi was to travel over eight hundred leagues; to visit hundreds of outposts, missions, and ranches along the frontier; to see the wild Indians of the north; and to gain a first-hand acquaintance with the primitive conditions of the confines of New Spain. The impressions he received during this journey were strong and lasting. It is safe to assume that from this time dates his deep interest in history and his profound admiration for the heroic virtues of the missionaries. He may have been interested in history before, but we have no evidence of any historical writings by him prior to 1778. It must have been after his return to Mexico that he began to collect actively all the documents he could find on the history of the provinces he had just visited. In fact, he must have secured, during this trip, some of the documents which now form the archive of San Francisco el Grande in the National Library of Mexico.[20]

Morfi kept a careful diary of the expedition from the date it set out, noting day by day the distances traveled; the direction of the march; the nature of the country traversed; the social and economic conditions that prevailed in the various cities, towns, villages, and even ranches; and the peculiarities that appealed to him. In each place where the expedition halted he quickly but systematically searched the local archives for data concerning the history of the place, so that his diary is a mine of information for all the important cities visited by him. Setting out from Mexico, the expedition passed through Tula, Querétaro, San Miguel el Grande, Zacatecas, Fresnillo, Sombrerete, Durango, Mapimí, Parras, Saltillo, Monclova, San Juan Bautista de Rio Grande, and San Antonio de Béxar. From here the expedition started on its homeward journey, but instead of going to Mexico City it made its way toward Chihuahua, the seat of government for the newly erected Provincias Internas. The diary of Morfi ends with the entry for February 24, 1778, made at a place called Las Cruces, on the border of the present states of Chihuahua and Coahuila. Morfi continued his trip to Mexico from this place, while Croix must have gone on to Chihuahua.[21]

Speaking of the significance of this diary as a social document, Vito Alessio Robles, well-known historian of Mexico, says:

> A reading of this diary gives us a fairly accurate idea of the social conditions of northern New Spain at the close of the eighteenth century. Morfi, in simple and direct style, discusses the extent of its wealth and its problems. He describes the physical aspects of the country, the quality of the farm lands, and the types of cultivation best suited to each. He makes observations on the flora and fauna; he describes briefly the geologic formations; he recounts the vicissitudes experienced by the different settlements; he comments upon their condition at the time of his visit; he tells us the customs of the inhabitants; he records the rivalry and animosity of the Spaniards, *criollos, mestizos,* and Indians; and he informs us of the discipline observed by the local troops. His style, naturally calm and agreeable, becomes caustic and cutting when he speaks of the large landed estates, which he condemns with bitterness, attributing to them the backwardness and the misery of America. Caustic indeed he is when he lashes without pity those who exploit the Indians. Morfi's observations on the agricultural system in vogue on the large landed estates, on absentee landlordism, on the inadequate wage of the peons, and on the injustices of the ranch commissaries are, in addition to being interesting, a revelation of the deep-rooted, age-old causes that have retarded the agricultural development of Mexico to this day.[22]

This able summary of the kind of information we find in Morfi's diary, and the brief analysis of his personal reactions to the conditions observed as portrayed by the changes in his style, give an excellent insight into the character of the man. The padre colector, who copied the diary, admitted the natural charm, the pleasing manner in which the items of information are presented, and the elegance that characterized all of Morfi's writings.[23] These same qualities will be observed in his *Historia,* where the narrative runs smoothly, where thousands of details are woven into the story with consummate skill, and where, as in the diary, there are blinding flashes of righteous indignation at what he considers the false accusations against the missionaries. There are, too, glowing and eloquent passages in praise of their virtues and their heroic efforts to bring to the fold the thousands of Indians that roamed the wild plains of Texas. But this will be discussed when the *Memorias* and the *Historia* are compared.

From Las Cruces, Morfi must have returned alone to Mexico city. The diary ends abruptly with the entry of February 24, 1778. He did not tarry on the way, for by March 31 he seems to have been back in Mexico. On that day Croix wrote him a letter from Chihuahua, his headquarters, requesting him to check with all care a map of the Interior Provinces which he was sending to him, to note all errors and corrections, and make a new drawing which he wished to forward as soon as possible to the king with a detailed report of everything concerning the territory just inspected. Croix closed the letter with a request that Father Morfi should send to him, together with the corrected drawing of the map, his diary of the expedition in order that he might send it to his majesty.[24] For some unknown reason it seems that Morfi did not send Croix the desired diary. If he did, and Croix transmitted it to Spain, it must have been lost or misplaced, for in the royal order of February 21, 1790, in which the viceroy was instructed to send sixteen documents needed for the projected history of the Spanish colonies in America, the "Viage de Indios y Diario del Nuevo Mexico" is specifically listed as number fifteen of those wanted.[25] It was not until two years after this order was issued that this document was finally copied and included in the *Colección de Memorias para la Historia de Nueva España,* made by Fray Manuel de la Vega under the general direction of Father Francisco García Figueroa, of the convent of San Francisco.[26]

Little is known of the activities of Morfi after his return to Mexico. He seems to have buried himself in his cell, among his papers and documents, which grew daily in number and which appear now to have absorbed all his interest. Some time after his return he must have been relieved of his class in theology, as by 1781 we find him referred to as Lector Jubilado, that is, retired or pensioned lecturer. But his interest in sacred oratory does not seem to have waned with his interest in history, for during his last years he wrote a book on eloquence. This was not an original work, rather it was a translation with some notes and observations. It remained in manuscript until 1795, twelve years after his death, when it was printed in Madrid in two volumes. The title of the work in English reads, *Dialogue on Eloquence in General and on that of the Pulpit in particular by the Archbishop of Cambrai, with a Letter on Poetry and History, translated into Spanish.*[27]

Some time in 1782 Morfi was elected guardian of the Convento Grande de San Francisco, the highest honor he could have received from his order, for the Convento Grande was the mother house of the Franciscans. It was a fitting tribute to Morfi's great learning, his high merits, and his exemplary virtues. The exact date of the election is not known, but the facts seem to indicate that it was either late in 1781 or early in 1782.[28] Be that as it may, on March 29, 1782, we find Father Morfi, who is referred to as father guardian of San Francisco, delivering the most important sermon of Lent on Good Friday at the cathedral of Mexico. The viceroy, who was not known particularly for his piety, attended the service and is reported to have listened with interest. This may be taken as evidence of the esteem in which Morfi's ability as a sacred orator was held. When it is remembered that the cathedral had among its canons and priests many distinguished men of letters and able orators, it is the more remarkable that the guardian of San Francisco should have been asked to preach on this solemn and important occasion.[29]

Only one other reference to a public appearance of Morfi has been found. On August 15, 1782, during the celebration of the feast of the Assumption of the Blessed Virgin, held in the cathedral, the sermon was again preached by him. This was a memorable day in the history of the cathedral. Its numerous stately columns were decorated with colorful silk hangings—"the first time they were ever adorned," declares the chronicler.[30] In the midst of these joyous surroundings, Morfi seems to have delivered his last sermon. If he again appeared in public, the fact has not been recorded.[31]

A little more than a year later he breathed his last. The event is recorded in the "Diario Curioso" in these words: "The twentieth day of October, 1783, at half past nine in the morning, died the father guardian of San Francisco, Fray Juan [Agustín] Morfi, the greatest man the province [of the Santo Evangelio] had, and the best orator in the kingdom [of New Spain]. This was on

Monday."[32] His death was the result of a malignant fever.

But the end found Morfi in the midst of his historical studies. The diligence with which he had gathered materials for the history of almost all of the Interior Provinces is evidenced by the papers which he left in his cell. When an inventory of these was made it was found that there were seventeen different *legajos* (bundles or groups) of documents neatly arranged in the following order: six on New Mexico; one on Texas; one on Nuevo León and Seno Mexicano (modern Tamaulipas); one on Coahuila; one on California; one on Nueva California; one on San Gregorio de Filipinas; one on missions in general; one consisting of the diary of the señor comandante general, Caballero de Croix; one of letters of Salvatierra; one labeled *Historia de Texas,* consisting of a manuscript all in the handwriting of Father Morfi, *casi mediado* (almost half finished); and a rough draft with two copy books (*cuadernos*) of additions. Besides these seventeen groups listed, there were three diaries.[33] This reveals better than anything the industrious habits of Father Morfi, his untiring efforts in assembling the sources for the history of all northern Mexico, and the broad interest of the collector. The list does not give us, however, any idea of the number of documents contained in each of the groups mentioned. But if each of these contained as many as the original one on Texas, it will have to be assumed that their number ranged from four to eight thousand pages in each group or legajo. Those relating to Texas, found by the writer, somewhat scattered but sufficiently assembled to identify them as having formed the original collection gathered by Morfi on the subject, make up more than eight thousand.[34]

That Morfi should have gathered so vast a collection of sources in the short space of five years, 1778–1783, may seem incredible. It should be borne in mind, however, that a considerable number of these documents were already in the general archive of San Francisco el Grande. Once his interest was aroused in the history of the various provinces he had visited, it was natural that Morfi should have turned first of all to the rich archive of his order, for had not the sons of Saint Francis traversed the length and breadth of New Spain from Guatemala to beyond the confines of Sonora and Arizona, and from California to eastern Texas? But he seems to have collected some materials while on his trip with Croix and to have made notes on others. There is evidence that soon after his return he began to make a systematic effort to collect such data as he considered necessary to complete the information found in what he calls "our private archives."[35] He prepared lists of these and sent them to the other Franciscan monasteries. Before the end of 1778 he made a list of thirty documents "needed to complete the history of Texas,"[36] which he sent to the Franciscan college of Querétaro, and perhaps he sent similar lists to the college of Guadalupe of Zacatecas. This would have been logical, as these two colleges supplied all the missionaries for Texas, and in their archives the principal documents relative to the history of this province were most likely to be found.

But Morfi did not spend all his time collecting and sorting documents. He seems to have devoted some time to copying and to making notes and extracts. Some of the materials which he collected or copied were secured by the distinguished Mexican collector, historian, and bibliophile, Señor Alfredo Chavero, who declared that he had some of these bound into three volumes which he labeled, "Misiones y Viajes."[37] Among the items he collected there is a fourth volume, consisting of three hundred and sixty-six folio leaves, all in the handwriting of

Morfi, in which was contained a copy of the *Historia política de Nueva España por el Oidor Zurita,* on the title page of which appears the signature of Morfi. Still another volume, all in his own handwriting, consists of a copy of the *Relacion de Ixtlixochitl,* with three hundred and eighty folio leaves. In this volume there was also a copy of the *Breve Compendio* of Bonilla.[38]

It was Bonilla's *Breve Compendio* that caused Morfi to undertake his *Historia,* here presented for the first time, and which until found by the writer had been mistakenly thought to be the same as his *Memorias para la Historia de Texas.* In his summary of events to 1772, Bonilla imputes the failures of the various attempts to colonize Texas to the missionaries, whom he sharply condemns for the San Xavier-San Sabá fiasco.[39]

Morfi, who, after his visit to the Interior Provinces with Theodore de Croix, had become convinced of the unselfish labors of the missionaries and had been filled with admiration for their heroic virtues, now undertook to vindicate his brethren in Texas by presenting the facts. He was by nature impulsive; injustice and unfairness aroused in him the deepest emotions; and, accustomed to crush his opponents with cold, unanswerable logic, he set out to prove not only the innocence of the missionaries, but the guilt of those who accused them, proclaiming at the same time the profound injustice of the accusation. One has only to read his relentless and bitter refutation of Rivera's report to realize the intensity of his feeling in the matter and the impatience he experienced with officials who, as he thought, had sacrificed the salvation of souls to material considerations. It is in such instances that he declares, " In twenty-seven years that I have been in America I have known many who have been most zealous of the royal treasury, but I have known few who, after having proved their zeal by reducing expenses, have not ended by soliciting royal aid, or promotion in rank, or an advance in salary. In the meantime America grows worse." [40] Still, if the reader is open-minded, he cannot fail to be impressed with the irresistible force of Morfi's logic, even while condemning his caustic remarks.[41]

It is evident that, before he wrote his *Historia,* Morfi first collected all the material possible. This he organized roughly in his *Memorias para la Historia de Texas,* preliminary to the final work, qualifying this first draft or tentative arrangement by the word *Memorias,* meaning notes. That he finished the *Memorias* there is little question, though this work necessarily lacks the unity and sequence of the corrected narrative. It was not until he had gathered everything he could find and organized it after a fashion, with the definite purpose in mind of proving how the blunders of the officials, the haphazard policy of the government, and not the missionaries, were to blame for the repeated failures in Texas, that he commenced to write his *Historia.* Unfortunately, death prevented him from finishing his work and giving it the polish which, as the padre colector declares, characterized all his writings.

Four different copies of the *Memorias* are known. The first is entitled, *Memorias para la historia de la provincia de Texas escritas por el R. P. F. Juan Agustín Morfi, lector jubilado, é hijo de provincia del Sto. Evangelio de México.* This consists of four hundred and twenty-eight folio leaves, all in the handwriting of the author.[42] The second copy, entitled *Memorias para la historia de Texas escritas por el R. P. F. Juan Agustín Morfi, lector jubilado de la provincia del Sto. Evango. de México* (*ca.* 1781), consists of four hundred and sixty-two folio leaves, written in a large, bold hand.[43] The third copy of the work is that made by Fray Manuel de la Vega in 1792 under the direction of Father Fray Francisco García de Figueroa, in response to the royal order of 1790. The title is exactly the same as that of the copy in the Bancroft Library just described, and the work seems to be the same, except that it is bound in two thick volumes.[44] The fourth copy bearing the misleading title, *Historia de la provincia de Texas por Fray Juan Agustín Morfi,* is in fact a partial or incomplete copy of the *Memorias,* consisting of two hundred and forty-two folio pages, all written in the characteristic small and even hand of Morfi. It has two maps of San Antonio not found in any of the copies described, but it ends abruptly on page 243 in the middle of a sentence of paragraph 10, Book VIII.[45] There is a possible fifth copy, described by Garrison, but this is also incomplete. It was a careless reference to this copy that inspired the confusion between the *Memorias* and the *Historia,* in 1790. Ever since that time much misunderstanding has existed with respect to the identity of the two works and, since only the first was known, it has been strongly suspected that, as in the case of the *Historia del Nuevo Mexico* mentioned by Morfi in his *Memorias,* it was never written.[46] The royal order of 1790 called for "el fin de la Historia de Texas" of Father Morfi and since that time it has been thought that this was the same as the *Memorias.* But Garrison is the first to point out that this order did not refer at that time to a different work. "It seems, however," he declares, "that the incomplete work relative to Texas, containing three hundred and sixty-seven folios in eleven books, which was sent in 1788, was the 'memorias' of Morfi."[47]

The *Memorias* was divided into books, and the paragraphs of each book were numbered separately, beginning with one. The complete known copies of this work contain fourteen books. The one sent to Spain in 1788 consisted of only the first eleven books, while the copy in the Library of Congress, to which reference has been made, has only eight.

614

[illegible] 360 leg. [illegible] al N.N.E.

Situacion, y confines de Texas [illegible]

1. La Provincia de Texas, o Nuevas Filipinas, dandole su principio
por el Sur, en la Bahia de el Espiritu Santo, que está en los 28
grados de latitud Boreal, y su termino al Norte en el Pueblo de
Sn. Teodoro de los Taovayases, situado en los 33 grados de la misma, ocupa un espacio de 200 leguas. La misma
o alguna mas extension tiene de Oriente a Poniente desde
el Presidio de Sn. Antonio de Bexar, hasta el abandonado de
los Adaes. Y considerandola por el N.N.O. no se han reco-
nocido hasta ahora sus limites. Confina por el medio dia
con el Seno Mexicano, y Colonia del Nuevo Santander: por
el poniente con el Nuevo Reyno de Leon, y Provincia de
Coahuila; por el N.O. y N.N.O. con el Nuevo Mexico, y la
Zona glacial; y por el Oriente con las Colonias Inglesas,
y la Luisiana.

Temperamento

2. El temperamento es excelente ni demasiado frio, ni extremadamente caluroso. Rara vez se ve el cielo cubierto de nubes un dia entero, sin que por eso deje de llover a sus tiempos con abundancia. La serenidad de las noches es igual a
la de los dias: el rocio contribuye a la fecundidad del País,
sin que sea necesario preservarse contra su malignidad. En
el hibierno suele nevar en ocasiones, y helar con frequencia, pero ni este, ni aquella son tan rigorosas que impidan
el cultivo, o molesten al Colono. Jamas se ha conocido allí
el terremoto o los uracanes: y las epidemias son rarisimas:
una salud robusta es el patrimonio de los habitantes que lle-
gan a la mas extrema vejez sin los achaques de la decrepitud.

Termina, p. 257

THE FIRST PAGE OF MORFI'S HISTORIA DE TEXAS

The manuscript of the *Historia de Texas* consists of two hundred and thirty-eight folio pages, all written in the characteristic small even hand of Morfi, with numerous corrections, additions, and marginal notations by the author himself, who seems to have read and reread the manuscript several times, adding such information as he found in the course of time. It is not signed, and there is no mark of identification other than the handwriting to indicate that it is the work of Morfi. The title page was added by someone later. This is explainable by the fact that the author had not finished the work and consequently had not made the final copy with the title he intended to give to his finished history.

Together with the manuscript of the *Historia* were found two small cuadernos (copy books) labeled "Additions." In the text of the *Historia* are found frequent marginal notes that read, "see sheet of additions," pointing out that at such places the additional information is to be incorporated in the text. These additions have been made in the present edition.

Throughout the manuscript, the paragraphs are numbered consecutively from one to six hundred. There are no divisions into chapters or books. Along the left-hand margin, at the top, the author places with scrupulous care the year, beginning with 1673 and continuing throughout the narrative, to 1779. In the same manner he has placed marginal topical headings to guide the reader to the information desired. Whenever Morfi departs from strict chronological order, he notes it in the text and justifies it by declaring that he does it "in order not to interrupt the course of the narrative."[48] Both the marginal topical headings and the marginal dates have been preserved in the presentation of the *Historia* as paragraph headings.

The manuscript clearly indicates that it was still in process of composition, and some difficulty has been experienced in deciphering a few of the corrections and additions. Had he had the time to recopy this work and put it in final form, many inconsistencies in the agreement and sequence of tenses, a few dates, and other confusing details would have been elucidated by the author. For example, the numbering of the paragraphs is confused in several instances. Beginning with paragraph 241, the initial 2 has been replaced by 1 and the subsequent paragraphs numbered consecutively, except for this error, to 200. But beginning with 301 the error seems to have been detected by the author and corrected in the rest of the manuscript. In two or three instances consecutive paragraphs have been numbered alike, and in one case several numbers have been skipped. All such irregularities have been noted. The naturally small handwriting becomes almost microscopic at times in the interlinear corrections and additions, so that the reading of the manuscript presented some problems in interpretation.

The *Historia* differs from the *Memorias* in organization, treatment, length, and style. Though following a chronological order in both works, Morfi has compressed his information much more in the first than in the second. He has conscientiously tried to reduce to a minimum the irrelevant and superfluous details in the *Historia* and to avoid all repetitions possible. By this means he succeeded in reducing the voluminous *Memorias* from four hundred and sixty-two folio leaves, to two hundred and thirty-eight pages, or one-fourth of the original length. How Morfi accomplished this may be deduced from a comparison of the space allowed to corresponding subjects in the two works. For example, in the *Memorias* he allows two whole books, or almost ninety folio pages, to a description of the various Indian tribes, their customs and habits, and their beliefs. In the *Historia* he gives all the essentials concerning the Indians in twenty-six para-

LIBRO I. 1.

Imposicion del nombre — 1. La Provincia de Texas, como otras muchas de ambas Americas recibió este nombre por la mala inteligencia de una voz. Quando el Capitan Alonso de Leon se encontró la primera vez con los Indios de aquellos territorios, lo recibieron estos graciosamente saludandole con la palabra *Texia*, que en su idioma quiere decir *Amigo*, y desde entonces ellos y su Provincia fueron con alguna corrupcion llamados Texas.

Situacion y confines — 2. Dista de Mexico al N.N.E. 360 leguas poco mas, ó menos. Tiene su principio al Sur en la Bahia del Espiritu Santo, que está en los 28 grados, con corta diferencia, de latitud boreal, y se dilata al Norte hasta el pueblo de Sn Teodoro de los Taovayases, ocupando un espacio de mas de docientas y cinquenta leguas N.S. La misma, ó alguna mayor extension tiene de oriente á poniente, desde el rio de Medina, que la separa de Coahuila, hasta el abandonado Presidio de los Adaes, por donde se une con la Luisiana. Confina por el medio dia con el Seno Mexicano: Por el oriente con la Luisiana, y Colonias Inglesas: por el N. N.N.O. y N.O. con el Nuevo Mexico y tierras incognitas: y por el poniente con las Provincias de Coahuila, Nuevo Reino de Leon, y Colonia de Santander.

Temperamento — 3. Su temperamento es excelente, ni demasiado frio, ni extremadamente caloroso. Por el invierno suele nevar en ocasiones, y helar con frequencia; pero jamas es con tanto rigor que impidan el cultivo ó molesten gravemente al Colono. Rara vez se vé el cielo cubierto de nubes todo un dia; sin que por eso deje ordinariamente de llover á sus tiempos con abundancia. La serenidad de las noches es igual á la de los dias: el rocio contribuye á la fertilidad del Pais, sin ser necesario precaverse contra su malignidad. No se conocen alli los terremotos, y solo rara vez se experimentan huracanes.

THE FIRST PAGE OF MORFI'S MEMORIAS

graphs, which occupy little more than fifteen pages.[49] Likewise in making a summary of the establishment of the French on the Gulf coast, Morfi reduces the two books given to this subject in his *Memorias,* to fifty-five paragraphs in his *Historia.* Feeling that he has taken considerable time to relate the adventures of the French in the establishment of their settlement on Matagorda bay, Morfi explains the necessity for this apparently long digression: "So closely are the events of the history of Louisiana connected with those of Texas that it is not possible to describe what took place in the second without giving at least a brief summary of the first." [50]

In general, it may be said that the *Historia* is much more concise and to the point than the *Memorias.* In the first hundred paragraphs we have a complete and detailed description of the province of Texas, of its rivers and numberless creeks, of its settlements, and of the native tribes, based on the most authoritative accounts known up to the time of Morfi's death. Modern historians have used the same sources and come to the same conclusions as Morfi, in many instances. This coincidence proves the soundness of the author's judgment and his unusual ability to analyze the facts and arrive at a fair conclusion.[51] In the remaining five hundred paragraphs he traces the history of Texas from 1673 to 1779 with a wealth of detail not to be expected in so short a space. He summarizes the early exploration of the Mississippi and the final settlement of La Salle's unfortunate colony on Matagorda bay; he then retells in rapid succession the various attempts of the Spaniards to find the French colony by land and by sea; the first occupancy of Texas and its abandonment in 1693; the renewal of interest in the province with the sudden appearance of St. Denis at the presidio of San Juan Bautista; the Ramón expedition of 1716; and the permanent occupancy of Texas. To the

Aguayo expedition and its significance in the early history of Texas he devotes considerable space, giving interesting details in connection with the establishment of the presidio at Los Adaes, the farthest outpost of Texas, until its abolishment in 1772. He then points out the fundamental weaknesses in the reforms of Rivera and the evils that followed the adoption of his ill-advised policy. The incursions of the French throughout the entire period, the efforts of the English to establish trade among the Indians of Texas, the misfortunes of the missions of San Xavier and San Sabá, the unsettled and confusing policy adopted by different governors and the government in Mexico with regard to the Apache and the nations of the north, and many other incidents treated in part by others, are summarized intelligently. Throughout the *Historia,* Morfi tries to give a connected narrative, bringing together all the important details and omitting the non-essential and superfluous. But his primary object was to prove, by presenting the facts, the unselfish character of the missionaries and the injustice that was done to their good name by the statements and insinuations of Bonilla in his *Breve Compendio*. That Morfi succeeded in his purpose will have to be admitted by the impartial reader, for nowhere will the record of the heroic efforts of the sons of Saint Francis to bring to Christianity the thousands of natives be found presented more fairly.

From time to time Morfi pauses in his narrative to lament the failure of the Texas missions as a result of the changing policy of the Spanish officials and the personal ambitions and petty jealousies of the local presidial captains. "The province declined from day to day, so that though we still call ourselves its masters, we do not exercise dominion over a foot of land beyond San Antonio." [52] Speaking of the destruction of the San Xavier and San

Sabá missions, he exclaims: "The new missions were destroyed, the hostility of the nations of the north continued, the Lipans did not cease their depredations, and the entire province was thrown into turmoil and strife by the Spaniards themselves." [53] In his condemnation of the officials he is particularly severe in his denunciation of Rivera, Bonilla, and Viceroy Casafuerte. His frankness in imputing the blame for the failures in Texas to the Spanish officials explains his lack of popularity as a historian after his death and the harsh opinion of the officials concerning his work.[54]

The difference between the *Memorias* and the *Historia,* in the final analysis, is that the first was the basis for the second. A comparison of the two shows, as already indicated, that in the essential points there is no difference; that the fundamental facts are common to the two works; but that the treatment, the organization, and the presentation of the subject matter are as different as the preliminary draft of any document and its final copy. It is because of this that a recent historian remarked, in comparing a passage quoted by Pichardo, supposedly from the *Memorias:* "This version of Morfi's writing differs so greatly from the photostat copy of the original in the University of Texas Library that one must conclude that either Pichardo altered the text at random or copied from a different text." [55] As a matter of fact Pichardo seems to have used the unfinished copy of the *Historia.* He had access to the archive of San Francisco el Grande, and for his purpose the shorter work was much more convenient. How extensively Pichardo utilized the work of Morfi may be deduced from the fact that he quotes him in the first volume of his *Treatise on the Limits of Louisiana and Texas,* just published, in discussing the following subjects: English traders in Texas, St. Denis' activities in

Texas, the La Salle expedition and settlement, Peñalosa in New Mexico and his relations with the French court, Ibarbo's exploration of the Gulf coast, the death of La Salle, French traders among the Indian nations, activities of Blancpain, and the history of New Mexico.[56] No wonder that Bancroft declared, speaking of Morfi's work, that "his historical memoirs [are] the standard authority for Texas history" down to the date of his death.[57]

In presenting the *Historia de Texas* in English all possible care has been exercised to translate the original text with accuracy. Special effort has been made to preserve, as far as possible, the style of the original, which varies with the subject matter. In descriptions and straightforward narration the language is simple and direct. In argument and controversial points it becomes impulsive, combative, and at times caustic. There are good examples of all the forms of debate, from the respectful refutation to the most sarcastic ridicule. Throughout the text all additions or variations from the original have been indicated by the use of brackets. These have also been used to enclose explanatory matter generally placed in parentheses. The punctuation of the original has in most cases been disregarded. Long paragraphs have been broken up for the sake of unity, but the numbering has been preserved at the head of the original paragraphs. It will be found, therefore, that a considerable number of paragraphs are not numbered. These can always be identified as having formed part of the first numbered paragraph immediately preceding.

Some of the additions made by Morfi in the margins of the original manuscript have been incorporated in footnotes when it has not been possible to determine with accuracy the point at which they were to appear in the text. All the notes are by the editor, unless otherwise indicated. In the annotations the aim has been threefold: to give, wherever possible, the original source used by Morfi or to corroborate or correct his statements with other reliable sources; to give such additional information as was thought useful for a better understanding of the text or to supplement the original text; to indicate other sources than those used by Morfi where the reader may find the same subject treated from a different point of view. An effort has also been made, in editing the text, to compare the citations given by Morfi with the sources he used or with other copies of the documents quoted, either in English or in Spanish.

In annotating the manuscript the collection of documents in the archive of San Francisco el Grande has been found invaluable. It has revealed also the accuracy with which Morfi used his sources, as it has been found uniformly true that his statements are invariably based on trustworthy authority. In this respect the extensive collection of transcript copies of documents from the archives of Mexico and Spain made by members of the department of history at the University of Texas was found of great value. It is worthy of note that many of the documents found in the transcripts from different archives and collections are included in the collection generally designated throughout as the archive of San Francisco el Grande, where in many instances the original autographed copies are preserved. This proves the contention of the writer that Morfi collected his materials not only from the archives of his order, but from other official sources.

The *Historia* presents a connected narrative of the principal events in the history of Texas from 1673 to 1779. It is far more detailed than Bonilla's *Breve Com-*

pendio and wider in scope than any work now available on the subject in Spanish or English.[58] Though avowedly undertaken for the purpose of defending the work of the missionaries, the account is fair on the whole and presents a unified and coherent story of the history of the province of Texas during a space of one hundred and six years.

CARLOS E. CASTAÑEDA

NOTES TO INTRODUCTION

1. Garrison, "The Archivo General de Mexico," in *The Nation,* May 30, 1901; Bolton, *Guide,* pp. 20–21; Beristain y Souza, II, pp. 301–305; Leduc, Diccionario, pp. 667–668; Nicolás León, *Bibliografía Mexicana del Siglo XVIII,* II, p. 1123; Alfredo Chavero, "Fray Juan Agustín Morfi," in *Anales del Museo Nacional de Mexico,* 2ª época (1904), I, pp. 52–53; Hackett, *Pichardo's Treatise,* I, *passim;* Bolton, *Texas in the Middle Eighteenth Century,* p. 469; Bancroft, *North Mexican States and Texas,* I, p. 631; and others too numerous to mention.

2. Ambrosio Sagarzurieta to Viceroy José Iturrigaray, December 31, 1806. Hackett, *Pichardo's Treatise,* I, p. 11.

3. Bancroft, *North Mexican States and Texas,* I, pp. 631–632.

4. In the *Memorandum* of the papers found in his cell after his death, all of which were deposited in the archive of San Francisco el Grande, collections of documents relative to all these provinces were found. Father Fray Manuel Lejarza, archivist, duly signed a receipt for these papers on December 31, 1783. Bolton, *Guide,* p. 207.

5. Beristain y Souza, II, pp. 301–302; *Enciclopedia Universal Ilustrada,* XXXVI, p. 1058; Leduc, *Diccionario,* pp. 667–668.

6. Fr. Francisco Antonio de la Rosa y Figueroa, *Promptuario General,* MS., p. 152. Father Figueroa had access to the official records and prepared with great care a detailed list of all the Franciscans of the Santo Evangelio province from the time of the Conquest to 1770. In this list he declares that Morfi was "Asturiano," meaning a native of Asturias. Galicia adjoins Asturias, but the people of the two provinces differ fundamentally. In Asturias it is not uncommon to find many descendants of the Irish who migrated to this province. It is very probable that Morfi's original name was Murphy, which was changed to the Spanish form he used.

7. See paragraph 316 of the text.

8. Rosa y Figueroa, *Promptuario General,* MS., p. 152. Beristain y Souza and all the others who have followed him say that he was a friar when he arrived from Spain. The Spanish friars who came this way were, in reality, transfers, and are usually designated in the records as *Gachupines.* Those who, though Spaniards by blood and birth, joined the order in Mexico were designated as *hijos de provincia,* while those who were born in Mexico and joined the order there were designated as *Criollos.*

9. *Ibid.,* p. 152.

10. This college has the distinction of having been the first college in America and the first in which Latin grammar was taught to the natives. It was opened on January 6, 1536, and was the result of the efforts of Fray Juan de Zumárraga, the first bishop of Mexico. For a brief summary of its history, see C. E. Castañeda, "Historia de Todos los Colegios de la

Ciudad de México," in *Nuevos documentos ineditos o muy raros para la historia de México,* II, pp. 1–18.

11. Beristain y Souza, II, p. 304. Beristain claims to have seen the original quarto manuscript in the old library of the college of Tlaltelolco at the time he was preparing his bibliography in 1816. The manuscript has since been lost. In 1904, Señor Alfredo Chavero declared he could not find this work anywhere. Chavero, "Fray Juan Agustín Morfi," in *Anales del Museo Nacional de Mexico,* 2ª época (1904), I, pp. 52–53.

12. Nicolás León, *Bibliografía,* II, p. 1123. The full title of the sermon was *La Seguridad de Maria Santísima de Guadalupe. Sermón Panegírico que en la fiesta que anualmente hacen los Señores Labradores, implorando su Protección Dixo el Día 17 de mayo de este presente año en la Iglesia de su Santuario el R. P. Fr. Juan Agustín Morfi, Lector de Sagrada Theologia en el Convento principal de N. S. P. S. Francisco de esta Corte. Dedicado a la misma Soberana Señora por los Caballeros de la Congregación. . . . Año 1772.*

13. *Loc. cit.*

14. Bolton, *Guide,* p. 75. A copy of this decree and the instructions given to the new commandant general are found in the archive of San Francisco el Grande.

15. Theodore de Croix was born in Lille, June 30, 1730. He had seen service in Spain and America prior to his appointment as commandant general and had risen from an ensign to the rank of general. His uncle, Don Carlos Francisco de Croix, took special interest in him and had him as a companion when he was governor of Galicia in Spain and when he came to Mexico as viceroy. For details of his life, see Ch. X, n. 33, of the text.

16. José Gómez, "Diario Curioso," in *Documentos para la historia de Mexico,* 1ª serie, VII, p. 15.

17. *Real Instrucción dada al señor Don Teodoro de Croix . . . con fha. de 22 de Agosto de 1776.*

18. El Caballero de Croix to father provincial Fray Isidro Murillo, Mexico, July 25, 1777.

19. Morfi, "Viage de Indios y Diario del Nuevo Mexico," in *Documentos para la historia de Mexico,* 3ª serie, I, p. 307.

20. In 1867 the official archive of the Convento Grande de San Francisco, the mother house of the Franciscans in Mexico, passed, at least in good part, into private hands. It was not until 1922 that, by a fortunate coincidence, it was recovered and placed in the National Library of Mexico, where it is now kept. In January, 1931, the writer made a survey of this archive to locate all the documents relative to the early history of Texas, as a result of which more than ten thousand pages of manuscript material were listed, rearranged, and copied. Most of these documents were doubtless gathered by Morfi, and not a few were copied in his own hand. Photostat copies of the entire collection relative to Texas were

made by the writer and are now in the University of Texas Library. Most of this material had not been listed before.

21. This diary is the "Viage de Indios y Diario del Nuevo Mexico," published in *Documentos para la historia de Mexico,* 3ª serie, I, pp. 305–487. The father collector, Fray Francisco García Figueroa, in accord with the royal order of 1790 for the collection of all documents pertaining to the early history of New Spain, had copies of many made by Fray Manuel de la Vega. These compose the thirty-two volumes of *Memorias para la Historia de Nueva España.* In a note appended to the diary the padre colector says: "Though in the list and in the royal order this work is designated as 'Viage de Indios y Diario del Nuevo Mexico,' it is in reality the diary of the route followed by the Señor Comandante D. Teodoro de Croix from Mexico to the province of Texas, in company with the R. P. Fray Agustín Morfi who describes in this writing all the peculiarities which offered themselves to his observation with that logic, amenity, and elegance proper to the good judgment, learning, and good taste that distinguish all his writings." *Ibid.,* p. 306.

22. Vito Alessio Robles, "Notes on the Diary of Morfi," MS. in possession of the writer.

23. See opinion of the padre colector cited in note 21, above.

24. El Caballero de Croix to Fray Juan Agustín Morfi, Chihuahua, March 31, 1778.

25. Garrison, "The Archivo General de Mexico," *op. cit.*

26. This *Colección,* generally referred to as *Memorias,* forms the nucleus for the "Sección de Historia" of the Archivo General de Mexico, and consists of thirty-two volumes. The "Viage de Indios" is found in volume III of the collection. For a complete description and table of contents, see Bolton, *Guide,* pp. 22–32; consult also Garrison, "The Archivo General de Mexico," *op. cit.*

The original copy in Morfi's own handwriting remained in the Archivo de San Francisco, where it was in 1904, according to Señor Chavero. The writer did not see it when he made the survey of this archive. Chavero, "Fray Juan Agustín Morfi," *op. cit.*

27. Beristain y Souza, *Biblioteca,* II, pp. 304–305. The title in Spanish is, *Dialogo de la elocuencia en general y sobre la del Púlpito en particular del Sr. Arzobispo de Cambrai, con la carta de este sobre la Poesia y la Historia, traducido al castellano.* Imp. en Madrid por Ramón Ruiz, 1795, 2 tom. 8°.

28. In August, 1780, there was a considerable disturbance at the Convento Grande de San Francisco as a result of a contested election. The former guardian refused to allow his successor to take office, whereupon the friars forcibly deposed him and locked him in the convent prison. The sympathizers of the deposed guardian appealed to the viceroy, who sent his alcalde and a notary public to investigate. There followed many recriminations, but finally the matter was settled and order reëstablished

on August 23 of that year. Just what part Morfi took in this scandal is not known, but he must have been entirely inactive or his name would have crept into the records. There was much dissatisfaction and a new election must have been held a few months later, of which there is no record, and Morfi must have been chosen as the most acceptable to all parties, for we have conclusive evidence that early in 1782 he was acting guardian. José Gómez, "Diario Curioso," *op. cit.*, 1ª serie, VII, pp. 91–92.

29. *Ibid.*, 1ª serie, VII, p. 133.

30. *Ibid.*, 1ª serie, VII, p. 143.

31. There are more than thirty different chronicles in the García Library, concerning the various religious orders in Mexico, some printed and others in manuscript. A careful examination of these has revealed no other mention of Morfi. The records and available material for the history of the Franciscan order in Mexico, which are very voluminous, are extremely meager for the years 1778–1790.

32. José Gómez, "Diario Curioso," *op. cit.*, 1ª serie, VII, p. 169. These documents, which contain much valuable information, were poorly edited and are full of typographical errors. In the entry cited, the last name is given as *Margil,* but it is evidently intended for Morfi. In substantiation of this fact may be cited the notation at the end of the copy of the *Memorias para la Historia de Texas* in the Biblioteca de la Real Academia de la Historia of Madrid, which reads: "To here the Reverend Father Morfi, who died before finishing this work as the result of a malignant fever, while he was guardian of the Convento Grande de Mexico, on October 20, 1783." Fray Marcellino da Civezza, *Saggio di Bibliografia Geografica, Storica, Etnografica Sanfrancescana,* p. 412.

33. The *Memorandum* of the papers left by Father Morfi was made by Fray Manuel Lejarza, archivist of the province of Santo Evangelio, who signed a receipt for all these papers on December 31, 1783, when they were deposited in the archive of San Francisco el Grande. Bolton, *Guide,* p. 207. It was the manuscript history listed here, together with the *cuadernos* of additions, that the writer discovered in January, 1931, while making a survey of this archive.

34. See notes 20 and 33. These documents doubtless formed the greater part of the original legajo mentioned in the text above. They easily fell into a chronological arrangement that paralleled the order followed by Morfi in his *Historia.* It was this fact that enabled the writer to verify all the statements in the *Historia* with relative ease.

While the writer was copying this material, Dr. France V. Scholes, then of the University of New Mexico and now of the Carnegie Institution of Washington, found and listed more than twelve thousand pages of material relative to New Mexico, which were perhaps parts of the collection made by Morfi. At the same time a group, consisting of two bundles of about fifteen hundred pages each and labeled, "Misiones de California," evidently collected by Morfi, was noted. The writer was informed that copies of these had been made for the University of California.

35. See paragraph 378 of the text.

36. This list was found by Bolton in the archive of the college of the Holy Cross of Querétaro, the missionaries of which were the most active in the Christianization of the Indians of Texas. Bolton, *Guide,* p. 388.

37. These may be the same which made up the legajo found in Morfi's cell under the designation "Misiones." See list of documents cited by Bolton in his *Guide,* p. 207.

38. These different items are described by Señor Chavero in "Fray Agustín Morfi," *op. cit.,* 2ª época, I, pp. 52–53. For the full title of Bonilla's work, see the bibliography. A translation and critical edition of this compendium was made by Elizabeth Howard West and published in *The Quarterly* of the Texas State Historical Association, VIII, pp. 9–78.

39. West, *op. cit.,* VIII, pp. 46–56. "Bonilla's work was somewhat unfavorable to the friars, and in several parts is sharply criticised by Morfi," declares Bancroft in his *North Mexican States and Texas,* I, p. 632n. The padre colector, in his brief note at the close of the compendium of Bonilla, likewise comments, "the Reverend Father Morfi, author of *Las Memorias para la Historia de Texas,* took pains to combat some points of this Compendium"; see West, *op. cit.,* VIII, pp. 71–72.

40. See paragraph 316 of the text.

41. For one of the best examples of Morfi's argumentative style, in which he displays all the skill of the trained logician, see paragraphs 302–315 of the text. Here he takes up the report of Rivera and points out all its weaknesses.

42. This copy was described in 1904 by Señor Alfredo Chavero (*Anales del Museo Nacional de Mexico,* 2ª época, I, pp. 52–53), who examined it personally.

43. This copy is in the Bancroft collection, University of California. In a letter describing the work, Dr. H. I. Priestley, Librarian, says: "Ours is an eighteenth century MS. with goose quill pen, on handmade paper. The writing is quite large, and the copy is perhaps taken from an earlier and smaller one." H. I. Priestley to E. W. Winkler, Berkeley, November 27, 1931. Bolton, in his *Texas in the Middle Eighteenth Century,* p. 469, says that he is editing the manuscript for publication, but up to the present it has not been printed.

44. This copy is in the Biblioteca de la Real Academia de Historia of Madrid. It is carefully described by Civezza in his *Saggio di Bibliografia* . . . , p. 412.

45. This copy is in the Library of Congress. There is a photostat copy in the Library of the University of Texas, where it has been consulted and examined by the writer. The narrative takes the reader through only a part of De León's expedition of 1689.

46. "If, by chance, Father Morfi actually wrote that which he here

promises, these papers absolutely are not in existence. It is even very probable that he did not succeed in executing this work, having been prevented by death," declares Pichardo. Hackett, *Pichardo's Treatise,* I, p. 158.

47. Garrison, "The Archivo General de Mexico," *op. cit.*

48. See paragraph 208 of the text.

49. See paragraphs 71 to 97 in the text.

50. See paragraph 173 of the text.

51. Throughout the text attention has been called to all such instances.

52. See paragraph 316 of the text.

53. See paragraph 479 of the text.

54. Sagarzurieta's low estimate of the worth of the *Memorias,* which he declared were mere copies of other documents and had the disadvantage of being poorly copied, was the result, in part, of Morfi's condemnation of the viceregal officials, and partly due to the fact that he was referring to the *Memorias* and not to the *Historia.* Furthermore, he was interested at the time in the question of the boundary, and Morfi gives little attention to this matter either in his *Historia* or his *Memorias.* See notes 2 and 40; Hackett, *Pichardo's Treatise,* I, pp. 10–12.

55. *Ibid.,* I, p. 172, n. 2.

56. *Ibid.,* I, *passim.*

57. Bancroft, *North Mexican States and Texas,* I, pp. 631–632.

58. The only other two general works on the history of Texas during the Spanish colonial period, besides that of Bonilla, are Bolton, *Texas in the Middle Eighteenth Century,* and Hackett, *Pichardo's Treatise on the Limits of Louisiana and Texas.* The first is a series of monographic studies ably put together but not covering the history of Texas prior to 1720; while the latter, though having a fund of information on the history of Texas from the earliest times, is in fact not a history but an argumentative brief to prove Spain's title to Texas and as such has definite limitations as a history of Spanish Texas.

LIST OF MORFI'S WRITINGS AND LETTERS

IN this list are included (*a*) all original writings by Father Fray Juan Agustín Morfi found by the writer or attributed to him by others; (*b*) all documents copied in his own hand; (*c*) all letters written to him.

A. Writings of Father Fray Juan Agustín Morfi

Descripción de la Ciudad de Querétaro y de sus alrededores, tomada del "Diario del Viaje a la Provincia de Texas" con el Caballero D. Teodoro de la Croix. Escrito en el año de 1777 Por el R. P. Fr. Juan Agustín Morfi del orden de S. Francisco de la Provincia del Santo Evangelio de México. Querétaro. Tip. y Lib. del Sagrado Corazon, 1913. Port. 13 pp.

Descripción geográfica del Nuevo Mexico: escrita por el P. Fr. Juan Agustín de Morfi, Lector Jubilado de la Provincia de S. Evangelio de México, Año 1782.

This is a manuscript in folio in the Biblioteca de la Real Academia de la Historia, Madrid. Civezza, *Saggio di Bibliografia,* p. 413. There is a copy in volume XXV of *Memorias para la historia de Nueva España* in the Archivo General of Mexico, Bolton, *Guide,* p. 27; and another in the British Museum, Mexico Tratados Varios. Add. MSS. 17,563, ff. 71–94. This description of New Mexico has recently been published by A. B. Thomas in *Forgotten Frontiers,* pp. 87–114.

Desordenes que se advierten en el Nuevo Mexico y medios que se juzgan oportunos a repararlo para mejorar su constitución y hacer feliz aquel reyno.

This manuscript is in the Archivo General de Indias, Seville, 103–4–18 (A. B. Thomas, *Forgotten Frontiers,* p. 371). Bolton lists a similar manuscript under the short title, *Desordenes de Nuevo Mexico,* as No. 8 in volume XXV of *Memorias para la historia de Nueva España.* Bolton, *Guide,* p. 27.

Diálogo sobre la elocuencia en general y sobre la del Púlpito en particular, del Sr. Arzobispo de Cambrai, con la carta de éste sobre la Poesía y la Historia, traducidos al castellano. Imp. en Madrid por Ramón Ruiz, 1795. 2 tom., 8°.

Described by Beristain y Souza in *Biblioteca Hispano Americana,* II, p. 305.

Diario del viaje a la Provincia de Tejas con el Caballero de la Croix.

According to Beristain this manuscript and the *Noticias históricas del Nuevo México* were both in the Secretariat of the viceroyalty in 1816 when he was preparing his bibliography. This may be the same or a different copy of the "Viage de Indios y Diario del Nuevo Mexico" listed here and printed as indicated. Beristain, *Biblioteca,* II, p. 305.

Historia de la Provincia de Texas, 1673–1779.

This manuscript was left unfinished, together with two small *cuadernos* of additions. It was discovered by the writer in January, 1931, in the archive of San Francisco el Grande, now in the National Library of Mexico, and forms the subject of the present study. It was listed as one of the documents found in the cell of Father Morfi after his death. Bolton, *Guide,* p. 207.

Informe del P. Morfi sobre el viage de los Padres Domínguez y Escalante hacia Monterrey y California. 7 ff.

This manuscript is in the handwriting of Morfi, according to Chavero. It is published in *Anales del Museo Nacional de México,* 2ª época (1904), I, pp. 52–53.

Memorias para la Historia de la Provincia de Texas Escritas Por el R. P. Fr. Juan Agustín Morfi, Lector Jubilado, é Hijo de la Provincia del Sto. Evangelio de México. MS. folio, 428 ff.

This copy, which is described by Chavero, was in the handwriting of Morfi. Chavero, "Fray Juan Agustín Morfi," in *Anales del Museo Nacional de México,* 2ª época, I, pp. 52–53. There are four other manuscript copies of this work, all different. For a discussion and description of each, see the Biographical Introduction.

La Nobleza y Piedad de los Montañeses. Demostrada Por el Smo. Cristo de Burgos. Sermon, Que en su Primera fiesta, celebrada en el Convento grande de N. S. P. S. Francisco de Mexico el dia 3 de Mayo de 1775. años Predicó el P. Fr. Juan Agustín Morfi. Dedicado por los Caballeros que componen la Muy Ilustre Mesa A todos los nobles naturales y originales de la Montaña. Reimpreso en Mexico. En la Imprenta del Lic. D.

Joseph de Jáuregui. Calle de San Bernardo. Folio; port. in two colors, 19 p. 1. unnumbered, 1–37 pp. text.

Described by Nicolás León in his *Bibliografía Mexicana del Siglo XVIII*, II, p. 1123.

Noticias en forma de diario, sobre el Parral. 7 ff.

This manuscript is entirely in the handwriting of Morfi. Chavero, "Fray Juan Agustín Morfi," in *Anales del Museo Nacional de México*, 2ª época (1904), I, pp. 52–53.

Noticias históricas del Nuevo México. 1 tom. MS.

Described by Beristain in *Biblioteca Hispano Americana*, II, p. 305.

Padrón de Texas, Septiembre 28, 1778.

This manuscript is entirely in the handwriting of Morfi and seems to have been compiled by him. Archive of San Francisco el Grande.

La seguridad del Patrocinio de María Santísima de Guadalupe. Sermon panegyrico que en la Fiesta que anualmente hacen los Señores Labradores, implorando su Proteccion Dixo el dia 17 de Mayo de este presente año en la Iglesia de su Santuario el R. P. Fr. Juan Agustín Morfi, Lector de Sagrada Teología en el Convento principal de N. S. P. S. Francisco de esta Corte. Dedicado á misma Soberana Señora por los Caballeros de la Congregacion Impreso con las licencias necesarias en México, en la Imprenta de la Biblioteca Mexicana del Lic. D. Joseph de Jauregui, en la Calle de San Bernardo. Año de 1772. 4° port. 13 p. 1. unnumbered, 12 pp. text.

Described by Nicolás León in his *Bibliografía Mexicana del Siglo XVIII*, II, p. 1123.

Tractatus de Fide, Spe et Charitate. MS. 4° Ann. 1766.

According to Beristain, this manuscript was in the library of the college of Tlaltelolco in 1816. Beristain, *Biblioteca Hispano Americana*, II, p. 305. It could not be found, however, in 1904. Chavero, "Fray Juan Agustín Morfi," in *Anales del Museo Nacional de México*, 2ª época (1904), I, pp. 52–53.

Viaje de Indios y Diario del Nuevo Mexico, escrito por el R. P. Fr. Juan Agustín de Morfi, 1777.

Several copies of this manuscript are known. One is in the Biblioteca de la Real Academia de la Historia, Madrid (Civezza, *Saggio di Bibliografia*); one in volume III of *Memorias para la histo-*

ria de Nueva España (Bolton, *Guide*, p. 22); and one described by Chavero, consisting of 290 ff. (*Anales del Museo*, I, pp. 52–53). This work has been published in *Documentos para la historia de México*, 3ª serie, I, pp. 307–487.

B. Documents Copied by Fray Juan Agustín Morfi

Apuntes sobre el Nuevo Mexico. MS. 12 ff.

This manuscript is in the handwriting of Father Morfi. At the end appears the name of Antonio Bonilla, written also by Morfi. It is contained in a volume of 388 folios, the remainder being in the handwriting of Fray Manuel de la Vega and consisting of a collection of royal decrees and orders concerning New Mexico. The manuscript was in the possession of Alfredo Chavero. *Anales del Museo Nacional de México*, 2ª época, I, pp. 52–53.

Breve Compendio de los sucesos ocurridos en la Provincia de Texas desde su conquista o reduccion hasta la fecha. Por el Teniente de Infanta. Dn. Antonio Bonilla. Mexico, 10 de Noviembre de 1772. 52 ff.

A copy of this work by Bonilla was made by Morfi, in whose handwriting it appears. *Anales del Museo*, 2ª época, I, pp. 52–53.

Expedición de Anastacio de Mézières por orden del Comandante General y correspondencia con el mismo.

Copies in the handwriting of Morfi consisting of 34 folio leaves. In Archive of San Francisco el Grande.

Historia política de Nueva España, pr. el Oidor Zurita. MS. 366 ff.

Bound in one volume, all copied by Morfi in his own hand. The first folio has an index and at the end is the signature of Morfi. Chavero, "Fray Juan Agustín Morfi," in *Anales del Museo*, 2ª época (1904), I, pp. 52–53.

Misiones y Viajes.

A collection of documents made and copied by Morfi, gathered by Chavero and bound in three volumes. *Anales del Museo*, 2ª época (1904), I, pp. 52–53.

Relación del Nuevo México, por el P. Gerónimo de Zárate Salmerón.

A copy, entirely in the handwriting of Morfi, was in possession of Chavero. *Loc. cit.* Printed in *Documentos para la Historia de Mexico*,

3a serie, IV, Mexico, 1856; translated and published in *Land of Sunshine,* XI, XII, Los Angeles, Nov. 1899–Feb. 1900, and in Bolton, *Spanish Exploration,* pp. 268–280.

Relaciones de Ixtlixoxhitl. 308 ff.

One volume, in the handwriting of Morfi. Chavero, "Fray Juan Agustín Morfi," *op. cit.*

C. Letters Written to Fray Juan Agustín Morfi

Barbastro, Fray Antonio, to Morfi, concerning the death of Father Garcés. January 3, 1777.

Listed by Bolton in his *Guide,* p. 22.

Croix, Teodoro de, to Morfi, Chihuahua, March 31, 1778, asking for a copy of the diary kept during the tour of inspection.

The original of this letter is in the archive of San Francisco el Grande.

Fages, Pedro, to Morfi, February 12, 1782.

Listed by Bolton in his *Guide,* p. 22.

Vélez Escalante, Fray Silvestre, to Morfi, giving a summary of the history of New Mexico, April 2, 1778. 12 ff.

This document has been printed in Maas, O., *Las Ordenes Religiosas,* II, pp. 37–47, Barcelona, 1929, and a translation in *Land of Sunshine,* Los Angeles, March–April, 1900. Bolton, *Guide,* p. 22.

Chapter I

GENERAL DESCRIPTION OF TEXAS

1. *Location and boundaries.* The province of Texas, or New Philippines, lies approximately three hundred and sixty leagues [1] from the city of Mexico. It is two hundred leagues from Espíritu Santo bay on the south, situated at 29° north latitude, to the town of San Teodoro of the Taovayases,[2] 35° north latitude. Its extent from San Antonio de Béxar on the west to the abandoned post of Los Adaes on the east is more or less the same. On the south it is bounded by the gulf of Mexico and Nuevo Santander [Tamaulipas]; on the west by the Nuevo Reyno de León and the province of Coahuila; on the north and northwest by New Mexico and the frigid zone; and on the east by the English colonies and Louisiana.

The misinterpretation of a native phrase, as in the case of Peru, Michoacán, and others, gave to this province the name of Texas, by which it has been known since 1688, when the Indians greeted the Spaniards with the word *Texia,* the ordinary salutation with which they welcome their friends, meaning "friend." [3]

2. *Climate.* Its climate is excellent, neither too cold nor too warm. Seldom is the sky covered with clouds for a whole day, though it rains abundantly at times. The heavy dews contribute to the fertility of the land, but it is not necessary to take precautions against their evil effect. In winter, snow and frosts are frequent, but neither one nor the other is so severe as to hinder the cultivation of the soil or molest the settlers. Storms and earthquakes have never been known in this country, and epidemics are very rare. The inhabitants are blessed with

sound health and live to a ripe old age without suffering the infirmities of declining years.

3. *Fertility*. The fertility of the soil exceeds all exaggeration. Wheat, barley, corn, beans, chick-peas, pepper, melons, watermelons, excellent potatoes, cotton, cane, all kinds of vegetables, and, in a word, whatever is planted yields abundantly. Besides the plants common to Europe, there are many others peculiar to the country, of which we shall speak in their place. Nothing proves the fertility of the land and the richness of the soil more than the incredible number of wild horses and cattle found everywhere. It is the multitude of rivers, creeks, and lakes that is responsible for its great fecundity. Up to the present twenty-five large rivers, six hundred and fifteen springs and creeks, and fifty-seven lakes have been counted.

[Generally speaking, all the rivers and creeks run from the northwest to the southeast. Consequently, the traveler who wishes to reach Los Adaes from Coahuila must necessarily cross them on his way [4]]. The San Sabá river rises twelve leagues west-northwest of the old presidio that bore its name,[5] and, after running seventy leagues to the northeast, empties into the Guadalupe.[6] It is joined along its course by six creeks.

The Chanas river [7] has its source in the same direction and is joined by eighteen creeks along its course of fifty leagues to the east before it empties into the Colorado.

The Medina runs twenty-seven leagues from its source before it joins the San Antonio.[8]

4. *Creeks*. The creeks nearest Béxar are the Cíbolo, nine leagues northeast of San Antonio; the Salado, four leagues northeast; the San Cleto, seven leagues east-northeast of the Cíbolo; the San Benito, nine leagues east-northeast of San Joaquín; the San Joaquín, two leagues [east] of San Cleto; the San José, seven leagues east-

northeast of the crossing on the Guadalupe; [9] and the Arcón, four leagues, according to the marquis of Aguayo.[10]

On the first of these [the Cíbolo] was placed a small detachment to protect the approaches to Béxar and La Bahía.[11] On the second [the Salado] there is a cave seventy varas deep [12] and eight wide, the entrance to which is visible on the top of a high hill that forms one of its banks. The cliff resembles a wall from which the depth of the creek can be better appreciated. The dome of the cave is upheld by eleven pillars that rise from the ground. It is curiously incrusted with marine shells that have retained a beautiful lustre. It was in this cave that De Mézières held a meeting in 1772 with the chiefs of the northern tribes that accompanied him to San Antonio to negotiate a peace with the governor of the province.[13]

San Antonio river. The San Antonio river rises one league from the villa of San Fernando. Both the villa and the presidio were situated at the point where the San Pedro creek enters the river, along the banks of which five missions were established, all of which the river waters without suffering much diminution in volume. It then flows on to the sea and enters the bay twelve leagues from the Guadalupe.[14] It runs for a hundred leagues in a southeasterly direction and is joined by nine creeks and two springs.

Alarcón river. The Alarcón has its source to the northwest and is joined by thirteen creeks. It enters the Guadalupe after flowing for twenty-six leagues. The banks of this river, called by the marquis of Aguayo, San Pascual Baylón, are covered with sabines, walnuts, poplars, mulberries, and many grapevines.[15] The woods continue for a league.

5. *Guadalupe river.* The Guadalupe river [16] bears this name for ten leagues before it reaches three copious

springs that increase its volume by a third. Twenty-two leagues beyond it is joined by the San Marcos.[17] The marquis of San Miguel de Aguayo, who crossed it a quarter of a league from its source during the dryest season of the year, declared that it was more than a vara deep and fairly wide. Its water is so clear that the pebbles in the bottom can be counted. He noticed at its source maiden-hair ferns and *doradillo*.[18] The river flows through beautiful meadows and is bordered by thick and delightful woods in which cedars and cypresses predominate, according to De Mézières.[19]

6. *San Ybón.* About three-quarters of a league from the preceding stream is the San Ybón. It rises in a group of hills to the north, and its bed, at the point where the marquis crossed it, is deep, its volume being at that time equal to that of the Guadalupe. It is claimed that in time of rains it rises rapidly and becomes impassable. Its banks are covered with rich vegetation, but not as luxuriant as that of the preceding stream.[20]

7. *Peñuelas.* Four leagues from the San Ybón is the creek called Peñuelas, in the bed of which water is found all the year in pools or ponds.[21] The country between the two streams is level and dotted with mesquites. To the north of this creek begins the range of hills that forms the cañon of the San Sabá where the Lipans live.[22]

8. *Inocentes.* At a distance of two and a half leagues of level and heavily-wooded land, through which it was necessary to send a party ahead to open the road, is the Inocentes river,[23] as large as the Guadalupe. Its banks are so densely covered with vegetation that the sun cannot penetrate it.

9. *San Rafael.* The San Rafael creek is one league to the northeast of the Inocentes. The land is level and well wooded. Its stream is permanent the greater part of the

year and there is always water in the large pools in its bed.[24]

10. *San Isidro.* At a quarter of a league to the northeast, through open country, with low hills and beautiful valleys, is found the spring called San Isidro, surrounded by a pleasant grove.

11. *San Bernardino.* The small creek called San Bernardino by the marquis of Aguayo is five and three-quarter leagues beyond San Isidro.[25]

12. *Garrapatas.* One league of level land beyond is the Garrapatas river, a permanent stream. At the crossing by the upper road followed by the marquis there is a rocky ridge across the stream that forms a pleasing waterfall.[26]

13. *San Marcos.* Three leagues from the preceding river by the road followed by Aguayo, or eight from the Guadalupe, by that of De Mézières, is the celebrated San Marcos river, which he says is "a worthy rival of the San Xavier in respect to the convenience which it offers for settlement." [27] It has its source in a large rocky bluff from which so much water flows out of a large mouth that it at once becomes a river. In its vicinity there are several caves with wonderful formations; here, steps, an altar, frontal, candlesticks, and a font; there, curtains, festoons, flowers, images, and niches, all so clean that they appear to be the work of art. There is no lack of benches to invite the spectator to contemplate at leisure the figures, some sacred, some profane, upon which nature has spent so much care that Europe may well grieve at not being endowed with their equal.[28] The vegetation on the banks of this river is very luxuriant and the volume of its waters twice that of the preceding streams.

14. *San Juan de Dios.* A small creek flows a quarter of a league from the San Marcos, bordered by many trees, especially mulberries, that yield twice as much fruit

as those in Spain. An observation taken at this point showed that it was 30° north latitude.[29]

15. *Santa Quiteria.* After two leagues of beautiful plains and gentle hills is found Santa Quiteria creek. Its bed is deep and its banks are so encumbered with trees that it is difficult to cross.

16. *San Francisco.* A short distance beyond is San Francisco creek. It borders on the San Sabá range of hills.

17. *Animas.* Two leagues to the northeast, the country consisting of open and treeless hills, devoid of underbrush, is the creek called Las Animas, the banks of which on either side are covered with dense vegetation.[30] A quarter of a league beyond is another creek bordered with trees. Both creeks appear to have their sources close at hand and they flow into the Colorado.[31]

18. *Colorado river.* Ten leagues from the San Marcos, according to De Mézières, is the Colorado river, the source of which is to the northwest above the San Sabá in a high and rough range of hills, where the Brazos also has its source. Both run parallel to the Sabine, but the Colorado, which is joined by four rivers and seventeen creeks, runs one hundred and thirty leagues east-southeast before it reaches the bay. It flows with such rapidity that it continually tears away its banks, forming bars out of the silt which it carries and losing itself in a series of lakes, without leaving trace of its entrance or permitting navigation. Near its crossing, on the Bucareli road, is seen a hill called Iron hill, because of the abundance of this metal which it contains. At the foot of this hill flows a creek, sufficient for industrial purposes. There is excellent stone for ovens and firewood for foundries.[32]

19. *San Xavier* [*San Gabriel*]. Five leagues from Las Animas, or ten from the Colorado, according to De Mézières, is the San Xavier river,[33] the banks of which

are thickly covered with vegetation, like the preceding ones. Though it is not very broad, its stream is ordinarily half a vara deep. In view of the controversy which, as we shall see later, arose with regard to its merits, I shall allow De Mézières to describe its good qualities, quoting from his report. Let me note first, however, that Aguayo declares that its stream was half a vara deep in the two branches that he crossed, which would make the volume of its main stream one vara. "The San Xavier rises in the hills which extend westward from the Tuacanas to the vicinity of the extinct presidio of San Sabá. It receives the waters of the San Andrés, and other smaller tributaries, and joins the Brazos. There is an abundance of oyster shells, some broken, some whole, others scattered, but the greater part of them so closely and firmly amalgamated that they appear to be of the remotest antiquity.

"Few rivers can compare with the San Xavier in the clearness of its waters or in abundance of fish. The surrounding country could be irrigated to avoid the uncertainty of the weather, and mills could be erected. The number of wild horses and cattle that graze here and which could be utilized as beasts of burden or as food is incredible. The buffalo is not lacking, for variety; while with thyme, lavender, sage, winter savory, and other aromatic plants, the goats and sheep would thrive. The fragrant flowers that abound in the fields offer splendid facilities for the culture of bees. Hogs could be fattened freely with the acorns, without the costly expense of grain. Prime oil could be obtained from the nuts, and the bears will furnish a not inferior quality of lard. In the woods will be found, in addition to abundant game, lumber, and in the quarries, all kinds of stone for building.

"The proximity of Béxar, of the Tuacanas [Tawakoni], the Indians of San Theodoro, the Panis-Mahas, and other friends, will result in frequent visits, trade, assistance, confidences, and reconciliations. [The settlement of this river] will bring about the quieting or punishment of the Comanches; will furnish the shortest and safest communication with the adjoining Louisiana; and, finally, will arouse in the subject greater desire to traverse, visit, and settle this extensive territory, at sight of which I have been unable to refrain from rapture and ecstasy, which, indeed, would be occasioned in the most stupid and indifferent." [34] At a gunshot's distance, the land being thickly wooded, there is a large lake with much water.[35]

20. *San Ignacio.* Four leagues northeast of San Xavier [San Gabriel], after crossing a heavily wooded creek, is San Ignacio creek. There are a number of low and high hills between the two.[36]

21. *San Fernando.* To reach the San Fernando one travels five leagues northeast and crosses twenty small creeks. This river has good and abundant water and heavy vegetation. Half a league beyond is another similar stream.[37]

22. *Espíritu Santo.* Four leagues northeast of San Fernando, the country being open, with gentle and beautiful hills, dotted with mesquite trees for a league's distance, is the Espíritu Santo river. It has abundant water and is sometimes impassable by the road followed by Aguayo.[38] This river is the lower branch of the main stream of the Brazos, on the old road to the Texas. The San Xavier, Las Animas, and most of the other streams mentioned, join the Brazos above the old crossing and make it impassable by the lower road. De Mézières declares that the land between this river and the Colorado abounds with game and wild cattle. The country is level and covered with beautiful and excellent pastures and many medicinal plants. There are several creeks and much good timber in the woods, as well as many tasty fruits.[39]

Two leagues beyond the crossing of Aguayo, the river divides itself into three branches.[40]

22a. *The Brazos.* The Brazos river has its source to the northwest. Besides its other branch it has four large tributaries, and thirteen creeks join its main stream. It runs for two hundred leagues, east-southeast, to its mouth. Its lower branch has its origin in a large lake. The upper branch carries a larger volume of water and empties directly into the sea eight leagues below the Trinity.[41] Between the Brazos and the Trinity, eighteen leagues to the north of Bucareli,[42] is located a ranchería of Quitseys Indians in a wide and fertile valley. The road that leads to this delightful place is over steep and rocky hills, deep glens, creeks, lakes, and bogs, but all is covered with beautiful vines, weighted down with delicious fruit. There are also viperine, *contrahierba,*[43] sassafras, and *camotitos.*[44] The latter have more than once saved Bucareli from hunger.

Fifteen leagues to the west of this ranchería is the place called La Tortuga [the Tortoise], of which we shall speak in the paragraph on the Tancagues Indians [Tonkawa]. The country throughout the whole distance is suitable for cultivation, consisting of woods and plains separated from one another by frequent brooks.

Sixteen leagues beyond, in the same direction, and over similar country and woods, is the abode of the Tuacanas [Tawakoni] on the Brazos whose lands will be described in their place. At this point the river is navigable part of the year. The portion of the river between the first and second ranchería of the Tuacanas [eight leagues beyond] is especially attractive, one of its banks consisting of pleasant hills and the other of beautiful meadows.

It is eighty leagues from this place to San Theodoro on Red river or the river of Natchitoches. The beauty of the lands that lie between cannot be exaggerated if one considers the number of creeks and springs that encourage the irrigation of the adjacent plains, the woods that beautify their banks, the rocks that, making their bottoms firm, facilitate the construction of dams; and, finally, the abundance of all kinds of game. From the banks of the Brazos, where the Tuacanas live, to San Theodoro on the Natchitoches [Red river] there runs to the right of the road an unbroken forest, very appropriately called by the natives the Grand forest. It extends for eighty leagues and is from one to three leagues wide throughout. It is very dense and seems to have been placed by providence expressly to guide the ignorant traveler and to afford protection to the weak on this dangerous road.[45]

According to reports made by Ybarbo, the Brazos does not lose itself in lakes, as many of the other rivers do on the coast, but enters proudly into the Mexican gulf, defying the sea with its high banks that encourage the establishment of a fort to defend its entrance, at the same time that it invites [the explorer] to examine the vast unsettled lands through which it flows.[46]

23. *San Norberto.* Two leagues north-northeast from the second branch [47] of the Brazos is San Norberto creek.

24. *San Antonio de Padua.* Five leagues northeast of San Norberto is the creek called San Antonio de Padua, the tree-covered banks of which can be seen from a distance, the land being open and hilly. The view is beautiful, though the land is cut at intervals by very deep ravines which must be, in reality [in time of rains], torrents.[48]

25. *San José.* The land to the north is level and open, with good pastures and many flowers as far as the San José, the banks of which are formed of whitish earth and resemble the benches of an amphitheater with ledges showing the successive wearing away by the current. It is bordered by lofty trees that invite one to rest.[49]

26. *San José de los Apaches.* A short distance beyond the San José is another beautiful brook called San José de los Apaches, because of its proximity to the lands inhabited by these Indians.[50]

27. *San Joaquín y Santa Ana.* For seven leagues to the northeast the country continues similar in all respects to that already described, there being a mesquite grove near the creek called the San Joaquín and Santa Ana, and the vegetation along its banks being as dense as that of the preceding ones.[51]

28. *Jesús Nazareno.* A short distance from this creek is a river called Jesús Nazareno, which is the second main branch of the Brazos. Two leagues above the point where Aguayo crossed it, another stream from the west joins it and the two form a large river along the banks of which there are many lofty and beautiful trees.[52]

29. *Santa María lake.* Two leagues to the east-northeast, through shady and delightful woods, is lake Santa María. It is about a quarter of a league across and its water is good though not very deep.[53]

30. *San Jorge.* For three leagues to the east-northeast the country continues woody, with pleasant clearings, to the edge of a wide plain. To the southeast the land is rich and is covered with mesquite and many live oaks. There are some stretches of sand and some deep and rough ravines. At a distance of five leagues, after crossing a creek without a name, is found the San Jorge [Saint George], a permanent stream.[54]

31. *San Juan de los Jumanos.* Four leagues to the southeast, over not too heavily wooded land, with high hills covered with grass and flowers, is the creek called San Juan de los Jumanos.[55]

32. *Patrocinio de Nuestra Señora.* The woods continue to the southeast, increasing in density and with some

ravines, to a muddy creek. Six leagues beyond is the creek named Patrocinio de Nuestra Señora.[56]

33. *Angel de la Guarda.* After three leagues of mesquite wooded land, a prairie is reached, more than a league in width, at the end of which begins a heavy forest of high trees through which runs a beautiful stream. A high hill is then crossed, beyond which the woods continue, chiefly oaks, followed by a mesquite grove that ends in a rather narrow clearing where the hot spring called Angel de la Guarda is found.[57]

34. *Nuestra Señora del Camino.* A small creek is crossed to the east-southeast before entering a dense wood of walnuts, oaks, grapevines, plums, and medlars, which extends for about two leagues to where there is a very clear creek. This is bordered by poplars, willows, and vines. Our course lay along the stream for the space of two more leagues before we camped at a place called Nuestra Señora del Camino.[58]

35. *Nuestra Señora de Guía.* A forest of oaks and walnuts continues to the northeast for the space of a league and a quarter, so thick that it was necessary to cut out a path. There are a few creeks and at the end of the wood is a lake in a peaceful meadow, beyond which the forest continues, chiefly of oaks and live oaks. An elevated plain is next encountered, broad and pleasing, dotted with groves of oaks and live oaks, and four leagues beyond is the creek called Nuestra Señora de Guía.[59]

36. *Nuestra Señora de la Estrella.* To the east there is a light wood through which three creeks flow. There are many plums and oaks. The land is sandy for a distance, then two other creeks with very steep banks are crossed. The land beyond resembles volcanic rock, is heavily wooded, and has many nettles. Nine leagues be-

yond the last creek mentioned is Nuestra Señora de la Estrella.[60]

37. *San Buenaventura.* For nine leagues the wood continues, consisting of lofty trees and heavy thickets of chaparral, the land being broken and rugged, with many bogs and shallow lakes. Veering to the south the road is made easier because the ground is higher and firmer. Before reaching San Buenaventura, however, three creeks must be crossed. At this point the two roads, the new and the old, or the upper and the lower, come together. The latter is the one closer to the coast or more to the south, the former is the one farther to the north.[61]

38. *Nuestra Señora del Rosario.* After crossing the San Buenaventura one comes to a lake called Santa Anna, commonly known as " las cargas," because the provisions that were being conducted for the relief of the missions in 1719 were hidden on its banks for eight long months without having been discovered during all that time by the Indians who frequently traverse those regions, nor having been spoiled by the rains, the sun, or the floods. The road lies through light woods with several openings. Two small creeks are crossed, and four leagues beyond is Nuestra Señora del Rosario which carries more water than the two preceding streams.[62]

39. *Carrizo.* For two leagues the light woods of live oaks continue, then the country is level and clear as far as Carrizo creek, the banks of which are steep and difficult to cross, particularly in time of rains.[63]

40. *Santa Clara.* The country is level as far as Santa Clara creek, called by some " de las cruces," because of the many crosses placed on the trees in its vicinity.[64]

41. *San Fernando.* Beyond Santa Clara the land is rugged, more thickly wooded, and with a few hills and clearings till San Fernando creek is reached.

42. *Nuestra Señora del Buen Suceso.* There is a wide plain which extends for six leagues, at the edge of which is the small creek called Nuestra Señora del Buen Suceso. Though this stream is small it is permanent.[65]

43. *Santa Rosa.* The five remaining leagues to the Trinity are lightly wooded with lofty trees, and there are a few clearings or openings. In this distance two boggy creeks are crossed before coming to the valley of Linares, where there are two lakes before Santa Rosa creek is reached.[66] The woods of oaks, walnuts, and pines continue with few clearings to the famous Trinity river, which is five leagues from Buen Suceso.

44. *Trinity river.* It [the Trinity] flows down from the northwest, having its source in the land of the Taovayases. It rises in three springs and is joined by many others immediately. Three creeks join their waters to its stream and it flows in an easterly direction to the sea. It is said that, notwithstanding the fact that the main flow spreads out considerably, the river is deep enough at its mouth to permit the navigation of two-masted ships. Its mouth is one hundred and fifty leagues from its source. It carries considerable water and is said to have its source to the northwest, being formed by two creeks that soon flow into a spacious basin where they are joined by many others. After winding continuously it enters the sea. (See paragraph 532.) Its bottom is filled with fine pebbles.[67]

45. *San Juan.* A league beyond the Trinity is San Juan creek, a good stream with shady banks.

46. *Santa Efigenia.* The next four leagues are covered with open woods, chiefly pines, walnuts, live oaks, oaks, and vines. Before reaching Santa Efigenia two small creeks are crossed.[68]

47. *Santa Coleta.* The country is somewhat rolling, with many trees, chiefly walnuts, pines, and chestnuts. After crossing two small creeks, the Santa Efigenia (*sic*)

[Santa Coleta] is reached, seven leagues from Santa Efigenia.

48. *San Pedro.* Three leagues beyond, the land and the woods being similar to those described, San Pedro creek is reached. It was here that the presidio and missions of the Texas Indians were situated.[69]

49. *Laguna del Presidio.* A short distance beyond, after passing some hills and ravines similarly covered with trees, are the plains where the presidio de los Texas,[70] established in 1716, was built. It was near a lake of fresh water formed by a spring in its center. Four leagues beyond is the Neches river.

50. *Neches river.* The Neches river has its source near the pueblo of the Navedachos [Nabedache] to the north-northwest. It flows eighty leagues from the Angelina, a stream that joins it farther down, and together they enter the sea with sufficient water to afford easy access to vessels. At the close of 1777, an English packetboat took refuge in its mouth and was robbed by the Attacapa Indians. Up to the present the whereabouts of its cargo has not been determined. Probably it fell into the hands of the Indians. Its mouth is fifteen leagues beyond the Trinity and marks the boundary between Louisiana and Texas on the coast.[71]

51. *Arroyo de San Francisco.* Two leagues beyond the Neches is the creek of the old mission of San Francisco to which the presidio was moved the second time in 1716.[72]

52. *Nuestra Señora de las Nieves.* The woods, chiefly oaks and grapevines, continue, two more creeks are crossed, and where a broad plain begins, four leagues from the Neches, is Nuestra Señora de las Nieves.[73]

53. *Santa Bárbara.* The woods continue, interspersed by a few plains, then a small stream is crossed, its banks covered with wild flowers and, after passing a plain that extends for about two leagues, Santa Bárbara creek is

reached. This stream is swollen the greater part of the year and the Indians keep a canoe there to cross it, though this is not necessary in the dry season. It is less than half a league from the abandoned mission of La Purísima Concepción [74] and about five from Las Nieves creek.

54. *Angelina river.* The Angelina river is eight leagues from the Neches and is of almost the same volume. It runs through the land of the Texas Indians, which is very fertile. The river is not navigable. It has its source about twenty leagues above the crossing of the road to Los Adaes and it joins the Neches about the same distance below.[75]

56 [*sic*]. *Atoyaque.* The Atoyaque river is crossed ten leagues from Nacogdoches and thirty from its source. It is joined by the creek of Los Ais and flows into the Angelina. Its rock bed offers facilities for the construction of dams. On its banks are found enormous cedars [junipers], and game is very abundant.[76]

57. *San Francisco de Sabinas.* The Sabine river is thirteen leagues from Los Adaes, twenty from Natchitoches, and its source is forty [from San Theodoro]. In addition to El Lobanillo, three other streams join it. It has its source above the said San Theodoro, in the neighboring plains, and flows south-southeast for a distance of two hundred leagues to the gulf of Mexico, into which it empties near Opelousas, in Louisiana. Its navigation is practical only in canoes or very small boats and only near its mouth, either because of its small volume or its frequent and dangerous rapids. Its floods are periodic, both in winter and spring, and greatly to be feared as they spread for a distance of as much as three leagues. There is no other river that causes so much damage.[77]

58. *Los Adaes.* The Paraje de los Adaes [Place of Los Adaes] is on the stream that bears its name and is seven leagues from Natchitoches. Though the lands lack

irrigation, they are extremely fertile, abounding in good pastures, wood, quarries, and salines. The Spaniards did not avail themselves of these advantages, a fact the celebrated marquis of Altamira deplores.[78]

59. *Laguna de los Adaes.* Between Natchitoches and Los Adaes, about a league from the presidio and four from Natchitoches, is the lake of Los Adaes [Spanish lake]. It is two leagues in circumference, and the Cadodachos river [79] flows through it and joins that of Natchitoches [Red river]. The latter stream is navigable for sixty leagues, the distance between the two presidios of Louisiana.[80]

60. *Red river.* The Rio Vermejo or Natchitoches [present Red river] is the boundary between the two adjacent provinces of Texas and Louisiana.[81] It has its source in the mountain ranges of New Mexico, four days' journey above [the land of] the Taovayases. Its upper stream is divided into three branches that come together near the pueblo of San Theodoro. The branch farthest to the north has a large and beautiful saline near its source. The volume of its waters, however, is small, except in time of floods, which last only a short while, because its descent is very rapid. Other rivers empty into its basin and this makes it navigable. It flows east-southeast for five hundred leagues from its source to its junction with the Mississippi, sixty leagues above New Orleans. It affords easy communication between Natchitoches and the neighboring Indian nations, as well as with that metropolis [New Orleans].[82]

61. It is not to be wondered at that by the lower road one should not find many rivers, creeks, and springs, for these join each other and combine on their way to the sea. The lakes multiply in number, because the coast that forms the southern limits of the province is very low.[83]

62. The coast region is not only insufficiently known,

but the almost total ignorance concerning it reflects upon the activity of the garrisons stationed there and has been detrimental, perhaps, to the best interests of the state.[84]

63. The land south of the town of the Tuacanas [Tawakoni] [85] is superior to the rest of the province, with broad plains, rich pastures, delightful woods, and abundant water. De Mézières crossed seven streams, besides the San Andrés, in a distance of fifty leagues, and these were at such proportional distances from each other that they seemed to have been placed there on purpose for the convenience of the traveler.

64. There is not, in the entire province, a river, creek, brook, lake, or pool, no matter how small, in which trout, *pullón,*[86] catfish, sardines, carp, eels, barbel, sea fish, robalo,[87] turtles, alligators, and other kinds of fish are not found in incredible numbers, to say nothing of the seashore where fishing is unexcelled. Otter and beaver are also found in all the rivers and streams. The number of ducks, wild geese, and cranes, of all kinds, that are seen as soon as the cold weather begins, and that remain here until the heat drives them farther north, is surprising. Along the banks of the streams and the outskirts of the woods the droves of wild turkeys are so numerous that they disturb the traveler with their clucking. The number of magpies, quails of all kinds, and wild hens, is incalculable.

65. The fields are covered with thyme, lavender, sage, maiden-hair ferns, celery, wormwood, indigo plant, viperine, wild sweet potatoes, antidotal herb, sassafras, flax, wild marjoram, a species of wild onion—very tasty,—and a plant that resembles the lettuce and is eaten as a salad, which is very good. There are found also a great variety of blackberries, strawberries, rose bushes similar to those of Castile, wild potatoes, and a thousand other aromatic plants and species of grass that attract the wild

horses and cattle which multiply so rapidly that one cannot journey through the province without meeting herds of two, three, and even four thousand head at a time.[88]

66. The woods and forests consist mainly of oaks of various kinds, poplars, willows, elms, mulberries, black and white walnuts, cedars, cypresses, mesquites, chestnuts, pines, *zozocoxote*—a tree resembling in quality the wood of the sweet gum tree,—hazel nuts, figs, peaches, and other fruit trees common to the missions and settlements, laurel, tamarisk medlars, which in season offer the traveler a variety of fruits, and above all, grapevines. These are so abundant and of such excellent quality that to form an idea [regarding them] it is necessary to hear what De Mézières, who admired them during his journey from the Navedacho [Nabedache] to the Quitseis, has to say. For the space of fifteen leagues, the distance traveled, he declares that the country is made up of gentle hills and valleys, with many permanent streams, and vines in such quantity and so distributed that they seem more the result of industry than of nature. Some creep along the ground, and their fruit serves as food for frugivorous animals; others climb the highest trees, the branches of which, though they keep the generous warmth of the sun from them, do not impede the fruit from reaching a certain degree of ripeness, pleasing to the taste. The most common is the muscatel, of which he says: " we dismounted every little while, appearing more like vintagers than soldiers. If cultivation and industry should come to this spot, I believe it would gain renown among the vineyards of highest grade." [89]

There is also a tree which is not very large and that bears a fruit that greatly resembles the bergamot pear, but so poisonous that whoever eats of it dies immediately. There is another tree of similar nature, a twig of which was used by a soldier to stir his mush. He no sooner tasted it than he became swollen, and his life was saved only by the strenuous and efficient efforts of his companions.[90]

66 [*sic*]. The abundance of fruits accounts for the multiplicity of all kinds of game. Thus one sees an incredible number of rabbits, hares, goats, wildcats, deer, boars, bears, and buffalo—the most useful animal to the Indian. In addition to furnishing meat that deserves first rank for its flavor and healthfulness, its brains serve to soften leather; its horns to make spoons, cups, and ornaments for the head or the home; the shoulder blades to dig and cultivate the soil; the ligaments to string the bows; the hoofs to make glue used in tipping the arrows; the bristles to make rope; the wool to make belts, ribbons, and other dress ornaments; the skin to make saddles, rope, shields, tents, shirts, boots, and shoes [leggings and moccasins], and coverlets against the cold or rain.

There are snakes and water serpents that are very dangerous; also spiders, such as the poisonous monilla;[91] all kinds of mosquitoes, yellow jackets, and horseflies, especially one called Apache, whose sting is worse than that of a bee. There are numerous gnats and countless ticks.[92]

NOTES TO GENERAL DESCRIPTION OF TEXAS

1. The Spanish league is roughly estimated to be the equivalent of three miles. A statute or land league is equal to 4.83 kilometers, a nautical or marine league to 5.56 kilometers. The Spanish judicial league, so generally employed in land measurements in the Southwest, is equivalent approximately to 2.65 miles.

2. San Theodoro de los Taovayases was on Red River. "The point seems to have been not far from the present town of Ringgold," declares Bolton. De Mézières named it San Theodoro in honor of Theodoro de Croix, commandant general of the Provincias Internas. Bolton, *De Mézières*, I, p. 114. Espíritu Santo bay is modern Matagorda bay.

3. The first to relate the incident to which the name *Texas* is attributed was Fr. Damian Mançanet in his letter to Don Carlos de Sigüenza y Góngora, undated, and until recently the only account of the De León expedition. "Some of them—and among these was their captain —came out and embraced us, saying: 'thechas! thechas!' which means 'friends! friends!'" Casis, "Carta de Don Damian Manzanet a Don Carlos de Sigüenza sobre el descubrimiento de la Bahía del Espíritu Santo," Texas State Historical Association, *The Quarterly*, II, p. 287.

Morfi evidently used the version of this incident found in Espinosa's Crónica, in which *Texia* is used instead of *thechas*. Espinosa, *Chrónica Apostólica y Seráphica*, p. 408.

4. This sentence is taken from Morfi's *Memorias*, because it seems to have been inadvertently left out of the final copy of his *Historia*. Morfi, *Memorias para la Historia de Texas*, MS., Libro I, p. 2.

5. The presidio of San Sabá was founded in 1757, but its real name was presidio of San Luis de las Amarillas. "It was founded on the San Sabá River, near modern Menardville." Bolton, *De Mézières*, I, p. 64.

6. The San Sabá joins the Colorado. It is strange that Morfi should have fallen into this error, for the Lafora map of 1771, which he must have known since he quotes from the report of the marquis of Rubí frequently, shows the San Sabá entering the Colorado. Lafora accompanied Rubí in his expedition and drew the map on his return. *Mapa de la frontera de Nueva España . . . por el Ingeniero D. Nicolás de Lafora*, Mexico a 30 de agosto de 1771.

7. The Chanas is the modern Llano river which, as Morfi correctly observes, empties into the Colorado. Bolton, *De Mézières*, I, pp. 65, 299.

8. "The Medina river forms the dividing line between the provinces of Coahuila and Texas. . . . Its bed is very deep as the result of the violent and frequent torrents that flow into it during the rainy season and of the soft nature of the soil. In time of drought the stream becomes intermittent, but there are always large pools or lakes where the traveler can provide himself with water and fish." Morfi, *Memorias*, Libro I, p. 3.

The Medina was considered the western boundary of Texas for a time. Hackett, *Pichardo's Treatise,* I, pp. 7, 64, 90, 96. As late as 1815 the Medina is shown as the dividing line between the two provinces in the *Mapa de las Provincias Internas* made for Arredondo. The Puelles Mapa Geográfico of 1807, however, shows the Nueces river as the dividing line.

9. Reference is made here to the main crossing on the *camino real* that ran due northeast of San Antonio, generally known as the upper road. Bolton, *Map of Texas and Adjacent Regions in the Eighteenth Century.*

10. A careful examination of the diary of the Aguayo expedition shows no such river or stream listed. In Morfi's *Memorias* there is no mention of such a creek, though Morfi observes that De Mézières called the Alarcón the "Arcón," adding "this is excusable, particularly in a Frenchman." Morfi, *Memorias,* Libro I, p. 4; Peña, "Derrotero de la Expedición," ff. 7–8. Further confusion as to the identity of this creek arises from the fact that the Guadalupe river referred to may not be the present Guadalupe. See note 18.

11. "On its banks the wretched fort of Santa Cruz, built with wooden stockades around it, was established. Here a detachment from the presidio of San Antonio was placed to protect the approach to that city and La Bahía." Morfi, *Memorias,* Libro I, p. 4. Lafora's map shows the presidio or fort, as does Bolton in his *Map of Texas.*

12. A vara is approximately 33 inches.

13. Morfi had access to many of the reports of De Mézières. In the archives of San Francisco el Grande, now in the National Library of Mexico, more than 200 pages of copies from De Mézières' reports and letters were found by the present writer, together with the copy of the *Historia.* From the frequent references to De Mézières' work among the Indians it is safe to deduce that Morfi made free use of these copies. Bolton published most of the De Mézières reports in his *De Mézières and the Louisiana-Texas Frontier, 1768–1780.*

14. At the time Morfi wrote this description it was not known that the San Antonio joins the Guadalupe before it reaches the bay. The Lafora map of 1771 shows the two rivers entering the bay separately, as does the Pichardo map, *El Nuevo Mexico y Tierras Adyacentes,* of 1811. Puelles, in his Mapa Geográfico of 1807, however, shows the two rivers joining as they enter the bay of Espíritu Santo. Austin's map of 1829 indicates more accurately the San Antonio joining the Guadalupe before the latter enters the bay. Lafora, *Mapa de la Frontera;* Pichardo, *El Nuevo México y Tierras Adyacentes,* 1811; Puelles, *Mapa Geográfico,* 1807; Castañeda, *Three Manuscript Maps of Texas by Stephen F. Austin.*

15. Peña, in his "Derrotero" of the Aguayo expedition, says (p. 7): "We reached a stream, which, having no name, the Governor called San Pascual Baylón." On the same day, May 17, the expedition crossed three different streams. Buckley, in her excellent study on the Aguayo expedi-

tion, has tentatively identified two of the three streams: San Pascual Baylón, the Guadalupe, and the San Ybón. The Guadalupe she declares is the present Comal, crossed by Aguayo almost at the site of present New Braunfels, and the San Ybón she believes is the present Guadalupe. Nothing is said about the San Pascual Baylón. Buckley, "The Aguayo Expedition into Texas and Louisiana, 1719–1722," Texas State Hist. Assn., *The Quarterly,* xv, pp. 36–37. Of the various maps examined, only the Lafora map of 1771 shows a river designated as "Alarcón."

16. This is the river identified as the Comal. Buckley, *loc. cit.*

17. The reference here is to the present San Marcos. Peña, "Derrotero," f. 7; Buckley, *op. cit.,* xv, p. 37; Bolton, *De Mézières,* II, p. 284.

18. The description given here fits the Comal, as Buckley points out. Evidently Morfi believed this stream was a part of the Guadalupe main stream. He follows the "Derrotero" of Peña very closely. Buckley, "Aguayo Expedition," xv, pp. 36–37; Peña, "Derrotero," f. 7. *Doradillo* is evidently a species of *Asplenium,* the spleenwort.

19. Bolton, *De Mézières,* II, pp. 284, 315. Reference is made to the published account by Bolton as more accessible than the manuscript copy of the same reports used by Morfi.

20. This river has been identified with the main stream of the present Guadalupe. Buckley, *loc. cit.;* Peña, "Derrotero," f. 7. This river is not designated by the name given to it by Morfi in any of the maps examined.

21. This stream is the lower branch of the San Marcos. Buckley, *loc. cit.*

22. The Lipan Indians were one of the Apache tribes. "Till after the opening of the eighteenth century the Apache tribes, especially the Lipan, regarded as their own the territory from the upper Nueces and Medina Rivers to the upper Red and Colorado, while their range between summer and winter might cover many hundred miles. . . . By the middle of the century the more usual haunts of the Lipan were the districts about the San Sabá River, in west central Texas." Bolton, *De Mézières,* I, pp. 24–25.

23. This has been identified as the main stream of the San Marcos. Buckley, *op. cit.,* xv, p. 37.

24. This is the present Plum creek. *Loc. cit.*

25. "We traveled . . . to a small creek which, not having a name, the governor called San Bernardino." Peña, "Derrotero," f. 8.

26. Since Morfi used chiefly the diary of the Aguayo expedition for this description it is safe to assume that this stream is Onion creek, crossed by Aguayo near present-day McKinney falls. Buckley, "Aguayo Expedition," p. 38, n. 2; Peña, "Derrotero," f. 8. The stream evidently derived its name from an abundance of ticks encountered there.

27. Bolton, *De Mézières,* II, p. 283. This is the present San Marcos. Buckley, *op. cit.,* p. 38; Hackett, *Pichardo,* I, p. 483.

28. Morfi has followed almost verbatim the description given by De Mézières in his letter to Croix of September 25, 1779. Bolton, *De Mézières,* II, pp. 283–284.

29. The name given to this little creek does not appear in the diary of the Aguayo expedition from which the statement about the latitude is taken. Peña, "Derrotero," f. 9.

30. This is the present-day Brushy creek. Buckley, *op. cit.,* p. 38, n. 4.

31. There is some confusion here due to Morfi's use of the diary of the Aguayo expedition and the reports of De Mézières alternately. Here he means the present Colorado as described by De Mézières. In his *Memorias,* he has the San Xavier before the Colorado; in making the final draft of the *Historia,* he followed the same order; but, after revision, he changed the numbering of paragraphs 18 and 19 to correspond to the altered order of the rivers. Peña, *loc. cit.;* Morfi, *Memorias,* Libro I; *Historia,* MS., pp. 5–7.

32. The river described here is the present Colorado, as noted by De Mézières, from whose report Morfi quotes freely. Bolton, *De Mézières,* II, p. 283. Morfi used copies of the reports of De Mézières, as shown by the documents found together with his *Historia.*

33. This is the present San Gabriel. Bolton, *op. cit.,* II, pp. 281, 283. Hackett, *Pichardo,* I, pp. 483, 489–490.

34. The passage quoted here is also found in Bolton, *De Mézières,* II, pp. 281–282; a MS. copy is in the archive of San Francisco el Grande. The Panis-Mahas here mentioned were evidently the Wichita, although the term was more applicable to the related Skidi Pawnee.

35. Peña, "Derrotero," f. 9.

36. From this point Morfi follows closely the course taken by the Aguayo expedition. "We stopped at a creek which, having no name and being near the San Xavier, the governor called the San Ignacio." Peña, *loc. cit.*

37. These two streams have been identified with the modern Salado and Lampasas. Buckley, *op. cit.,* p. 39.

38. This is the present Little river. Buckley, *op. cit.,* p. 39, n. 1. It has also been identified with the Brazos. Hackett, *Pichardo,* I, p. 468.

39. Bolton, *De Mézières,* II, pp. 187–188.

40. Peña, "Derrotero," f. 10.

41. As usual, Morfi has used the Aguayo diary and the description of De Mézières and tried to harmonize them. Little was known at the time about the location of the mouth of the Brazos. For a full discussion of this subject, see Hackett, *Pichardo,* I, pp. 385–388.

42. Bucareli, better known as Nuestra Señora del Pilar de Bucareli, was established in 1774 by the exiles from Los Adaes under the leadership of Gil Ybarbo. "The site designated . . . was on the right bank of the Trinity River, at Paso Tomás, a place which was apparently at the cross-

ing of the San Antonio Road and the La Bahía Road over that stream." Bolton, *Texas in the Middle Eighteenth Century,* p. 405.

43. An antidotal plant, *Dorstenia contrayerba.*

44. A species of sweet potatoes that grew wild. The name is the Spanish diminutive form of Aztec *camotl.*

45. The entire description of the country between the Brazos and the Trinity is based on the reports of 1778 of De Mézières to Croix. In places Morfi follows the originals almost word for word, while in others he makes minor changes. Bolton, *De Mézières,* II, pp. 188–201; archive of San Francisco el Grande.

46. Antonio Gil Ybarbo, *alcalde mayor* of Bucareli, made several explorations of the coast region about the mouths of the Colorado, the Brazos, and the Trinity between 1776 and 1778. For a complete discussion of his findings, see Hackett, *Pichardo,* I, pp. 384–391.

47. The second branch referred to here is not the main stream of the Brazos, but the Lampasas from which the Aguayo expedition set out on June 6, after a wait of three days on account of its swollen condition; this creek is only three-quarters of a league from the branch identified as Little river, and two leagues from the second or Lampasas. Peña, "Derrotero," f. 10; Buckley, "Aguayo Expedition," p. 39, n. 1; Hackett, *Pichardo,* I, pp. 338, 491, 538.

48. Peña, "Derrotero," f. 10; Hackett, *Pichardo,* I, p. 338.

49. Peña, "Derrotero," f. 10.

50. Both Aguayo and Rivera passed this stream. It is believed by Pichardo to be the one on which La Salle was murdered. Peña, "Derrotero," f. 10; Hackett, *Pichardo,* I, pp. 344, 388, 541.

51. Peña, "Derrotero," f. 10; Hackett, *Pichardo,* I, pp. 338, 541. Pichardo suggests the possibility of this being the site where La Salle was murdered. He suggests the same possibility in the case of several other small streams in this section.

52. According to Peña's diary, it was only half a league from the crossing to the point of juncture with the other river identified as the Bosque. According to Buckley, the point where Aguayo crossed the river was near the present city of Waco. Peña, "Derrotero," f. 11; Buckley, "Aguayo Expedition," p. 40.

53. Peña, "Derrotero," f. 11.

54. The unnamed creek referred to is the one called by Aguayo San Silverio Papa. Morfi either did not read the Peña diary carefully or the copy he used was defective, for he has followed the Aguayo expedition from the crossing of the Brazos to this point. After crossing the Brazos, Aguayo took an almost due north course, retracing his steps a few days later from San Silverio Papa. Peña, "Derrotero," f. 11; Hackett, *Pichardo,* I, pp. 339, 528; Buckley, "Aguayo Expedition," p. 40.

55. As stated in the preceding note, after going about fifteen miles northeast of present-day Waco, the Aguayo expedition retraced its steps,

following closely the eastern bank of the Brazos river. The creeks mentioned in this and the preceding paragraph, therefore, are small tributaries on the east side of the Brazos. Buckley, "Aguayo Expedition," p. 40.

56. Peña, "Derrotero," f. 11.

57. *Loc. cit.;* Hackett, *Pichardo,* I, p. 339.

58. Morfi has quoted directly from the Peña diary without changing even the person of the original version. Peña, "Derrotero," f. 11.

59. The description of the country in this paragraph is based entirely on the diary of the Aguayo expedition.

60. Peña, "Derrotero," f. 12.

61. The San Buenaventura has been identified with the Navasoto river. Father Maçanet first learned the name from the Indians who, he claimed, called it *Nabatsoto.* Espinosa, in 1716, was the first to call it the San Buenaventura, the marquis of Aguayo keeping the name. Rivera called it the Navasoto in 1727, and this name was kept by Solís in 1767. Buckley, "The Aguayo Expedition," p. 41.

62. Hackett, *Pichardo,* I, p. 340; Peña, "Derrotero," f. 13.

63. *Loc. cit.*

64. *Loc. cit.*

65. *Ibid.,* ff. 13–14.

66. In the manuscript Morfi has placed a note after Santa Rosa, on the margin, that reads "See map; the Navasoto river, not a very large but very rapid stream with beautiful banks (Solís)." All efforts to locate the map that must have accompanied the manuscript proved futile. None of the maps that are available give any information that would identify this creek with the Navasoto (see note 61). Solís, in his diary, under date of April 27, refers to the Navasoto in the words cited by Morfi, but it is evident that he is referring to the present Navasoto. Forrestal, "The Solís Diary," Texas Catholic Historical Society, *Preliminary Studies,* I, no. 6, p. 26.

67. In the *Memorias,* Morfi gave much more space to the geographic description and the habits and customs of the natives. In the final copy of his *Historia,* he tried to boil down the detailed information of his *Memorias* (notes), and it is for this reason that, as in the above paragraph, there is some confusion and, at times, awkward repetitions. His description of the Trinity in the *Memorias* is so much better that it seems advisable to include it here. "This river of the Holy Trinity has its source to the northwest, above the Pueblo of San Theodoro of the Taovayases (whose lands it waters). It rises in three springs which come together in a large bed that permits it to receive the numerous creeks that enrich it. Its bottom is made up, in several places, of flint stones or little pebbles. It is navigable the greater part of its course, which is one hundred and fifty leagues to the sea, where it empties to the east. It is subject to frequent and terrific floods during the rainy season or the melting of the snow. It is not difficult to avoid their consequences by selecting a high

place along its banks, but the indolence of the settlers of Bucareli was responsible for their being surprised by a flood that destroyed their wretched huts. The bar at the mouth of the river, where it enters the sea, though it does not offer facilities for a good port, permits the entrance of two-masted ships." Morfi, *Memorias,* Libro I.

It was De León that gave this river its name. Terán knew it was the Trinity, but, with his penchant for changing names, called it Encarnación del Verbo. Espinosa, in 1716, named it San Juan Bautista, but Ramón, Rivera, Lafora, and Solís consistently called it the Trinity. Buckley, "Aguayo Expedition," p. 42.

68. Peña, "Derrotero," f. 14; Hackett, *Pichardo,* I, pp. 335, 340.

69. The old mission of San Francisco de los Texas was first established in 1690, about four and a half miles from the mouth of the San Pedro and seven or eight miles from the crossing. Bolton, "Native Tribes . . . ," in Texas State Hist. Assn., *The Quarterly,* XI, p. 265.

70. Reference here is made to the Presidio of Nuestra Señora de los Dolores founded by Ramón in 1716. It was refounded by Aguayo in 1720. "The Presidio was one league from the mission (Concepción) which in turn was half a league from the Angelina. It occupied an advantageous position on a hill, overlooking the country." Buckley, "Aguayo Expedition," p. 48.

71. On the margin, next to the name, Morfi has added the following note: "It forms a small island at its mouth, about two hundred varas in diameter, firm and easily fortified, with no other approach than that of the river. See map." As already stated, the map referred to by Morfi has not been located. The map drawn by Ibarbo after his exploration of the coast region in 1777 shows a small island at the mouth. Hackett, *Pichardo,* I, p. 388.

72. The reference is taken from the diary of the Aguayo expedition (Peña, "Derrotero," f. 16) and refers to the reëstablishment by Ramón, before the second abandonment of 1719.

73. *Ibid.,* f. 17.

74. Of the East Texas missions this was the only one that had not been totally destroyed after the abandonment of 1719. It was refounded by Aguayo on August 8, 1720. The Santa Bárbara mentioned here is the present Angelina river. For the exact location of the mission, see Bolton, "Native Tribes," *op. cit.,* XI, p. 269; Buckley, "Aguayo Expedition," p. 47; Peña, "Derrotero," ff. 17–18.

75. Speaking of how this river came to be named, Morfi declares, in his *Memorias,* "It took its name from an Indian maid of the Texas nation who had been baptized and reared in the mission of San Juan Bautista, on the Rio Grande, in Coahuila, who, after having returned to her country, proved very useful to the Spaniards because of her knowledge of the language and her good services in winning the goodwill of her people for the Spaniards." It is interesting to note that the associa-

tion of this woman with the name of the river, attributed by Buckley to Bolton (*Aguayo Expedition*, p. 42, n. 5), was known to Morfi at the time he made his notes. St. Denis' companions found a woman named Angelique among the tribe of the Hasinai in 1712. Later, in 1720, Belle-Isle was befriended by this same woman, and her two sons guided him back to Louisiana. Margry, *Découvertes et établissements des Français dans l'Ouest et dans le Sud de l'Amérique Septentrionale;* also Bolton, *De Mézières,* II, pp. 262–263.

76. Paragraph no. 55 is deleted in the original, though the enumeration is not changed. It reads, "At the foot of the hills of the old mission of the Nacogdoches there is a beautiful large stream to which Bucareli was moved but to little advantage because they could not irrigate their lands."

It seems that the Atoyaque was first named by Rivera (Rivera, *Diario,* entry for September 11); Solís, in 1767, says that it was "a large river with pleasant, shady banks" (entry for May 4); De Mézières describes it thus: "The Atoyaque River flows fifteen leagues from that of Sabinas, ten from Nacodoches, thirty from its source, and an almost equal distance from the Angelinas River, which is farther up. Its bottom is of stone; it abounds in fish, and its banks are covered with very high cedars, which furnish the best of timber for building and are the haunts of much wild game." Bolton, *De Mézières,* II, p. 309.

77. It may be said that this description follows closely that given by De Mézières, though there are some notable additions, such as the information concerning the number of tributaries, which De Mézières does not mention. Bolton, *De Mézières,* II, pp. 256–257, 307–308. For a detailed discussion of its course and mouth, see Hackett, *Pichardo,* I, pp. 371–375.

Opposite the margin and obviously intended as an annotation to be added to this paragraph, Morfi has the following observation, taken mainly from the diary of the Aguayo expedition.

"A short distance beyond the Sabinas is a small stream called San Nicolás Tolentino. There are several glades with high trees and many rivulets. Six leagues beyond is the brook called Santa Rosa de Lima. The woods and the creeks continue, and eight leagues beyond is San Agustín Creek in the vicinity of a lake." Peña, "Derrotero," ff. 19–20.

78. The first mission founded here was San Miguel de los Adaes. It was abandoned in 1719, as a result of the French hostilities. Aguayo refounded the mission with the same name on October 12, 1721. At the same time he established the presidio of Nuestra Señora del Pilar. This was situated "one-half league beyond where the mission had formerly stood, by a spring or brook, on the side of a hill, where it could command the surrounding country." A garrison of one hundred men with six cannon was left here by Aguayo, showing the importance attached to this farthest outpost of the Texas frontier.

As to the location of the mission it was "opposite, one-fourth of a league from the presidio, with a creek intervening." Father Margil de Jesús remained in charge of this mission. The arroyo between the mission and the presidio has been identified with the Hondo. Buckley declares the location was near the present town of Robeline, Louisiana. Buckley, "Aguayo Expedition," pp. 52–53; Peña, "Derrotero," pp. 20–22. The ground plan of the new presidio and the location of the creek are given in the "Derrotero."

79. A careful examination of the diaries of the various expeditions and of numerous maps shows that Peña is the only one to refer to a *Caudodachos river* as flowing through the lake of Los Adaes, generally known as Spanish lake. Of all the maps examined the only one showing this lake with a small stream flowing from it to the present Red river is the Spanish draft of the Austin map of Texas of 1829. Castañeda and Martin, *Three Manuscript Maps of Texas by Stephen F. Austin.*

80. Morfi has mentioned only Natchitoches, but must mean the distance between this post and the country of the Cadodacho Indians, which was approximately sixty leagues up the river from Natchitoches, as indicated, and was the farthest outpost of the French on Red river.

81. That this was considered by Spain as the boundary of Texas, Pichardo proves several times. Hackett, *Pichardo,* I, pp. 8, 96, 402.

In explaining the origin of the name Natchitoches, Pichardo points out that it is due to the Indian word *nacicit,* which means, in the Indian language, "a place where the soil is the color of red ochre." The name was applied by the Indians to a small creek that ran into the main stream, because its course lay through red soil, a thing equally true of a part of Red river. Hackett, *Pichardo,* I, pp. 496–497.

82. In the main Morfi follows the data given by De Mézières in his various reports of his expedition to Red river. Bolton, *De Mézières,* II, pp. 184, 204.

83. At the time Morfi was writing his history very little was known about the coast region of Texas. In chronological order the expeditions undertaken to explore the coast were led by the following: (1) Barreyro, 1727, who by order of Rivera explored the coast from Espíritu Santo bay eastward for about 180 leagues, supposedly to the Neches. He traveled, going and returning, 363 leagues. No copy of his report is known, other than the summary which Rivera makes of the expedition. Hackett, *Pichardo,* I, pp. 485–486; (2) Luis Cazorla, 1772, who explored the coast region from the Guadalupe to beyond Los Brazos, probably as far as the Trinity (quoted in full in Hackett, *ibid.,* I, pp. 392–397); (3) Gil Ybarbo, 1777, who made a reconnaissance of the coast between the Trinity and the Neches (map published in Hackett, *ibid.,* I, p. 388); (4) Evía, 1785, who explored the coast by sailing from the mouth of the Mississippi to the Rio de Tampico (see Hackett, *ibid.,* I, pp. 350–362). The reports of the second and third were, perhaps, accessible to Morfi, but the last one by Evía, which is the best and most detailed, Morfi did not see, as he died

two years before it was undertaken; consequently, his knowledge of the coast region is very meager and he had reason to deplore the lack of information on the subject.

84. Morfi realized fully the difficulties of making an accurate description of Texas and the confusing nature of the information available to him. In his *Memorias,* he very appropriately expressed his own misgivings and the reasons for some of the apparent contradictions with regard to the various streams and rivers, a thing that worried Pichardo also (see Hackett, *Pichardo,* I, p. xix) and has been something of a nightmare to all who have tried to identify the rivers since.

In his *Memorias,* he says: "Though in all that has been said we have kept before us the most accurate diaries available, particularly those of the very careful observer, Athanase de Mézières, no claim to infallibility in the description is made. The authors of the various diaries could not possibly have seen everything themselves. The information furnished them by the natives, whose natural distrust and malice is well known, added to the misinterpretation of the questions asked them and the confusing nature of their replies, constitute a powerful motive for doubting the veracity of the statements.

"Furthermore, I wish to state that if the names of the rivers and creeks given are compared with those that appear in some of the diaries, notable differences will, no doubt, be found. This is due to the fact that each expedition named them at will, not having at hand the diaries of their predecessors. I have taken the names more commonly used, and in each instance I have expressed the distance from one to the other, both to avoid error as far as possible and to describe the country, giving an idea of the land and supplying the lack of a map." *Memorias,* Libro I.

85. The town of the Tuacanas was situated on the Trinity, about 31° 52′ north latitude and 91° 55′ longitude (See Bolton's *Map of Texas*). Speaking of this town De Mézières says: "I arrived at the pueblo of the Tuacanas, after crossing the large Trinity River, which, when high, forms a peninsula where the village is located. It has only one very narrow entrance, which leads to the plains, for the woods become sparser thenceforward. The houses are thirty-six in number, the warriors one hundred twenty, with women in proportion, and an infinite number of children of both sexes. These people are horsemen. . . . They speak the same language as the Iscanis, Ouedsitas [Wichita], and Taouaïazes, and are considered to be the same nation." Bolton, *De Mézières,* I, p. 289. For a discussion of the Tawakoni, see next chapter; cf. also Bolton, in Hodge, *Handbook of American Indians,* II, pp. 701–704.

86. A species of catfish, locally called yellow cat.

87. The name is spelled the same in English as in Spanish; any of several pikelike marine fishes of the West Indies and tropical America constituting the family *Centropomidae.*

88. In a marginal notation Morfi added: "There are also flowers of

all colors, red, white, purple, blue, pastel shades, yellow, varicolored, striped, etc."

89. The description of the country between the Nabedache and the Quitseis follows closely the report of De Mézières. Cf. Bolton, *De Mézières,* II, pp. 264–265.

90. The information about these two poisonous trees is added as a marginal note in the original manuscript, intended to be incorporated in the text, where a mark appears at the place where it is to be inserted.

91. This name is applied locally to the tarantula, but was in reality the dangerous black widow.

92. This paragraph on snakes, spiders, bees, and ticks was placed as a marginal note in the original manuscript, but as in the case of the poisonous trees, it was intended to be incorporated in the text.

Chapter II

SPANISH SETTLEMENTS AND NATIVE TRIBES

67. The entire European population of so vast and fertile a province [1] is reduced to the villa of San Fernando, which, together with the presidio of San Antonio de Béxar, constitutes a town so miserable that it resembles a most wretched village. The governor of the province and the parish priest reside there. By adding to the inhabitants of this town those of the missions established in its vicinity [including all Christian Indians], and the garrison of the post of Santa Cruz on the Cíbolo, as well as all those living on the ranches in the surrounding country, the total number of souls is 2060.[2]

68. Thirty-two leagues to the southeast is the presidio of La Bahía and the missions of Espíritu Santo and Nuestra Señora del Rosario, with a combined population of 695 souls.

69. On the banks of the Trinity, one hundred and twenty-five leagues east-northeast, was established the new town of Nuestra Señora del Pilar de Bucareli, with 347 inhabitants,[3] who, because of the carelessness with which they chose the location for their establishment and the failure to irrigate their lands, are today dispersed and forced to live among the Indians, as we shall see later [in the course of this history].

70. There are, besides, on the coast and throughout the country, many Indian nations which I shall attempt to describe without following any particular order other than that in which they occur to me.[4]

71. *Maritime tribes: Karankawa.* The Carancaguases or Carancagues [Karankawa] nation is vile, cowardly, treacherous, and very cruel. The number of warriors of

this nation does not exceed, if it actually reaches, one hundred and fifty men.[5] They generally wander about individually, the nation residing either on the mainland along the coast when cold weather makes it seek shelter, or on the islands in the bay of Espíritu Santo when warm weather permits fishing. They spend most of the time on the islands, where fish are very abundant throughout the year. These Indians gather frequently on an island formed at the mouths of the Brazos and the Colorado, where, according to their testimony, are found anchors, bells, pots, artillery, and other wreckage from the vessels that not infrequently are dashed against its shore. The horrors of such misfortunes are increased by the barbarous cruelty with which these wretches assassinate the miserable survivors that escape the rage of the waves. Many of them speak Spanish with great fluency, being, in many instances, apostates from our missions.

72. *Attacapas and Orcoquisas.* The Attacapas[6] are of Louisiana, but they range in different places. The Orcoquisas[7] are friends of the Attacapas and make their home in the vicinity of the mouths of the Neches and the Trinity.[8] These Indians have no fixed home; they do not cultivate the soil; they are few in number, and are of little importance. They live along the coast, protected by other nations in the interior, who defend them from their enemies, for which reason they never bear arms except against the wretches who are shipwrecked on the coast. They live near to and are the allies of the Xaranames.

73. *Xaranames.* The Xaraname nation[9] is cowardly, vile, and nomadic. These Indians would be unworthy of notice were it not for the cruelties they practice upon the Europeans that are wrecked on the coast. They were congregated in the mission of Espíritu Santo,[10] near La Bahía, but after embracing Christianity they ungratefully

became apostates and took refuge among the Tuacanas [Tawakoni].[11] For sixteen years they persisted in their apostasy, until 1778, when Athanase de Mézières visited the pueblos of this nation [the Tawakoni]. Seeing them there, he expostulated with the chiefs of the Tawakoni, pointing out how wrong it was for them to receive and give protection to the renegades. With the consent of the nation, he sent all the apostates, under the escort of Lieutenant Menchaca and the care of Father Garza,[12] to the town of Bucareli. From there more than one hundred returned to their original mission where they remained, with the exception of twenty who fled a second time.[13]

74. *Cocos and Mayeyes.* The Cocos and the Mayeyes[14] are two distinct nations that now live together and whose members have intermarried. The twenty families that fled from the mission established themselves on the coast, opposite the island that lies between the mouths of the Brazos and the Colorado. They number about fifty.[15]

75. *Nations of the East: the Ais.* The Ais or Ayses are likewise reduced to twenty families that occupy one of the most beautiful and fertile spots in the entire province near the Sabine.[16] They are given to all kinds of vices and to extreme drunkenness. They are generally hated both by the natives and the Europeans. In order to redeem them the mission of Nuestra Señora de los Dolores was founded,[17] but, being obstinate and lazy, they merely ate everything the missionaries brought or raised. They showed no inclination to work, nor did they ever give ear to the teachings of our doctrine, for which reason the mission was hopelessly abandoned.[18]

76. *Bidais.* The Bidai or Biday were greatly weakened and their number reduced by the last epidemic, during which Fr. Francisco José de la Garza baptized many children and adults.[19] These Indians are lazy and listless

and scarcely number one hundred warriors, having lost almost as many in their last affliction. Because of their indolence they are obliged to beg their sustenance from the settlers of Bucareli, in whose vicinity they live and to the inhabitants of which they are a great drain. Their friendship with the Apache-Lipans is of long standing, a fact that makes it necessary to treat them with caution, though in themselves they are not dangerous nor treacherous. Their friends supply them with arms and ammunition.[20]

77. *Texas, Nabedache, Adaes, Hasinai.* The Texas Indians are divided into different tribes variously designated as Hasinai, Nabedache, Nadocogo or Nacogodoche, and Texas. They all speak the same language, regard themselves as kin, and the members of the different groups intermarry freely.[21] The recent epidemic diminished their number greatly. The Texas now have only eighty warriors, the Nabedache fewer than forty, the Nacogdochitos have three hundred and make their headquarters about twelve leagues up the Atoyaque river, from where the Los Adaes road crosses it. Opposite them, on the other side of the river, there are almost as many Ahijitos.[22] Between Lobanillo spring and the Ais creek [23] there are twenty families of the Ais nation, and a few Adaes remain in the vicinity of the former settlement of that name.

The Texas occupy the lands about the Angelina, and the Nabedache the banks of the upper Neches. A short distance from the pueblo of the Neches a small mound is seen, said to have been raised by their forefathers for the purpose of erecting a great temple at its top, from which the surrounding country is dominated, to worship their false gods.[24] In order to convert these Indians to our religion the mission of Nuestra Señora de Guadalupe was established,[25] but it proved as fruitless as Dolores, because the Nacogdoches deserted, and, although the Texas and Nabedache remained, they never accepted our doctrine, nor did they ever renounce their heathen practices. The buildings of the mission are still preserved.[26]

The Texas are industrious and very friendly to the Spaniards. In Louisiana, they were always regarded with kindness, out of gratefulness for the help they gave to the settlers of Natchitoches when these were attacked by the Natchez, and found, in the Texas, allies who gallantly put the enemy to death and freed them from the peril.[27]

78. *Nations of the North: Tonkawa.* Fifteen leagues to the west of Bucareli there is an eminence called La Tortuga [the Tortoise] that dominates a wide and fertile valley. The Tonkawa nation is found in its vicinity, scattered about in groups who live in tents made of skins. It is a wandering nation that moves about at will, in obedience to its chiefs or captains. The total number of warriors is about three hundred, among whom are included many apostates.[28] They are daring thieves and were the principal aggressors in the destruction of the mission of San Sabá.[29] They are responsible for the death of the missionaries, as well as for the greater part of the insults endured by the presidios of Béxar and La Bahía. They would perhaps still continue their depredations were they not restrained by the example, influence, and threats of the Tuacanas [Tawakoni], and the Yscanis. Lieutenant Colonel Athanase de Mézières succeeded in persuading their chief, *Tosche,* alias El Mocho [the Maimed], because he had lost one ear in battle, to establish himself permanently and to build a pueblo with all his people in the vicinity of Bucareli in a delightful spot.[30] Governor Domingo Cabello won his goodwill still more completely, solemnly making him captain in the public square of San Antonio de Béxar, from which he

set out in 1779, resolved to carry out his establishment at the place agreed upon.[31]

79. *Tawaconi, among whom about ninety Yscani warriors live.* On the western bank of the Brazos river, about thirty-one leagues west of Bucareli, is the first pueblo of the Tawakoni [Tuacanas],[32] called Quiscat. It is situated on a fertile plain, well protected from the floods of the river by a high hill, from the base of which flows a copious spring that supplies the inhabitants with water and could be used to irrigate abundantly the extensive plains used for their crops, but they do not realize this advantage.[33] There are about one hundred and fifty warriors in this settlement.

80. Continuing up the same river toward its source, eight leagues west, is the largest and most important village of the Tawakoni, called El Flechazo. The river is very beautiful between the two villages, and is navigable part of the year, one of its banks being formed by pleasant hills and the other by very attractive meadows. The land here is even more fertile than at the preceding village and rich in everything needed for a prosperous settlement, such as timber, limestone, millstone, and other useful stones. So plentiful is the water that within a short distance eleven abundant springs have been counted, all of which could be combined without difficulty to obtain most desirable results. The number of Indians in [this town] is far in excess of that found at Quiscat.

81. The inhabitants of the two villages are equally industrious, docile, and friendly to the Spaniards, as they have proved on various occasions, particularly in the opportune relief they gave Bucareli, supplying it with food.[34] They suffered severe losses during the epidemic of 1778, so much so that the following year of 1779 they had only two hundred and fifty warriors.

82. *Taovayas, united with the Ovichita* [*Wichita*]. In

the same westward direction, at about eighty leagues from the villages of the Tawakoni, are found the Taovayas,[35] who reside in two villages or settlements, one on the north bank of Red river or the river of Natchitoches and the other across from this on the opposite bank.[36] The first has thirty-seven houses and the second one hundred and twenty-three. Each house has from eight to ten beds, from which it is inferred that the number of warriors exceeded eight hundred. The number of women and children of both sexes is very large. Their dress, which consists of long shirts, leggings or boots, and moccasins, is of skins, as are their shields, horse equipment, and camping tents. They are very industrious, and there is not a house in which four or five vessels filled with large quantities of beans and pumpkins are not seen. The latter they preserve from one year to the next by cutting them in long strips and weaving them curiously like mats. They also raise watermelons, melons, and tobacco in abundance.

83. They have many good springs that furnish them with drinking water and that invite them to irrigate profusely their broad fields. The brackish water of the river is a great attraction for the numerous cattle that graze along its banks and which they kill at all times. The river is also rich in all kinds of fish, but these the Indians do not relish. They have firewood right at hand in a beautiful forest next to their settlement. In this forest, which extends for eighty leagues from east to west and is three, four, and five leagues wide, bears and wild boars are found. Nor is there any scarcity of useful timber, such as poplar, ash, elm, and black and white walnut, the former valuable for lumber, and the latter for the oil extracted from its fruit. The quarries seem to challenge use, but the Indians utilize only the whetstone to sharpen their arrows, the grinding stones to make *metates,*[37] the white stone to make pipes, and flint to tip their arrows. These

advantages are offset by the enmity of the Osage, who wage constant war against them; the fear of the Apache, who threaten them at all times; and the treachery of the Comanche, who in the guise of friends visit them frequently only to rob them, all of which they pretend not to notice in order not to make more enemies than they now have.

84. The climate is moderate, neither too cold nor too hot. Finally, in order that nothing be lacking, they are provided with excellent salt from a bank in the river which has the peculiarity that when a portion of salt is removed the loss is restored in a very short while.

85. The government of the Indians is democratic, without the exclusion of women, and this justly so, since it is the latter who contribute more to the welfare of the republic. The women tan, sew, and paint the skins, fence in the fields, sow the grain, care for the cornfields, harvest the crops, gather and keep the seeds, cut and fetch the firewood, prepare the food, build the houses, and rear the children, never ceasing in their watchfulness for everything that contributes to the comfort and pleasure of their husbands. The men devote themselves entirely to the chase and to war. The former makes them wealthy, the latter famous. They become leaders [chiefs or captains] not by the deeds of their fathers, but by their own prowess, a fact that impels them to deeds of great daring. The belief in life after death contributes in no small measure to make them brave, persuaded that after death they will enjoy happiness proportionate to their deeds. They have little or no religion, the ridiculous superstitions with which they regard the fire being the only observable manifestation of this kind. They are cheerful, affable, and very docile in their manners, compassionate toward the sick, the orphans, and the widows, respectful to their elders, generous with strangers, kind to guests;

but in general they are more resentful of injuries received than grateful for benefits conferred. They are extremely cruel with the prisoners they take in war, but this practice seems more an ill-advised reprisal than natural cruelty.[38]

87. *Ovaes or Panis-Mahas.* The Ovaes or Panis-Mahas used to live on the remote and celebrated Missouri river, but a short while ago [39] they abandoned that place for various reasons to come to live with the Taovayas but, moved by their natural fickleness, they changed their mind and chose a place sixty [40] leagues from San Theodoro. De Mézières, having learned of this determination, sent word to them through some of their friends, pointing out the dangers to which they exposed themselves by moving so far away from friends and the natural advantages of good neighbors. They were persuaded to return and they decided to establish themselves in a convenient and fertile spot on the south bank of Red river, two and a half days' journey from San Theodoro and an equal distance from the Cadodachos. The river being navigable to this point will afford them an easy commerce; they will reënforce the cordon of friendly Indians opposed to the Osage; and it will in turn afford protection to the hunters from Louisiana, enabling them to enjoy the advantages of this opulent river, of which they are deprived at present by the hostility [of the Osage].

88. The Ovaes [Panis-Mahas] are docile, honest, and indefatigable. They cultivate the soil and apply themselves to hunting and to war. Their chief spoke with De Mézières and told him of many nations that inhabit the Missouri. He assured him that two moons' [two months] journey to the west-northwest over rough mountain ranges there is a large lake of brackish water on the banks of which there live various nations, that these are visited at certain times of the year by a people that come

in ships propelled across the lake by oar and sail, that [the strangers] wear long dresses, are of brown color, and have swords and firearms. In a word, all the signs given suggest Asiatics. This is an old report and so frequently repeated that it seems there is no longer any doubt of its truth.[41]

89. *Cadodachos.* The Cadodachos [Kadodachos] speak the same language as the Nasonis, Nacogdoches, Hasinai, Taovayas, and Natchitoches.[42] They are divided into four families: Beaver, Otter, Wolf, and Lion. They declare that in a hill, two leagues from their village, there appeared a woman whom they consider their goddess and call Zacado; that she reared their first parents, taught them how to hunt, fish, and make their houses and their dresses, and that when they had learned all these things she disappeared. The hill is still held in veneration by these Indians, and the Cadodachos are respected as the forefathers of the other nations. Such is the description given of these Indians by Caballero Macarti, in a letter he wrote from Natchitoches on November 17, 1763, to Governor Angel Martos de Navarrete, the original of which is kept in the archives of [San Antonio de] Béxar.[43]

90. *Cocos.* The Cocos,[44] friends of the Karankawa and similar to them in customs, lived in the territory that lies between the Colorado and the Brazos rivers. Fray Francisco Benito Fernández de Santa Anna congregated them on the San Xavier [Gabriel] river in the mission of [Nuestra Señora de] la Candelaria.[45] When the missions were moved from this river [46] the greater part of these Indians was transferred to the missions on the San Antonio river, some of the others joined different nations, and very few returned to their former lands, where they were absorbed by the neighboring tribes.

91. *Comanches, 5000 men distributed in five tribes with different names.* This nation is far superior to all

Mitote, ò baile de los Yndios Cumanches, y Apaches.

APACHE AND COMANCHE INDIANS SKETCHED BY
FRAY VICENTE DE SANTA MARIA

the others in the number of warriors, the extent of the lands they occupy, the modesty of their dress, the hospitality shown to visitors or those they meet, the human treatment of captives, and the valor they display, which is admirable even in their women. But the wandering life they lead mars so many good qualities and forces them to be professional thieves. They have attacked us fiercely in New Mexico and Texas, but nothing can compare with the mortal hatred they feel for the Apaches, with whom alone they are cruel when they succeed in capturing them.[47]

92. *Osage.* The Osage is a treacherous, cruel, thieving, and wandering nation that lives to the north of the Taovayas and Natchitoches. We do not know them yet, but they commit barbarous depredations in Louisiana, particularly in the lands along the Arkansas and the Natchitoches rivers.[48] It is against these Indians that the cordon of friendly tribes has been established.[49]

93. *Quitseis* [*Kichai*]. A ranchería of Quitseis was established eighteen leagues north of Bucareli by a group of these Indians that separated themselves from their nation.[50] It has about twenty warriors. They occupy a broad and fertile valley where they cultivate the soil and graze their horses. They have near at hand many salines from which they provide themselves with salt for their personal use and for sale, using it to cure the deer they kill (the meat of which is their main sustenance and the skins their chief article of trade). The principal village of this nation is fifteen leagues beyond [to the west], the country between consisting of rich woods and valleys in which the wild grapes, so admired by De Mézières for their delicate taste, abound. [See paragraph 19.] The greater part of the nation joined the Cadodachos.[51]

94. *Common friendship.* All the preceding nations, including the Tonkawa and the Comanches, are irreconcil-

able enemies of the Apache and Osage. They all use with great skill the bow and arrow, the lance, the sword, the dagger, and firearms. They carry shields, jackets, and caps made of leather, adorning the last of these with feathers and buffalo horns to resemble a helmet. In general they are accomplished horsemen and they apply themselves greatly to the raising of horses. They all visit one another and live on friendly terms among themselves, though the Comanches frequently break the relations because of their thefts. But this is soon made up, none of the nations caring to declare itself against so powerful an enemy, when they are all so much in need of his strength to repel the Osage. They secure powder, balls, guns, clothes, and trinkets from Louisiana in exchange for chamois and deer, bear, and buffalo skins, tallow, and lard.

95. *War and organization.* Each nation or village has its chief whom they obey and under whom they fight. No chief makes an effort to coerce his men to follow him, knowing full well that where there is no pay there can be no obligation. But the chiefs are not responsible either for the outcome of the expeditions undertaken with volunteers, though men to follow them are never lacking. They invite each other with tokens or gifts rather than with words. If a campaign is to be undertaken the leader gives a war dance and those that come must follow him. If the chief wishes to go on a hunting trip he invites [the braves] to a feast and those that partake of it accompany him. But in neither case is an inviolable obligation incurred. Those that volunteer for the march are free to stop anywhere on the road or to return home. In either case they are indifferently told they do well. In this manner they are enlisted, disbanded, or given leave, without any sense of duty or obligation, without hard feelings or recriminations. A chief has as much authority as his

eloquence, his fame, and the love of his nation for him command.

96. They carry no supplies when setting out on a campaign, as these are found in abundance everywhere in the province in the wild cattle, deer, bears, rabbits, hares, turkeys, etc. When these are not found they do not spare the skunk, the rat, or the snake. When everything fails them, their temperance and the fortitude with which they endure long fasts are astounding.

97. Great are the precautions observed while on the march, the warpath, and the chase, particularly in territory where there is even a remote danger from enemies. They examine the ground with the greatest minuteness, select advantageous locations to pitch camp, and set lookouts. They exercise great care both morning and night to sleep lightly and for short periods. They always rise with the dawn and whenever possible bathe themselves the first thing. They never stray far from the main body of their men to avoid being surprised alone [by the enemy].

98. When two nations are allies in war they call each other *Techan,*[52] which means comrade or friend. Among those who use this term a tie of friendship so close is developed that it is the general opinion that no one can violate the trust without the fear of incurring the penalty that perfidy and perjury merit.

99. *Traders or agents.* In each one of the friendly Indian villages a trader from Louisiana resides who is always expected to know their language, to be able to read and write, to be liked by the natives, and to be very prudent. He is to promote trade and to make the Indians keep the peace with their neighbors as well as with ourselves, to watch their movements, and to report the slightest occurrence in their village or those of the neighboring

nations, as well as any information as to [the plans of] enemies.

There are many other nations besides those already mentioned. Some of these were congregated in the missions; others do not deserve to be noted because of their idleness; still others disappeared or died out during the various epidemics; while some were absorbed by the nations described, such as the Nasones, Tatases, Quitseis, Yscanis, Yojuanes, Deadose, and Xanas [Xaraname].

100. *Villa de San Fernando and Presidio de San Antonio de Béxar.* On the west bank of the San Antonio river, about a league from its source, above the point where San Pedro creek joins the river, is situated the villa of San Fernando and the presidio of San Antonio de Béxar, with no other division between them than the parochial church. To the west of the presidio is San Pedro creek, in such a manner that the villa and the presidio are both situated within the angle formed by the juncture of the two streams.[53] The church building is spacious and has a vaulted roof, but the whole is so poorly constructed that it promises but a short life. The town consists of fifty-nine houses of stone and mud and seventy-nine of wood, but all poorly built, without any preconceived plan, so that the whole resembles more a poor village than a villa, capital of so pleasing a province. Its population is made up of islanders [*isleños*] [54] and families from the country.[55] The former have acquired control of practically the whole city government [*regimiento*]. They are indolent and given to vice, and do not deserve the blessings of the land. The soldiers' quarters, originally built of stone and adobe, are almost in ruins. The establishment of this villa, independently of the presidio, has cost the king more than eighty thousand pesos.[56] The streets are tortuous and are filled with mud the minute it rains. The presidio is surrounded by a poor stockade on which are

mounted a few swivel guns, without shelter or defense, that can be used only for firing a salvo. There is no other trade than that required to supply the needs of the commissary for the garrison and the meager wants of the wretched settlers. The parish priest looks after the [garrison of the] presidio, there being no chaplain, and receives a small pension for his services. The governor used to live in what was the jail or guard house, which afforded a poor residence at best.

San Antonio de Valero. On the east bank of the San Antonio, about two gunshots' distance from the villa, is the mission of San Antonio de Valero.[57] It consists of a small convent fifty varas square with an arched gallery around the court [patio] on the first and second floors, around which are built the necessary rooms for the missionaries with the corresponding porter's lodge, refectory, offices, and kitchen. On the second patio [backyard] there is a large room with four looms and the necessary spinning wheels to weave cotton cloth for shawls, and ordinary coarse cotton and woolen cloth for the Indians. Two other rooms, in which the raw materials and the tools are kept, adjoin the workshop.

The church [chapel] was ruined through the ignorance of the builder, but a new one, simple, roomy, and well planned, is being erected on the same place, though it is not finished.[58] In the meantime services are held in the sacristy, which is a small room, but very tidy and neat, with a small, new, golden altar on which is venerated a handsome image of the titular Saint Anthony.

The Indian quarters form a square about the mission with attractive porticoes, the whole being watered by a beautiful irrigation ditch bordered by various kinds of trees. Besides this, a well was dug to forestall the lack of water in case of being besieged by the enemy. To safeguard it the door [leading to it] is fortified. At the entrance to the convent a small watchtower was built, with loopholes for three swivel guns which, with other firearms and the corresponding ammunition, are carefully guarded.

This mission was founded with Xaraname, Payaye, Zanas, Ypanis, Cocos, Tops, and Karancawa Indians and from the time of its erection [1718] to the end of the year 1761, there were 1972 persons baptized, 1247 were administered the holy sacraments at their death, 454 were married, and there were at that time 76 families [at the mission], numbering 275 persons in all. But since that time their number has been greatly reduced and today [1778] it scarcely has enough [neophytes] to cultivate the fields, and the looms have been abandoned [for lack of workers].[59]

Purísima Concepción. One league south of San Antonio [de Béxar] and on the east side of the river is the mission of Nuestra Señora de la Purísima Concepción de Acuña, first founded in the land of the Texas in 1716, and later removed to its present site in compliance with a decree of his excellency, the marquis of Casafuerte, in 1730. The church is beautiful. It is thirty-two varas long and eight wide, built of stone and mortar, with vaulted roof, transept, cupola, and two belfries. The sacristy is also a handsome room with vaulted roof the same as the living room of the religious, which is large and comfortable, though not very high. This opens on a gallery. The Indian quarters are arranged in two parallel rows on either side of the convent, the square being completed by the granary on the other, thus forming a closed rectangle with only two doors that are well defended. From the time of its establishment [1731] to the year 1761 there were 792 persons baptized, 558 received Christian burial, and in that year there were 58 families, numbering 207 persons, chiefly Pajalates, Tacames, and Sanipaos.

This mission has also suffered great reduction in the number [of its neophytes].

San José y San Miguel de Aguayo. The mission of San José y San Miguel de Aguayo is slightly more than half a league from the preceding one. From the time of its establishment by the venerable Fray Antonio Margil de Jesús in 1720 to the present, it has been under the care of the apostolic fathers of the college of Nuestra Señora de Guadalupe of Zacatecas.[60] It is, in truth, the first mission in America, not in point of time but in point of beauty, plan, and strength, so that there is not a presidio along the entire frontier line that can compare with it.[61]

The living quarters and public offices form a square 216 varas on each side, but two of these measure 220 varas on the outside because the Indian houses, built next to them, are four varas in depth. There are four identical doors on the four curtains, over the top of each of which a bastion has been built to defend them, and on the sides of the hollow, or indentation, of each door, loopholes have been made through the walls of the adjoining rooms on either side where the most trusted Indians live that they may fire safely upon the enemy should the doors be stormed. On the west side, in front of the church, there is a fifth door with an iron grating and this is the only one that is open every day. It faces a wide plain from which the trees and brush were cut down for a good distance to prevent a surprise by the enemy.

From this door to the north corner a granary was built alongside, of stone and mortar, with three naves and a vaulted roof. There is also a loom in which rich blankets, cotton cloth, sackcloth, and other heavy cotton and woolen cloth worn by the Indians are woven. There is a carpenter shop, a blacksmith shop, a tailor shop, and everything needed in a well-regulated community. Lastly, everything is in such order and so well planned that even if the enemy were capable of laying siege, the besieged, having as they have their granaries well filled with food and plenty of good water in their wells, could afford to laugh at their opponents.

Next to the north side a new church was being built within the walls, which perhaps is finished by now as there was very little to be done when I saw it at the close of 1777. It is a beautiful temple with three vaulted naves, fifty varas long and ten wide with its transept. The corner stone was placed by Hugo Oconor on May 19, 1768. It has a beautiful cupola, though it is overcrowded with unnecessary ornaments. This building, because of its size, good taste, and beauty, would grace a large city as a parish church. The whole structure is admirably proportioned and strongly built of stone and mortar, chiefly out of a sandy limestone that is light and porous when freshly quarried but in a few days hardens and becomes one with the mortar, for which reason it is as useful for building as *tezontle*.[62] This stone is secured from a quarry near the mission of Nuestra Señora de la Concepción. The façade is very costly because of the statues and ornaments with which it was heavily decorated, detracting somewhat from its natural beauty.[63] In the center, and immediately over the main entrance, a large balcony was constructed which gives much majesty to the building, and the effect would have been enhanced if the hexagonal window that illuminates the choir, and is the entrance, had been made to simulate a door. In a word, no one could have imagined that there were such good artists in so desolate a place.

The sacristy of the new church, the place where the divine services are celebrated for the time being, has a door that opens into the living quarters of the religious. It is a handsome and cheerful room, large and well decorated, with vaulted roof, good light, and everything in good taste.

The convent or living quarters for the missionaries has two stories with spacious galleries. The one on the second floor opens out on the flat roofs of the Indian quarters and is very convenient. Two quadrants [sun dials] on vertical columns were set up there, made out of a species of limestone so soft when first brought from the quarry that it can be planed like wood but which, when exposed to the air, hardens and can be polished like marble. The figures of the façade of the church, the balustrade of the stairway of the convent, and an image of Saint Joseph that is on its pedestal, all were made more beautiful by the ease with which the stone is worked. There are enough rooms for the missionaries and for the convenience of a few guests, as well as the necessary offices for the religious, a large and well-ordered kitchen, a comfortable refectory, and a pantry. There is an armory where the guns, bows and arrows, and the lances are kept, with which to arm the neophytes in case of attack and to equip them as auxiliary troops in a campaign, in which case the mission provides them not only with arms, but with ammunition and supplies as well. In a separate room are kept the decorations and dresses with which the Indians bedeck themselves for their dances, introduced by the missionaries, now Spanish and now Mexican, that they might forget their native *mitotes* [pagan festivals].

The farm occupies an area about a league square and is all fenced, the fence being in good condition. For its benefit water is taken from the San Antonio river and distributed by means of a beautiful irrigation ditch to all parts of the field, where corn, beans, lentils, cotton, sugar cane, watermelons, melons, and sweet potatoes are raised. It has also a patch for all kinds of vegetables and there are some fruit trees, from among which the peaches stand out, their fruit weighing at times as much as a pound.

The mission was founded with Pampopas, Mesquites and Pastias, to which later were added Camanas, Tacames, Cannas, Aguastallas, and Xaunaes. These Indians are today well instructed and civilized and know how to work very well at their mechanical trades and are proficient in some of the arts. They speak Spanish perfectly, with the exception of those who are daily brought in from the woods by the zeal of the missionaries. Many play the harp, the violin, and the guitar well, sing well, and dance the same dances as the Spaniards. They go about well dressed, are abundantly fed, and arouse the envy of the less fortunate settlers of San Fernando, the indolence of many of whom obliges them to beg their food from these Indians who enjoy so much plenty and whose mission is in opulence, thanks to the labors and exertions of Fray Pedro Ramírez de Arellano, of the college of Nuestra Señora de Guadalupe of Zacatecas, who is in charge of this mission and is the president of all the missions in the province, and whose dedication, zeal, and religious spirit deserve all praise.

In March, 1768, the mission had 350 persons, of whom 110 were capable of bearing arms; 45 of these could use guns, and the rest bows and arrows. Since that time their number has been greatly reduced. There were 1054 baptisms performed up to that year, 287 marriages, and 359 burials.

San Juan Capistrano. A little more than a league from the mission of San José is the mission of San Juan Capistrano, originally established in the land of the Texas but moved to this place together with that of Concepción. The church is neat and in good order, though it does not compare with those described as to the building. The convent has four cells with a gallery, two offices, a refectory, kitchen, and workshop. The pueblo or Indian quarters do not compare with those of the preceding ones. The mission was founded with Orejones, Sayopines, Pamagues, and Piguiques. From the time of the establishment to 1761, there were 847 baptisms and 645 burials, there being 51 families with 203 persons that year. But like the others, it has steadily declined each year.

San Francisco de la Espada. One-quarter of a league from the preceding mission and three from the presidio of San Antonio, on the west side of the river, is the mission of Nuestro Santo Padre San Francisco de la Espada, companion mission of Concepción and San Juan Capistrano in point of origin, and like them removed at the same time [to its present site]. The church was demolished because it threatened to fall down, and services are being held in an ample room that has a choir and a sacristy, all very neat. The convent is laid out on a straight line, with four cells on the second floor and three on the first, galleries, workshop, and a good-sized granary, all made of stone, but ill-arranged and plain. The pueblo or Indian quarters consist of three rows of houses that form a square with the convent, a wall, likewise of stone, closing a portion of the enclosure where there are no houses. It was founded for the Pacaos, Borrados, and Mariquitas. From the time of its establishment to the year 1761, there were 815 persons baptized and 513 buried. Today there are 40 families with 133 persons.

Between the presidio, villa, and the five missions described they make up 514 families: 759 men, 613 women, 373 boys, 300 girls, 4 male slaves, and 11 female slaves, totaling in all 2060 persons, of whom 324 are Spanish, or as they commonly say "de razón" [literally "sensible"], 268 Indians, 16 mestizos, and 151 "de color quebrado" [literally "of broken color," meaning colored].

Nuestra Señora del Rosario. The mission of Nuestra

Señora del Rosario was founded in the vicinity of the presidio of La Bahía del Espíritu Santo in 1754. The presidio is to the east, at a distance of three or four leagues. The mission has good water, which it gets from the San Antonio river, on the banks of which it is situated, at a pleasing and fertile crossing. It is surrounded by good agricultural land, but the depth of the river bed precludes its being irrigated. The climate is unhealthful because of the heat and humidity, so much so that as soon as the south wind blows everything becomes dripping wet, even inside the houses, to such an extent that clothes appear as if they had been soaked in water, and the walls reek as if it were raining. The crops, though not so plentiful as in the other missions, are ample enough. The living quarters of the missionary, neophytes, and soldiers are good and comfortable. The whole is protected by a good stockade that insures it against surprises. The church is very handsome, made of wood plastered and whitewashed, the roof being made of beams and shingles curiously arranged to resemble paneling. Everything is neat and tidy. The altars, sacred vessels, ornaments, pulpit, confessionary, and everything that pertains to the divine service is of good quality, well kept, and carefully arranged, so that all inspires devotion. The mission was founded with Indians belonging to the Coxanes, Guapites, Carancaguases, and Copanes nations, though at present there are few members of any of them left, because the majority apostatized and fled to some remote river or shore, or to some [enemy] nation that received them graciously to increase their number with the runaways. From the time of its establishment [1754] to 1768 there were 200 baptisms, 110 burials, and 35 marriages.[64]

Espíritu Santo de Zúñiga. The mission of Espíritu Santo [de Zúñiga] was founded in the year 1720, at the same time the presidio of La Bahía [presidio de Nuestra Señora de Loreto] was established, and the mission followed the presidio, or better said, the presidio followed the mission in its various removals.[65] It is situated, likewise, on the banks of the San Antonio, which separates it from the presidio that lies in plain view and with which it has communication by means of a canoe. It is better than the preceding one [Rosario], being older, except as regards the church which is smaller but sufficiently ample [for its purpose]. The sacred vessels, ornaments, etc., are more numerous and are kept with the same care as at Rosario. The Blessed Sacrament was kept for a long time in the private oratory with the permission of the Rt. Rev. Fray Francisco Texada, bishop of Guadalajara, who visited this and the other missions.[66] The sanctuary lamp was filled with oil extracted from nuts, and this was also approved by the bishop. The Indians maintained a constant watch and kept a sentinel at the door of the oratory day and night. The offices and the living quarters of the missionary, the soldiers, and the Indians are clean and well kept. With regard to the temporalities, they are in a flourishing condition.

It was founded for Cujanes, Guapites, and Carancaguases, but most of these deserted, and Xaranames, Tamiques, and later Manos de Perro were congregated. It now has about 300 neophytes of all these nations, of whom 65 bear arms, 30 use guns, and the remaining 35 are armed with bows and arrows, lances, and *medias lunas*.[67] They are more civilized than those of Rosario and eat only beef or the flesh of such animals as are eaten by the Spaniards, but all have the same fondness for the barbarous customs of their forefathers and it is necessary for the missionaries to be continuously on the watch to guard against their inclination. From the time of its establishment to the beginning of 1768, there were 623 baptisms performed, 278 burials, and 88 marriages.

Presidio of La Bahía. The presidio of La Bahía [presidio of Nuestra Señora de Loreto originally] comprises 515 persons, including all ages and both sexes and counting the members of the garrison stationed there as well.

Bucareli. The settlement of Bucareli,[68] now disbanded, had 42 houses built of wood and was defended by a stockade. It had a population of 348.

Santa Cruz. The fort of Santa Cruz on the Cíbolo has seven persons living there now.[69]

Ranches. Rancho Chayopin has eight persons; La Patoguilla, three; Las Cabras, twenty-six; San Francisco, seventeen; Mora, twenty-six; Las Mulas, five.[70]

NOTES TO SPANISH SETTLEMENTS AND NATIVE TRIBES

1. The description of the settlements and the Indian tribes that forms the subject of this chapter refers to conditions as they were in 1777–78, at the time Croix made his inspection. Morfi accompanied Croix, who set out from Mexico city on a tour of inspection on August 4, 1777, and reached the Rio Grande on December 25, 1777. When Morfi describes the Spanish settlements he speaks from first-hand information. Croix turned back on January 14, 1778, after spending several days in San Antonio, and Morfi visited only that section of Texas lying between the Rio Grande and San Antonio. Morfi, "Viaje de Indios," in *Documentos para la historia de México,* 3ª serie, I, pp. 446–465.

2. In his *Memorias,* Morfi exalts the natural facilities and the beauty of Texas and deplores the indifference of the Spanish settlers. "In a country so vast, so fertile, so peopled with friendly and industrious nations, and whose coast offers all the advantages that one may desire to establish a sound and lucrative trade with Veracruz and our island possessions, what have we? It seems incredible! A miserable place called a villa, two presidios, one outpost, six wretched ranches, and seven missions, that would not occupy a space seven leagues square." Speaking of San Antonio proper he says, "I do not hesitate to say that in all New Spain there is not a more beautiful, more suitable, and more inviting place in which to establish and maintain a great city than that occupied by the villa of San Fernando and presidio of San Antonio de Béxar." *Memorias,* Libro IV.

3. The facts concerning the population of Texas, in which he includes only the Spaniards, mestizos, and Christian Indians, are summarized by Morfi in these words: "In conclusion, the total number of souls in the one villa, two presidios, one outpost, six ranches, and seven missions, including the dispersed settlers of Bucareli, is 3803 persons. There are 780 families in all: 1141 men, 902 women, 561 boys, 479 girls, 6 male slaves, 14 female slaves." *Memorias,* Libro IV.

4. It is of interest to note that in the treatment of the native tribes Morfi, anticipating modern historians, divided them geographically. As far as the writer knows, he is the first to do so. In his *Memorias,* Morfi gathered much detailed information which he very ably condenses in this chapter. For instance, in the *Memorias* he gives two whole books to the Indians and their customs, a total of eighty pages. In the present chapter he has condensed the original data, leaving out none of the essential details, but cutting off all superfluous material. The best short treatment of the native tribes in English now available is the summary presented by Bolton in his introduction to *De Mézières.* The more detailed description of the *Memorias* has since been published in a limited edition by Fred. C. Chabot under the title of *Indian Excerpts from Morfi's Memorias.*

5. The Karankawa included the Cujanes, Guapites, or Coapites, Cocos, Copanes, etc. They occupied the region embracing the Gulf coast and the littoral islands from Galveston bay to and beyond the mouth of the San Antonio. "They were fierce cannibals," declares Bolton, "and were regarded as particularly dangerous to mariners on that perilous coast." Bolton, *De Mézières,* I, pp. 19–20; Hackett, *Pichardo,* I, p. 388; cf. also Gatschet, "The Karankawa Indians," in *Archaeological and Ethnological Papers,* I, no. 2, 1891 (Peabody Museum Publications). This last study, long and detailed, contains many interesting facts.

6. This tribe occupied the lower Neches and Sabine rivers and the lands to the east. They really belong to the group of Indians that occupied western Louisiana. Bolton, *De Mézières,* I, p. 20. "The name of the tribe is Choctaw, signifying 'man eater,'" declares Swanton. In 1779 the tribe was estimated to number 180 warriors. There were 9 survivors in Louisiana in 1908. Swanton, *Indian Tribes of the Lower Mississippi Valley,* pp. 43, 45, 360.

7. This tribe, with the Bidai, Deadose, and Attacapas, forms the Attacapan group. The Orcoquisas occupied the lower Trinity in particular, down to the coast region, where a cape, Punta de los Orcoquisas, was named after them, and the river was often referred to by the same name. "They were of somewhat higher advancement than the Karankawa. They had little agriculture and lived mainly by hunting and fishing." Bolton, *De Mézières,* I, p. 20; cf. also his *Texas,* pp. 2–3; Hackett, *Pichardo,* I, pp. 379–380.

8. These facts are borne out by recent investigations and show how accurately Morfi used his sources and how logical were his conclusions.

9. The Xaraname (variously spelled Jaraname, or Caraname), Tamique, and smaller kindred bands lived on either side of the lower Guadalupe. They appear to be different from the four main groups of Indians: the Karankawa, the Coahuiltecan, the Bidai-Arcoquisa, and the Tonkawa. In 1772, they had 46 warriors and "a goodly number of women and children." Bolton, *De Mézières,* I, pp. 28, 291.

10. The marquis of Aguayo founded in 1722 the presidio of Nuestra Señora de Loreto and the mission of Nuestra Señora del Espíritu Santo de Zúñiga on Espíritu Santo bay on the site of the old French fort of St. Louis. In 1726, the mission was moved "to the Guadalupe River, some ten leagues away, among the more docile Xaraname and Tamique tribes. In 1749 the presidio and mission were again removed, this time to the lower San Antonio, at the present site of Goliad, whither the Xaraname were transferred with their mission." Bolton, *De Mézières,* I, pp. 31–32.

11. "Soon after the removal of their mission to the San Antonio—the exact date is not quite clear—the greater part of the Xaraname deserted in a body and went to live with the Tawakoni and Tonkawa, where they were found by De Mézières many years later." *Ibid.,* I, pp. 32–33. In his

next sentence Morfi seems to imply that the desertion took place about 1762.

12. On April 8, 1778, De Mézières wrote to Croix from the Tawakoni villages, "An object of the greatest importance being the conversion of the Xaraname Indians, their extraction from among heathen, and their restitution to the mission to which they belong, all of which, thanks be to God, has been accomplished, as I have the honor of informing your Lordship. . . ." Morfi has misread the remainder of the letter. Menchaca was not sent as an escort with the Xaranames but to carry post haste a special dispatch to San Antonio, while Fr. Francisco José de la Garza returned to Bucareli with the Indians, "the Xaranames desiring and having chosen him for their father with such eagerness," declares De Mézières, "that I found it impossible to deny them this consolation." Bolton, *Ibid.*, II, pp. 197–198.

13. Here he has reference to twenty families of Cocos that escaped from the mission rather than to the Xaranames. See next paragraph.

14. The Cocos were one of the Karankawan tribes and formed part of the coastal group of Indians. Though the Cocos and Mayeyes came to live together, they were two distinct tribes, as shown by recent investigations. "My researches have determined the linguistic affiliation of the Bidai, Deadose, and Arkoquisas with each other, and of the Mayeye with the Tonkawa," declares Bolton in his *De Mézières*, I, p. 19, note.

15. "Their nation (Orcoquisas or Arkoquisa) has gone down to occupy an island situated between the mouths of the Colorado and the Brazos . . . On the mainland, opposite this island, there are located twenty-four families of Cocos and Mayeyes, likewise fugitives from the missions of La Bahía del Espíritu Santo and San Antonio de Béxar." De Mézières to Croix, March 8, 1778, in archive of San Francisco el Grande.

16. The Ais tribe lay between the Caddo and the Hasinai groups. Though distinct from either, they have more in common with the Hasinai. In 1778, it had thirty warriors and occupied the territory in the vicinity of the Sabine. Bolton, *De Mézières*, I, pp. 22, 118; II, p. 166.

17. Late in the fall of 1716, two additional missions were established by the friars from the college of Zacatecas for the Ais and Adaes. Nuestra Señora de los Dolores, one of these, was well across the Sabine in what is now Louisiana, only seven leagues from Natchitoches. *Ibid.*, I, p. 38. It has generally been held that it was in the spring of 1717, but conclusive evidence is now available to show it was in 1716. Castañeda, *The Winning of Texas*, chapter II (In press).

18. By order of the king, Ripperdá issued instructions for the abandonment of Los Adaes and for "extinguishing at the same time the useless missions of Nacogdoches, Ays, Adaes, and Orcoquiza." Ripperdá to Unzaga y Amezaga, April 17, 1773. Bolton, *De Mézières*, II, pp. 29–30.

19. In 1777–1778, an epidemic broke out and spread from Béxar to Los Adaes and caused great loss of life among the natives. The Bidai nation

lost about 100 warriors. "Fr. Francisco José de la Garza zealously took advantage of the situation, in order that the souls [of the victims], most of whom died baptized, might be saved." De Mézières to Croix, March 18, 1778, in *Prov. Int.*, vol. 182.

20. Much concern was felt by Spanish officials over the friendship or alliance of the Lipan and Bidai, and strenuous efforts were made to prevent it. De Mézières was sent in 1772 to the nations of the north with particular instructions to frustrate such an alliance. Bolton, *De Mézières*, I, pp. 65, 96, 98.

Morfi is mistaken in believing that the Apaches supplied the Bidai with firearms. As a matter of fact it was the latter who supplied the former. Ripperdá, in a letter dated September 8, 1772, expresses the hope that De Mézières will stop the Apaches from getting arms "through the Bidai" by obliging them to declare themselves enemies of the Apaches. *Ibid.*, I, p. 346.

21. "West of the Sabine, on the Angelina and the upper Neches, was the compact Hasinai (Asinai, Cenis, or Texas) Confederacy, consisting of some ten or more tribes, of which the best known were the Hasinai, Nacogdoches, Nabedache, Nasoni, and Nadaco . . . The Hasinai were a settled people, who apparently had been long in the place where they were found at the end of the seventeenth century." *Ibid.*, I, pp. 20–21. For a more detailed description of this native group, see Bolton, "The Native Tribes . . .," *op. cit.*, XI, pp. 249–276; Casañas, *Relación, The Quarterly*, XXX, p. 206; and the several articles on the different tribes in Hodge, *Handbook of American Indians.*

22. I have found no other mention of this tribe, or division of a tribe, whose strength at this time entitles it to more notice.

23. This creek has been identified with the first eastern branch of the Angelina. Buckley, "Aguayo Expedition," XV, p. 48.

The information regarding the number of Indians was gathered by Morfi from among the various reports of De Mézières and those sent to Croix by other officials and Indian agents, copies of which were found in Morfi's papers, particularly for the years 1772–1779. Archive of San Francisco el Grande.

24. "This mound and its two less conspicuous companions still stand in Cherokee County about a mile and a half from the river and five miles southwest of Alto, in a plain known to some as Mound Prairie, undoubtedly the true Mound Prairie whose whereabouts has been debated." Bolton, "Native Tribes," XI, pp. 261–262.

The mound is shown on the Austin map of Texas, 1829, Spanish draft, reproduced for the first time from the original MS. copy in Mexico, in Castañeda and Martin, *Three Manuscript Maps of Texas.*

25. Nuestra Señora de Guadalupe was first established in 1716 by the Ramón expedition at the village of the Nacogdoches, primarily for these Indians and not, as Morfi implies, for the Nabedache. "This mission re-

mained on the same site until it was abandoned in 1773." Bolton, "Native Tribes," XI, p. 258.

26. Morfi refers to the year 1779, when he was writing, and he is borne out in his assertion by the following statement: "But when in 1779 (not 1778, as is commonly stated) Antonio Gil Ybarbo laid the foundations of modern Nacogdoches with his band of refugees from the Trinity River settlement of Bucareli, he found the Nacogdoches mission buildings still standing, settled his colony near them, and apparently reoccupied some of them." *Ibid.*, XI, p. 258.

27. The attack on Natchitoches occurred in 1729, and Morfi doubtless procured the information from the speech made by De Mézières to the chiefs of the principal northern tribes some time in October, 1770, in which he declared that "they should profit by the good example and inviolable fidelity of the friendly Cadodachos, whose hands, far from having been stained with our blood, had been dedicated, at the cost of their own, to the defense of our lives, when the ferocious Natchez threatened them by their invasion of Natchitoches, a deed worthy of the greatest applause, and one which for all time will receive the gratitude which it merits." Bolton, *De Mézières*, I, p. 210.

In the original draft of the *Historia*, Morfi has deleted five full pages of additional details on the Hasinai confederacy. Most of the material discarded was notes taken from Espinosa's *Chrónica*, Solís' *Diary*, and De Mézières' reports, for which reason Morfi deleted them.

28. "What were apparently the Tonkawa and Yojuane were encountered in 1719 by Du Rivage on the Red River seventy leagues above the Cadodacho, while at the same period tribes seemingly Tonkawan were living in central Texas near the Colorado . . . In the middle of the eighteenth century the best known divisions of the group were usually found between the Colorado and the Trinity Rivers, chiefly above the *Camino Real* leading from San Antonio to Los Adaes." To this group belonged the Tonkawa proper, the Mayeye, the Yojuane, and the "highly mixed band" of the Yerbipiame. Bolton, *De Mézières*, I, pp. 22–23.

29. The mission of San Sabá was founded in 1757 for the Lipan-Apache. It was located on the upper San Sabá river. "In 1758 a large force of Comanche, Wichita, Hasinai, and perhaps Caddos attacked and destroyed the mission, killing several Spaniards and two Franciscan friars." *Ibid.*, I, p. 49. More details of this bloody episode will appear in the course of this history.

30. The proposed site was La Tortuga. De Mézières to Croix, September 5, 1779, *Prov. Int.*, vol. 182.

31. Hostilities again developed between the Spaniards and El Mocho, however, and he never carried out his good intentions. He was finally murdered at the presidio of Bahía del Espíritu Santo on July 12, 1784. Bolton, *De Mézières*, II, p. 271, note.

32. The Tawakoni are a division of the Caddoan group, to which be-

longed the Jumanos, Taovayases, Wichita, Yscanis, and Kichai. These various tribes are collectively called by ethnologists the Wichita. Bolton, *ibid.*, I, p. 23.

33. This village was near present-day Waco. See Bolton, *Map of Texas*.

34. "They are very fond of us, as experience proves, now in the restoration of the . . . apostates, and again in the supply of provisions with which they have relieved Bucareli, without even reserving enough for their own use until the harvest." De Mézières to Croix, April 5, 1778, in *Prov. Int.*, vol. 182.

35. The Taovayas is one of the tribes now included in the general group designated as Wichita. They habitually lived on the Wichita and the upper Red river. "The civilization of the Wichita [including in addition to the Taovayas, the Tawakoni, the Yscanis, and Kichai] was essentially like that of the Caddo and the Hasinai, though they were more warlike, less fixed in their habitat, and more barbarous, even practicing cannibalism extensively." Bolton, *De Mézières*, I, p. 24.

36. These villages were near the present site of Wichita. In 1787, the ranchería was visited by Pedro Vial and his companions, who were sent from Santa Fe to Natchitoches by Governor Concha to explore a route between the two places. Hackett, *Pichardo*, I, pp. 325, n. 6, 528, n. 4; Bolton, *Texas*, pp. 128–130.

37. A *metate* is a grinding stone, cut or fashioned to grind maize by hand.

38. This is confirmed by the following incident. While traveling with a small party from the presidio of Béxar to that of La Bahía, Lieutenant Antonio Tremiño met a party of Taovayas with whom they were at war at that time. As they approached each other they opened fire and the latter, either more fortunate or more skilled [in the use of their arms], killed the few soldiers that accompanied Tremiño. At the first shots he lost his horse, but afoot, full of wounds, and with only his sword and shield, this officer kept up the fight for an hour by taking refuge behind a tree. The leader of the Taovayas, seeing this brave defense, made his followers cease fighting, and, approaching Tremiño, explained to him the futility of his stand against so many in the condition in which he was. Should they withdraw and leave him in possession of the field of battle, he would die from the wounds he had received already or perish from want, unable to reach help. The Indian entreated him to surrender, giving him assurances that he would be well treated. Tremiño agreed, and immediately the rest of the Indians made a stretcher out of willow branches and brush and placing him upon it took him to their country on their shoulders, giving him of the best they had while on the way. When they arrived in their village, they vacated a house for him and gave him Indians to wait upon and treat him. After he recovered from his wounds they gave him a woman, as if he were a native, and showed him so much

confidence that they allowed him to attend the most secret meetings of the chiefs and captains. But all these kindnesses and favors could not make Tremiño forget his country, his religion, and his family. For two years he stood it, but at last he fell into a melancholic mood that revealed his longing. The Taovayas noted this, and, realizing that his sadness was caused by his love for his family, they declared to him that he had never been considered a prisoner, that if they had kept him with them it was because they thought this gave him pleasure, and that if he was not pleased, he was free to arrange for his departure any day he desired. They presented him with some horses, gave him supplies, and escorted him to the outskirts of San Antonio de Béxar, where he would be safe from attack by the Apache. They took leave with the greatest tenderness, asking him not to forget them, and to visit them whenever he could, for war could not change the affection they had conceived for him. This was related to me by Tremiño himself in the presidio of San Antonio de Béxar where I met him. As a matter of fact, when Ripperdá negotiated a peace with the Taovayas, he commissioned Tremiño to visit them several times in their villages. He accompanied De Mézières in 1778, and he always met with the same warm affection, as evidenced by De Mézières. This incident reveals their true character. [Though this is paragraph 86 of the MS., it is marked on the margin "note." For confirmation of this story, see Bolton, *De Mézières,* I, pp. 50, 195, note; II, pp. 199, 205, 215, 322.]

After they concluded peace with us [a treaty was made with the Taovayas and signed on October 27, 1771; translated in full in Bolton, *op. cit.,* I, pp. 256–259] they openly manifested the love they have for us in their efforts to induce Spaniards to settle in their lands, offering to give them all the aid necessary for a new establishment; in the zeal with which they drove out of their territory two English traders after they were informed the English were our enemies, depriving them of their goods first; and, lastly, in the promptness with which they restored to De Mézières the two cannons that Parrilla abandoned to them after his defeat, and the thanks expressed to him for having named their villages San Theodoro and San Bernardo. [All the facts summarized here by Morfi are borne out by the reports of De Mézières. See Bolton, *De Mézières.*]

39. According to De Mézières, they came to Texas in 1777, for he wrote on April 19, 1778, to Croix that the Mahas had come down from the banks of the Missouri the year before. *Prov. Int.,* vol. 182.

40. De Mézières estimated the distance from the Taovayas to the place where the Panis-Mahas had made their settlement as seventy leagues northwest. *Ibid.,* f. 33.

41. In the summary of the various reports of De Mézières about these Indians and the story of the strange people that visited the nations on the lake we find this statement, "They are brown skinned, and in the opinion of De Mézières resemble Asiatics." Is this to be taken as a lingering

vestige of the long-cherished hope that India could be reached through the strait of Anian? *Prov. Int.*, vol. 182, f. 13.

42. "The Caddo . . . extended along both banks of the Red River from the lower Natchitoches tribe, in the vicinity of the present Louisiana city of this name, to the Natsoos and Nassonites tribes, above the great bend of the Red River in southwestern Arkansas and southeastern Oklahoma. The best known members of this group were the Cadodacho [Kadohadacho, Grand Cado], or Caddo proper, Petit Cado, upper and lower Natchitoches, Adaes, Yatasí, Nassonites, and Natsoos." The Caddo and the Hasinai were both divisions of the Caddoan linguistic stock and their culture, as well as their language, was similar. The failure to recognize the fact that there are two tribes of Natchitoches, the lower near the city of that name, and the upper in the big bend of Red river, has led to much confusion regarding the route of De Soto west of the Mississippi. Bolton, *De Mézières,* I, pp. 21–22; Hodge, *Handbook of American Indians;* Mooney, "Caddo and Associated Tribes."

43. A careful search of the Béxar archives, now in the University of Texas, proved futile in locating the original. A certified copy, sent by Martos y Navarrete to the viceroy from Los Adaes on November 23 of the same year, is found in the Nacogdoches archives, now in the State Library, under date of the original letter. This is a long argument to show the right of the French to the control of the Tawakoni and was written before either Navarrete or Macarti had heard of the cession of Louisiana to Spain.

44. See paragraph 74 of this chapter for a description and affiliation of this tribe.

45. Fray Benito Fernández de Santa Anna, president of the Queretaran missions at San Antonio and the San Xavier, first came to Texas in 1733. He spent more than twenty years in missionary work here. He was chiefly responsible for the founding of the three missions on the San Xavier. Nuestra Señora de la Candelaria was founded especially for the Cocos, whom he congregated with much toil. A detailed report of the founding of this mission and of the difficulties that had to be overcome was made by Fray Benito in 1748(?) from which Morfi has drawn the information. "Autos sobre las misiones de Texas," consisting of six documents, dated 1747–1750, all on the missions of the San Xavier river, in archive of San Francisco el Grande, vol. 4, pp. 207–244.

46. The removal of the San Xavier missions was approved by a *Junta de Guerra y Hacienda* on February 27, 1756. It was ordered that the presidio be removed to the San Sabá, that its garrison be strengthened to the number of one hundred men, and that all converted Indians be transferred to the missions contiguous to San Antonio de Béxar. This was partly accomplished by April, 1757. *Bonilla's Brief Compendium* (Tr. by Elizabeth Howard West) in *The Quarterly,* VIII, pp. 51–52.

47. The Comanche is a southern tribe of the Shoshonean stock, an off-

shoot from the Shoshoni of Wyoming. Speaking of the Apache and Comanche, Bolton says, "Though these two groups were quite distinct, [they] were the bitterest of enemies." Mooney gives the twelve divisions of the Comanche in Hodge, *Handbook of American Indians.* See also Bolton, *De Mézières,* I, pp. 24–25.

48. Osage is a corruption for *Wazhazhe* due to the mispronunciation of the French traders. It is the most important southern tribe of the western division of the Siouan group. Their main village was situated on Osage river, though they also had a settlement on the Missouri. Marquette is the first to note them in his autograph map of 1673. De Mézières says of them: "They appear insolent and proud and commit the greatest injuries . . . They never fail to demand that protection which favors and perpetuates their outrages, a sad example of which has just occurred in Louisiana." *Ibid.,* I, p. 304; *Handbook of American Indians,* II, pp. 156, 158.

49. After his expedition to the nations of the north in 1772, De Mézières urged, declares Bolton, "the Wichita, Taovayas, and the Tawakoni of the Brazos, to move inland, farther away from English influence, and to form a cordon of settlements, to be covered by a Spanish presidio, as a protection for themselves against the Osage and as a bulwark for the Spaniards against both the Osage and the English." Bolton, *De Mézières,* I, p. 97.

50. The information here is drawn mainly from the letter of De Mézières to Croix of March 13, 1778. *Prov. Int.,* vol. 182.

51. The Quitseis or Kichai were in reality "a Caddoan tribe whose language is more closely allied to the Pawnee than to the other Caddoan groups . . . They seem to have . . . intermarried with the Kadohadacho [Cadodachos]." In 1772, the main Kichai village was east of Trinity river, not far from Palestine, perhaps a little northeast. *Handbook of American Indians,* I, p. 682.

52. According to Maçanet the word with which the Spaniards were greeted by the natives was *Thechas.* The similarity of the words is to be noted as well as that of their meaning. See note 3, chapter I.

53. As stated before (see note 1 of this chapter), Morfi is describing San Antonio and the missions from his own personal observations. During his short stay in the city he visited in person all the missions and actively examined their records and archives for facts for his history. His power of observation and ability to condense his information with preciseness and vividness is clearly demonstrated in this description of the city and the missions in its neighborhood.

54. The original settlers of San Fernando came from the Canary islands, and were officially settled and organized as a villa on March 9, 1731. They were generally referred to as *isleños,* meaning "those who came originally from the Canary islands." The *Auto de fundación* was

found by the editor in the State Library of Guadalajara, a copy of which is now in his possession.

55. Presumably Morfi here means settlers from New Spain, who came after the original settlers, as there were no others sent from Spain. He could not mean *Texans,* for the only "familias del país" in that restricted sense were the Indians.

56. Approximately $40,000, if estimated at the modern rate of exchange.

57. This is the modern Alamo. It was founded in 1718. Bolton, *Texas,* p. 5.

58. That is, the new chapel was not finished in 1778, when Morfi saw it.

59. "By good fortune, reports of all the Texas missions, made in 1762, have been preserved. By an order of October 16, 1761, issued by Fray Manuel de Náxera, comisario general, a report was required on all of the Franciscan missions of New Spain. In response to the order, on March 6, 1762, the Queretaran missionaries in Texas dispatched a report directed to Fray Francisco Ortiz, guardian of the college of Santa Cruz. It gives us a most excellent view of the missions on the eve of the Louisiana cession." This report, so effectively described by Bolton, was used by Morfi in summarizing the work of the missions herein presented. A copy of it was found in the archive of San Francisco el Grande.

60. Fray Antonio Margil de Jesús founded the college of Nuestra Señora de Guadalupe of Zacatecas in 1707, which, together with that of Querétaro, generally referred to as the Colegio de la Santa Cruz de Querétaro, supplied all the missionaries that labored in Texas. Angel de los Dolores de Tiscareño, *El Colegio de Guadalupe desde su origin hasta nuestros días,* III, pp. 67–68.

61. Morfi had just been over the entire line from California to Texas with Croix on his tour of inspection and was in position to judge. See note 1 of this chapter.

62. *Tezontle* is a porous stone of volcanic origin extensively used in Mexico for building purposes during the colonial period. It is of a dark reddish color, very light and porous and relatively soft, but it hardens with time.

63. The façade has been accurately and carefully reproduced in the new church of St. Francis, at Waco, dedicated November 26, 1931. The church is a replica of San José mission and gives an excellent idea of the proportions and beauty of the original. It was erected to commemorate the return of the Franciscans to Texas to work among the Mexicans at the invitation of Bishop C. E. Byrne, of Galveston.

64. Morfi seems to follow closely the account given of this mission by Solís, from whom he must have drawn freely for his information. It is to be noted, however, that he is thoroughly correct in all the fundamental facts. See Bolton, *Texas,* pp. 316–324; Forrestal, *The Solís Diary.*

65. The presidio was unofficially founded by Domingo Ramón, who

was sent by Aguayo from the Rio Grande on January 16, 1720, with forty men to take possession of La Bahía, which he did on April 4 of the same year. The mission was founded at the same time, but it was not till March 24, 1722, that Aguayo personally dedicated the presidio and "made the formal grant of the mission . . . to the *padre* Agustín Patrón, of the College of Zacatecas." Buckley, "The Aguayo Expedition," pp. 55–56, 58.

66. Speaking of this bishop, Sierra says: "He visited twice his immense diocese, entering not only Nuevo León and Coahuila, but the remote province of Texas, an immense and unsettled territory, inhabited at that time by savage tribes. This difficult and painful trip, undertaken with all its corresponding privations, was the indirect cause of the death of señor Tejada, who contracted an illness during his last visit that carried him to his grave." His full name is Francisco de San Buenaventura de Tejada Diez de Velasco. He took possession of the bishopric of Guadalajara July 4, 1752, and governed the diocese till the time of his death, December 20, 1760. He was a member of the Franciscan order and had previously served as bishop of Yucatán and as auxiliary bishop of Havana and Florida, having visited Florida and having been responsible for rebuilding the old church of San Agustín some time between 1730 and 1735. Luis Alfaro y Piña, *Fundacion y descripcion de la Santa iglesia catedral de Guadalajara,* p. 11; Justo Sierra, *Francisco de San Buenaventura de Tejada Diez de Velazco,* in *Diccionario Universal,* VII, pp. 229–230.

67. No satisfactory translation for this expression has been found. Velazquez' *Dictionary* says that in a military sense the expression means, "Ravelin built before the angle or curtain of a bastion," while the old *Diccionario de la lengua* (Madrid, 1743) says the term was used sometimes to designate a shield or breastplate. This is the sense we are inclined to believe is intended in this passage.

68. For details about this settlement, see note 42, chapter I.

69. Concerning this fort near San Antonio, see note 11, chapter I.

70. Chayopines was ten leagues southeast of San Antonio. Efforts to locate or identify the other ranches mentioned here by Morfi have been fruitless. Bolton, *Texas,* p. 131. There were many ranches in Texas, mentioned from time to time in the various diaries. A study of these early establishments should be of interest in connection with the history of the development of ranching.

CHAPTER III

FRENCH INCURSIONS AND THE SPANISH EXPLORATION OF TEXAS

101. *River of the Palisades* [*Mississippi*], *1543*. The first information concerning the Mississippi was obtained in 1543 by the Spaniards who accompanied Hernando de Soto, who navigated the river, and, because of the many tree trunks that lay on its banks and were carried by the stream, called it [Rio de] la Palizada.[1] Those who saw it or heard of it did not realize its importance, occupied with discoveries and explorations which, in their opinion, were more useful, and they did not again think of it until they saw themselves forestalled by the French.

102. The French in Canada had heard through the Indians that to the west of their colony was a great river called by some Michasipi and by others Mississippi and that this river flowed neither north nor east, from which it was concluded that it must flow into the gulf of Mexico, if its course was to the south, or into the South sea, if it ran to the west.[2] In either case great advantages, no doubt, would result from its navigation.

103. M. Talon, intendant of Canada, who had already received his leave to return to France, did not wish to depart from America without ascertaining the truth concerning so important a matter.[3] He entrusted the enterprise to Father Marquette, a Jesuit missionary, and to a citizen of Quebec called Jolliet, a man of courage and experience.[4]

104. *1673, Jolliet-Marquette Expedition.* They set out in 1673 [May 15] [5] from the bay in Lake Michigan, and, having reached Fox river,[6] which empties into the bay [Green bay], they proceeded up the stream, in spite of the swift current that makes navigation difficult, and

ascended almost to its source.[7] Here they left the river and traveled overland for a distance, again embarking on the Wisconsin,[8] and, traveling always to the west, they came upon the Mississippi near 42° 30′ north latitude.[9] On June 17, 1673, they entered this famous river, the width of which, and more particularly the depth, seemed to them to correspond to the idea they had formed of the river from the description of it by the Indians. Allowing the current, which here is very moderate, to take them along, it was not long before they came upon three villages of the Illinois, situated a short distance below where the Missouri enters the Mississippi.[10]

105. *1673.* They were well received by these Indians and, after a few days of rest, continued down the river till they reached the country of the Arkansas in 33° north latitude. The lack of provisions and the small number of men in the expedition, there being only three or four besides the two leaders, did not permit them to penetrate farther.[11] Doubting no longer that the Mississippi flowed into the gulf of Mexico, they returned to the country of the Illinois, entered the river that bears this name, ascended it as high as Chicago [river], and from there continued to Lake Michigan, from which they had set out.[12] Here the two separated, Father Marquette in order to stay with the Miami Indians, a powerful nation that occupied the lower extremity of the lake, and Jolliet in order to go to Quebec to give an account of the expedition. The death of Father Marquette, which occurred in 1675,[13] and the absence of M. Talon, caused interest in the Mississippi to wane.

106. *La Salle, 1676.* But another Frenchman, who had come to America a few years before to enrich himself or gain fame in some honorable enterprise, realized that he could find no occasion more opportune to obtain

both [than this]. His name was Robert Cavelier, Sieur de la Salle. He spent his youth with the Jesuits, and the obligations contracted with this order excluded him from the inheritance of his family. He had courage and determination, but it is said that he was haughty and harsh, defects that prevented him from gathering the fruit of his labors.[14]

107. His first intention had been to search for a passage to Japan or China by way of the north or by going west of Canada, and, although destitute of everything necessary for so great an undertaking, he was wholly occupied with it when Jolliet returned to Montreal with the news of his discovery.[15] Not only did La Salle no longer doubt that the Mississippi entered the gulf of Mexico, after hearing him, but he conceived the hope that by ascending the river to the north the first object of his quest might also be accomplished. The count of Frontenac, who was his friend, promised him his help, and advised him to go to France to acquaint the government with his plans.

108. After his arrival in France he heard of the death of Colbert.[16] This misfortune made him fear for the success of his enterprise. Nevertheless he presented himself to the marquis de Seignelay,[17] who had succeeded the great man in the department of marine. The minister was so well impressed with the courage of La Salle and took such pleasure in his reports, that he secured for him all the favors desired from the king. His most Christian majesty granted him a patent of nobility and the seigniory of Catarocouy, near Lake Ontario, with jurisdiction over a fort of the same name,[18] which would be advantageous to his purposes, and invested him with very extensive powers for the establishment of commerce and the pursuance of his explorations.[19] The prince of Conti, whose acquaintance he had made,[20] became one

of his most enthusiastic protectors, asking no other return for his favor than to include in the enterprise a man whom he had honored with his patronage. This was the chevalier de Tonty, brother of a military officer in New France and son of the celebrated author of the Tontine.[21]

109. La Salle acceded to the petition of the prince, considering it but a new favor, and, in fact, he found many reasons later to congratulate himself on the good services of Tonty. He had served with distinction in Sicily, where he lost one of his hands. This he replaced with one made of iron which he used very effectively.

110. *1678, Return to Canada.* They sailed together from La Rochelle, on July 14, 1678, with thirty men, among whom they took care to include pilots and artisans. The voyage was successful, and they reached Quebec [safely], where they tarried for a short while, passing then to Catarocouy, seigniory of the Sieur de la Salle. He repaired the fort granted him [Fort Frontenac], which had no other defense than a stockade. He then advanced to the Niagara, where he established a second fort, which he called Crèvecour,[22] and placed it under the command of Tonty, leaving thirty men there. From here several expeditions were undertaken in which he suffered repeated misfortunes, to the extent that during one of these his own men tried to poison him. But this does not concern us.

111. *1680, Exploration of the Upper Mississippi.* Finally, desirous of carrying out his principal enterprise, La Salle charged M. Dacan [23] and Father Louis Hennepin, a Franciscan religious who had accompanied him from Quebec, to ascend the Mississippi above the Illinois, and if possible to its source. The two travelers left Fort Crèvecour February 28, 1680.[24] They ascended the Mississippi to 46° north latitude, where they were stopped by a very high waterfall that extended across the

whole breadth of the river. There Father Hennepin took possession of the land in the name of his most Christian majesty, called the falls St. Anthony, the river St. Louis, and the country through which it flowed Louisiana, names which happily have been preserved. Dacan started back, but because he wished to continue his explorations, Father Hennepin remained. He was captured by the Sioux who treated him kindly and came to esteem him for the knowledge of surgery this father possessed. He remained among them for a while and was voluntarily delivered to other Frenchmen who came into their lands from Canada.[25]

112. Various difficulties which arose detained La Salle at Fort Crèvecour until September [1680], when he was obliged to return to Catarocouy. While on the way, having noticed on the banks of the Illinois a site that seemed to him suited for the construction of a fort, he drew the plans and caused the chevalier de Tonty to come and take charge of their execution. Hardly had the work been started when, hearing of the insubordination of the French at Fort Crèvecour, he had to go to its rescue. In short, La Salle was kept busy, overcoming the new embarrassments that confronted him each day, until the year 1682.

113. *1682, Exploration of the Mississippi by La Salle.* Early this year La Salle went down the Illinois river, and on February 2, found himself on the Mississippi. On March 4, he took possession of the country of the Arkansas with all the ordinary formalities,[26] and on April 9, reached and reconnoitered the mouth of the river. Having completed this important discovery and taken care to establish the rights of France to the whole known course of one of the largest rivers in the world by acts of possession to which no objection could be raised,[27] he reëmbarked on April 11 and succeeded in

ascending the river as far as the Illinois, whence he proceeded to winter at Green bay, being unable to reach Quebec till the spring of the following year. A few months later he left New France to go to the court at Paris to give an account of his expedition.

114. *1683, Preparations for an expedition by sea.* In spite of the fact that his enemies had written disparagingly against him, he was received with such marked notes of esteem that he was encouraged to propose to the minister the plan he had been contemplating to explore the mouth of the Mississippi by sea, in order to open the way for French vessels, and to establish a settlement there. Not only was his project approved, but he was entrusted with the organization of the expedition.[28]

115. *1683, Terms and organization.* His commission declared that all the French and Indians found between Fort St. Louis on the Illinois and New Biscay [Nueva Vizcaya] were to be under his jurisdiction; that the commander of the squadron who was to conduct him from France to America was to be governed by his advice while *en route,* and was to give him all the assistance possible in effecting a landing, compatible with the safety of the king's vessels.[29] Four ships of different sizes were armed and made ready at Rochefort [30] in which 280 persons took passage with their equipages. There were, besides these, one Canadian family, the head of which was named Talon; one hundred soldiers; thirty volunteers, many of whom were of gentle birth; some maidens; several hired servants; and a few artisans; but the selection was poorly made. The greater part of the soldiers were wretched beggars; many were deformed or maimed and did not know how to use their guns. The artisans were no better, and experience soon revealed that no one understood his profession or trade.[31]

116. Among the volunteers were Cavelier and Moran-

get, two nephews of La Salle, of whom the first was only fourteen years old; three ecclesiastics of St. Sulpice, one a brother and the other a kinsman of La Salle, the third being named Mazulle;[32] four religious of the order of St. Francis: Fr. [Zenobius] Membré, who had accompanied La Salle in his previous explorations; Fr. [Maximus] Le Clercq, who had served in Canada for several years; Fr. [Anastasius] Douay; and Fr. [James] Marquette (of whom we have a very valuable relation), all destined either to remain in the new establishment or to labor among the Indians, but the fourth fell sick the first day out and was returned to land, for which reason he did not undertake the voyage;[33] and, lastly, a native of Rouen called Joutel, in whom La Salle recognized such probity that he made him practically his intendant [lieutenant].[34]

117. The four vessels were the *Joly,* a royal ship of about forty guns; a frigate of six guns, called the *Belle,* given by the king to La Salle; the *Amiable,* capable of carrying about three hundred tons burden, laden with all the effects [of the expedition]; and a ketch of about thirty tons burden, laden with munitions and merchandise.[35] The commander of the royal ship was named Beaujeu, his lieutenant was [M. le Chevalier] d'Aire, and his ensign was [le Sieur de] Hamel.

118. *1684, The expedition by sea.* The small fleet set out from La Rochelle July 24, 1684, together with the fleet which was going to the islands and to Canada. All the ships were to sail together under the orders of the commander [Beaujeu] until they reached the coast of Spain, but an accident[36] detained the *Joly* five or six days and separated it from the rest of the fleet. This did not prevent the expedition from reaching the island of Madeira by August 16. Jealousy over the question of authority between the commander and La Salle augured ill for

the success of an enterprise in which they should have shared honors, particularly when their rivalry resulted in the loss of the small ketch, captured off the coast of Santo Domingo by two Spanish pirogues. Nevertheless, after the expedition had reached a French port on this island,[37] it rounded the western extremity of Cuba and on September 28 [*sic*] [38] came upon the coast of Florida.

119. La Salle had been told that in the gulf of Mexico the currents flowed east, from which he deduced that the mouth of the Mississippi must be far to the west.[39] This error was the cause of all his misfortunes. It made him sail in this direction, making progress slow, and forcing him from time to time to approach the coast in an effort to detect the object of his quest.

120. *1685*. On January 10, 1685, he was very close to the mouth of the river, as it was afterwards ascertained, but, convinced that he was in the midst of Apalachee bay, he steered west without sending the longboat to reconnoiter the coast. A few days later, better informed by the Indians, he tried to return to the same place, but the commandant, though duty bound by the orders of the king to follow La Salle's advice, refused to hear him and the latter desisted from his purpose. The course was continued to the west and the fleet soon after reached the bay of San Bernardo, unknown to them. This bay is one hundred leagues west of the mouth of the Mississippi.[40]

121. *1685*. The ships anchored, and the longboats were sent to reconnoiter. They discovered a beautiful river,[41] at the bar of which there were only ten or twelve feet of water. After many explorations and many councils in which nothing was settled, because the moment one of the two leaders proposed anything the other immediately opposed it, La Salle, who did not think he was far from the Mississippi, and to whom the presence of the

frigate commander was irksome, decided to land at the place where they were.

122. The following day, which was February 10,[42] he sent orders to the commander of the fleet to unload the heaviest part of the cargo in order that the ship, being lightened, could cross the bar. At the same time, not having enough faith in the skill of this officer to entrust him with a maneuver that was difficult, he ordered the captain of the *Belle* to take charge of this operation. The commander [Beaujeu] regarded this as a slight and refused to obey. La Salle was embarrassed by this disobedience which he did not expect, and decided that the maneuver should be carried out in his presence. But, as he was about to supervise it, a lieutenant of infantry named Sablonnière and five or six Frenchmen who had gone for a walk to a wood nearby were captured by the Indians. This news obliged him to go to their rescue. As he withdrew from the bank of the river, turning to gaze at the bar, he saw the ship in motion, but maneuvering with such ill grace that it was threatened with destruction. The desire to save his men overcame his apprehension and he went in pursuit of the Indians, from whom he recovered the prisoners. A cannon shot which he heard [while engaged in this] warned him of the misfortune that had befallen his vessel.

123. In fact, he found the ship grounded.[43] There is no doubt that this accident was a premeditated design of Captain Aigron. The vessel had on board the munitions, utensils, tools, and everything that was necessary for the establishment [of a settlement]. La Salle, who regretted not having foreseen this loss, the greatest misfortune that could have befallen him, made haste to remedy the situation. Great was his astonishment to see part of those who had witnessed the misfortune standing idle. Nevertheless, with the longboat and skiff of the frigate,

which Beaujeu did not dare refuse him, he began to salvage by rescuing the baggage. He then thought of the powder, the provisions, and the liqueurs, and succeeded in taking about thirty barrels ashore. If the longboat of the frigate had coöperated efficiently in the rescue work, almost the whole cargo might have been saved. But it seems that this boat was purposely delayed, and, with night coming on, it became necessary to wait till the next day to continue the salvage. A short while afterwards the wind which blew in from the sea freshened, the waves rose and lashed the ship to pieces against the rocks, and much of its cargo was carried away by the strong currents. As the state of the vessel was unknown until day dawned, only thirty barrels of wine and gin and some flour, salted meat, and vegetables were saved.

124. *1685.* This loss was followed by others still more regrettable. The Indians were already beginning to crowd around, and all precautions were useless in preventing them from stealing part of what had been saved from the wreck. [This new loss] was not discovered until after the Indians had retired with their loot. They left some canoes on the shore, which the French took, a poor recompense for which they paid dearly. The Indians returned that night for their canoes, and, finding those who were guarding them asleep, they killed two—Orray and Desloges—wounded others, and made their retreat without other loss than that of their canoes, which they did not have time to take with them.[44]

125. So many misfortunes, coming together, discouraged many of those who had embarked on this expedition, especially when the most hostile began to discredit the conduct of the leader, declaring that the enterprise was foolhardy and rash. Far from being disheartened on this account, La Salle showed greater courage and resolution than ever. He had a storehouse constructed and sur-

rounded it with trenches. He then decided to explore the river, believing it to be a branch of the Mississippi.

126. *1685*. As the frigate was making ready to return to France, La Salle begged Beaujeu to leave him the cannon and mortars which he had on board and which had been placed there solely for the [protection] of the settlement. Beaujeu replied that these were in the hold of the ship and it would be necessary to unload everything to get them out, and that this operation required more time than he had at his disposal in order to avoid the dangers of the bad season on the return trip. Thus La Salle found himself reduced to the six small pieces on board the *Belle,* without a single ball for them.

127. Beaujeu gave him a still clearer proof of his ill will. Though the perfidy of the captain of the wrecked vessel was well established,[45] he received him on his ship with all his baggage, purposely to enable him to escape the punishment he deserved, and in open violation of his pledged word to La Salle not to take on board anyone without his consent. He set sail on March 15.[46]

128. *1685*. The number of Frenchmen left at the bay of San Bernardo [Lavaca] was 220. La Salle ordered immediately the construction of a fort, and left Joutel, with 120 men under his orders, to finish it, while he embarked on the river with the intention of ascending it as far as possible.[47] Among the fifty who were to accompany him, he took [M. de Cavelier] his brother, Father Chefdeville, two Franciscans, and many volunteers. His expedition, however, was interrupted immediately. The Indians came every night close to the fort that was being erected, and Joutel, who had instructions to keep them at a respectful distance, ordered some shots to be fired, the noise of which was heard by La Salle. He could not have been very far, as he at once repaired to the fort with six or seven men, and, finding Joutel safe, told him that

he had discovered a beautiful site; that it was his intention to build a fort at the place where he had left his force; and that he had actually given instructions to that effect before he left.

129. *1685.* He then set out to join his men, but upon his arrival he found that many of the workmen had allowed the Indians to rob them of their tools. They were supplied with others, but he soon discovered that they were no more able to use their tools than they were able to defend them. He was obliged to bring up [to the new fort] some of the artisans he had left at the first. This not only delayed the work, but it made the others who remained with Joutel conspire against him, irritated, perhaps, by the additional work placed upon them. Joutel discovered the plot in time to prevent disorder, and, having notified La Salle, was ordered to join him with all his men. In this manner the first fort was abandoned, but the work on the second was intensified. In spite of the disappointments which oppressed La Salle, and the many obstacles encountered, he was the architect of his enterprise, and, by setting an example of industry and firmness, he succeeded at last in inspiring emulation.

130. The new fort was called St. Louis.[48] It offered them protection against the attacks of the natives, whom they had come to regard as a very dangerous nation. These were the Clamcoats (Carancaguases), cruel, treacherous, naturally taunting, and very cunning. Having completed the fort, La Salle decided to reconnoiter the bay of San Bernardo with his vessel. He set out in October, leaving only thirty-four men in the fort under the command of the prudent Joutel, with orders not to receive any of those who accompanied him without a letter in his own handwriting.[49] Death had deprived him of many of his bravest followers, like [the Sieur de] Villeperdry and Le Gross, his quartermaster, who, being

bitten by a rattlesnake and not knowing the antidote, which is found everywhere in this country (the viperine), had his leg amputated; he survived the operation only a few days. These losses not only afflicted La Salle, but made him melancholic, and his sadness seemed to increase his natural haughtiness and aloofness.

131. *1686.* His absence lasted more than three months, during which no news of him reached the fort of St. Louis. At last, during the month of January, 1686,[50] very sad tidings were obtained through a Frenchman called Duhaut, whose brother, named Dominic, had remained at the fort without going with La Salle. The elder, who had gone with La Salle, reached the fort without a letter from his commander. He came alone, in a canoe, and in the night was heard calling his brother. The sentinel notified Joutel, who, fearing for a moment some fatal accident had befallen La Salle, went forward to meet him in order to be the first to hear the news, but Duhaut assured him that his chief was enjoying perfect health and confessed, of course, that he had returned without his permission. He gave an air of such simplicity to the account of his adventures that Joutel thought he was excused from acting harshly toward him. Here is his account.

132. He declared that when La Salle came in sight of the frigate [the *Belle*], he sent five of the best men with orders to the pilot, to sound the bay in a canoe. The pilot employed a whole day in this exercise, and that night, being tired, went ashore with those who had given him his orders. They lighted a fire and went to sleep next to it, without taking any precautions against the Indians. The barbarians, warned by the fire of the presence of strangers in their country, surprised them, killed all six while they slept peacefully, and destroyed the canoe.

133. *1686.* Seeing that the men did not return, La

Salle went in search of them and found their remains, partly devoured by wild beasts. He grieved much over the loss of the pilot, whose ability he knew well. Some days later he had occasion to regret it still more. His first care was to have the frigate moved to the bay and to load it with all the supplies necessary for his enterprise. He placed some of his men aboard with instructions not to leave the ship without orders from him, or to go ashore without an escort. He then took twenty men and crossed the river in two canoes, which he sank in the water after he saw himself on the opposite bank, continuing his march overland. A few days brought him to the river which he called Maligne.[51] A short distance beyond, Duhaut, having lagged behind the party, had the misfortune of getting lost. For a time he wandered aimlessly, and, without knowing how, he found himself one day in front of Fort St. Louis.

134. *1686.* As the story seemed plausible, Joutel did not doubt it and contented himself with watching the conduct of Duhaut. During the month of March, La Salle arrived at the fort with part of his men, having sent the rest in search of the frigate, though it is not stated where it had been left.[52] Though he did not find what he was looking for in this expedition, he was well satisfied to have discovered so beautiful a country. The sight of Duhaut, whom he suspected of desertion, surprised him greatly, but when Joutel informed him of the circumstances, he asked for no further explanations. The rest of his men arrived the next day, without having found the frigate, which grieved La Salle much, because he had placed on board all the linen, clothes, papers, and his best goods. Furthermore, he had intended to use the ship to explore some of the rivers he had discovered, sending her later to the French islands to bring some needed supplies. In it he would have followed the various streams

that flow into the bay in an effort to locate the Mississippi, until all hope of finding it was lost, and then he would have explored the gulf coast until he found its mouth.

135. After six weeks of useless solicitude, he decided, with his accustomed firmness, to set out in search of a new route. Scarcely had he left when Chefdeville, Sablonnière, and a few others of those who had been left on the frigate, arrived at the fort in a canoe with the clothes of La Salle, part of his papers, and a few supplies. They came to inform Joutel that the ship had been wrecked. The details of a loss which deprived La Salle of his only hope of reënforcement, after so many misfortunes, cannot be omitted. It seems that when the water on board became low, some men were sent ashore in the longboat to bring a fresh supply. As they were returning to the ship, they were detained by a high wind, and night overtook them before they could reach the vessel. Those on board, seeing the men trying to make their way back, lighted a signal lamp to guide them through the darkness. But the light went out shortly afterwards, and, not taking care to relight it or to replace it with another, neither the longboat nor those in it were ever heard of again. They waited for them uselessly several days. Finally, those aboard the frigate, compelled by thirst, tried to reach the river, but their extreme weakness and lack of skill prevented them from executing this maneuver properly, and the wind being contrary [to their purpose], the ship was grounded on the opposite shore of the bay. Without boats and in an unknown country, they could think of nothing but to build a raft to cross the bay. This was so poorly constructed that the first who attempted [to cross] were all drowned. Those left behind built a better one, placed on this all they could save from the ship, and crossed the bay. But the fear of the Indians prevented them from making their way back to the fort by land, and it was im-

possible to ascend the river in the raft. Consequently, they were extremely happy to find an old Indian canoe, which they mended and used in order to return to the fort.

136. Two months elapsed without news from La Salle, and his absence caused much dissatisfaction in the colony. The elder Duhaut, whose brother had gone with La Salle, placed himself at the head of the mutinous group, and Joutel was informed that he aspired to nothing less than his position. It does not seem that at this time he had yet formed the dark designs we shall presently see him put into execution. The authority of Joutel was sufficient still to restrain him until the return of La Salle, who came back to the fort at the end of August.[53]

137. The loss of the frigate afflicted him greatly but did not make him lose his courage in the least. He had penetrated as far as the country of the Asinais (which he calls Cenis or Asenis), with whom he made an alliance, but he had learned no more than he knew before of what he was trying to discover. The fruit of his expedition was reduced to five horses loaded with supplies and presented to him by the Asinais. Of the twenty men who set out with him, he brought back eight. Duhaut, the younger, and four others whom he had sent back to the fort, never arrived. One named Bihorel, who unfortunately lost his way, was, likewise, never heard of again. Another, named Dumesnil, was dragged to the bottom of a river and devoured there by an alligator, and four deserted while in the country of the Asinais.

138. Such repeated and endless misfortunes necessarily made a deep impression upon the settlement. La Salle paid little heed to them, having already formed his plan for a third expedition [in search of the Mississippi]. But the heat, which was excessive, obliged him to put it off until the month of October. In the interim, the Carancaguases, with whom no definite alliance had been pos-

sible, killed two of his men almost before his eyes, an incident that confirmed him in his determination to leave the country of this barbarous people. It was his intention to discover a route that should take him to the Illinois. He was about to set out when a serious case of hernia detained him. Joutel, seeing him in this condition, offered to make the trip with fifteen men, but the offer was rejected. La Salle believed his presence among the Illinois was necessary, and it was his purpose to send his brother from there to Quebec and thence to France to make a report.

139. By the end of December, he thought he had recovered his strength sufficiently to undertake the execution of his plans. Joutel desired to accompany him; consequently, Barbier, another of his trusted friends, was left in command of the fort. While La Salle was at the settlement, the defenses of the fort had been placed in condition to resist the attacks of the Carancaguases. He left sufficient supplies and ammunition for the settlers who remained, twenty persons in all, of whom seven were women. This number included the two Franciscan missionaries, Fathers Chefdeville, La Sablonnière, and a surgeon.

140. *1687, Last expedition of La Salle.* On January 12, 1687, La Salle set out from Fort St. Louis with twelve men,[54] whose names have been preserved because of the importance of the events [that followed]. They were M. de Cavelier, his brother; Moranget, and the young Cavelier, his nephews; Father Anastasius [Douay], the Franciscan; Joutel; Duhaut [the elder]; Marle; Xetot; l'Archevêque; an Englishman called James [Hiens]; Liotot, the surgeon; Teissier, a pilot; young Talon; Saget, servant of La Salle; and an Indian hunter [Nika].[55] The five horses of the Asinais were laden with the greater part of the baggage and supplies. Even though the march was made over one of the most beau-

tiful countries in the world, this did not prevent great suffering as a result of the water supply, which, owing to the floods occasioned by the rains, was very poor. Though Indians were encountered frequently, La Salle had the art of always winning their favor with his courteous treatment. The greatest obstacles were the rivers that had to be crossed. [To overcome this] La Salle invented a portable canoe which was carried on poles and proved very useful. In proportion as they advanced they found the country more populated. When they were forty leagues from the Asinais they learned that the Indians had a Frenchman living among them.

141. But the time of sorrow was at hand. On May 17,[56] while out on a hunting expedition, Moranget treated Duhaut, James, and Liotot with some harshness, and these three men decided to do away with him, as well as with the servant and hunter of his uncle, who were with him and might protect him. They communicated their design to l'Archevêque and Teissier, who not only approved of it but desired to take part in its execution. They did not disclose their plan to Marle, who was also a member of the hunting party and whom they wished to remove, if possible, from the scene. The following night, when the three unfortunate victims [Moranget, Nika, and Saget] were sleeping peacefully, Liotot began the bloody work by striking each one of them several times on the head with a hatchet. The servant and the hunter died instantly, but Moranget staggered to his feet, without strength to utter a word. The assassins forced Marle to finish the murder, threatening him with a similar fate if he refused, in order to make an accomplice of him, no doubt.

142. Realizing, then, that all their precautions would prove useless in deceiving La Salle and saving them from his vengeance, they determined to kill him. With this per-

fidious intention, they now thought of nothing but of falling on him and putting an end to his life and that of those who might try to defend him. But an unforeseen incident made them change their plans somewhat. A river which separated them from the camp was swollen by a flood that came up after they had crossed it, and this detained them a day or two. The delay, which at first seemed to them an obstacle to the execution of their plan, later turned out to have helped their designs. La Salle, worried at the delay of his nephew and his two companions, decided to go in search of them himself, rather than trust anyone with an undertaking that he felt was dangerous. It was observed that before he set out he seemed deeply perturbed, and that he asked whether Moranget had quarreled with anyone. He then called Joutel and entrusted the command of the camp to him, asking that a watch be kept; that no one be allowed to leave during his absence; and that fires be lighted to guide him on his return should he get lost.

143. *Murder of La Salle.* He left the camp on the 20th, accompanied by Father Anastasius and an Indian. As he approached the place where the murderers had camped, he noticed many crows [buzzards] that circled in the air a short distance away. This made him think that there was some dead animal in the neighborhood. He fired a shot, and the conspirators, who were unaware of his approach, doubted not that it was he and made ready their arms. The river still lay between them. Duhaut, Liotot, and l'Achevêque came over, and, as they saw La Salle slowly approach them, Duhaut hid among the weeds, while l'Archevêque went forward a little farther to meet him. A moment later, La Salle, recognizing him, inquired for his nephew. That same instant Duhaut fired a shot that pierced his head and caused him to drop dead.

144. *1687.* Such was the end of a man worthy, be-

cause of his ability, his valor, and his constancy, of a better fate.[57] There is no doubt, as Prévost reflects, that if his purpose had been only to establish a settlement at the [mouth of the] Mississippi, he could have accomplished it without so many misfortunes, and, perhaps, without exposing himself to the perfidy of his followers. Even if he had not penetrated to the country of the Asinais, or if these had not given him guides to lead him to the river, he could have reached it by sea. He knew that he was west of the goal he was searching for, and he cannot have forgotten the instructions given him at court, according to which he should have gone back [to the Mississippi]. But if Beaujeu prevented him from doing so, he still could have embarked in the frigate [after Beaujeu's departure] and gone in quest of the mouth of the river which he doubtless would have found, saving his men from misfortune, establishing a colony, and securing for himself a more glorious end, perhaps. But, it is said, declares Prévost, that he wished to approach, without delay, our possessions to acquire information concerning the famous mines of Santa Bárbara.[58] It is further added, says this author, that he obtained this idea in France, where it was so commonly entertained, that the obsession of realizing this chimera prevailed there for a long time and retarded the fruits that might have been secured from his misfortunes and failures. In a note on page 98, volume 26 (octavo edition), he remarks: "They even flattered themselves [in France] that they would attain it [the possession of the mines of Santa Bárbara] by an understanding with the count of Peñalosa,[59] but the extreme pretentions of this count thwarted the negotiations." Who was this man who called himself the count of Peñalosa and took refuge in France? And what were the propositions which he made to that government, and why were they not accepted? All these questions we shall explain in our history of New Mexico,[60] of which province this supposed count was governor. But let us return to our province of Texas.

145. *1688.* The murderers of La Salle found the punishment of their treachery in themselves. They killed each other for various reasons and at various times. Joutel, who also feared for his life, found, at last, the means of leaving the country of the Asinais, and, thanks to a guide furnished him by those faithful Indians, succeeded in reaching the country of the Illinois. [He was accompanied] by the two Caveliers, Father Anastasius [Douay], Marle, Teissier, and a young man from Paris named Bartholomey. They left the country of the Illinois March 21, 1688, and after many adventures reached La Rochelle on October 5 of the same year.[61]

146. When Joutel arrived in France, it was thought (justly) that it was too late to give aid to, or attempt to rescue, those who had remained at Fort St. Louis. In fact, the Carancaguases, who could not have remained long in ignorance of the death of La Salle and the dispersion of his followers, fell upon the French colony, when they were least expected, and killed all the settlers, with the exception of the three sons of Talon, their sister, and one Eustace de Bremont, whom they took as captives to their ranchería.[62] An Italian, who had come from Canada overland to join La Salle, saved his life by a very ingenious idea. Seeing that the Indians were determined to kill him, he said to them that they would be doing a great wrong to kill a man who carried all of them in his heart. This statement caused surprise to the Indians. The Italian then explained that if they would give him until the next day, he would prove his words; that this delay would in no way prevent them from doing as they pleased with him, being masters of his life. The time was granted. That night he fixed securely a small mirror upon his

breast and in this manner presented himself to the Indians next day. So great was the surprise experienced by the Carancaguases when they saw one another reflected in the glass, either in groups or individually, that, believing it was a window to his heart, they granted him his life.[63]

147. M. Prévost, either misinformed or prejudiced against us, which seems more likely, as we shall see later, declared that the Spaniards of New Mexico, whom the enterprise of La Salle had frightened, made several attempts to destroy his settlement; that they sent five hundred men to the Asinais, who captured several Frenchmen, among them Groslet and Yvetot, who were taken to Spain, whence they were sent back to New Mexico, apparently to work in the mines; and that the Italian was conducted as a prisoner to Veracruz, where he would probably not be released, lest he be destined for the same work [as his French companions]. It is strange that a man as well informed of our history in America as Prévost should suppose us so active in the defense of our possessions and so inhuman in our treatment of the unfortunate captives.[64] This manner of speech serves only to excite or promote a certain rancor between two nations that have many reasons for being friendly. The Spaniards of New Mexico had not heard of the expedition of La Salle up to that time [1689], nor were any forces sent from there, nor did those who went in his search number five hundred, nor were the French captives treated so inhumanly.[65] All these arguments we shall now see explained with clearness, granting that the truth of the statements can be proved by authentic documents found in the secretariat of the viceroyalty [of New Spain], where the marquis of Altamira [66] examined them while preparing his report of 1744. No one will give less

credit to the documents presented by a man of his character in a private report to the viceroy than to the declarations of the two ungrateful Talons.[67]

148. It was natural to expect that the baggage and papers of La Salle's ship, captured by officials in Santo Domingo, should have warned them. But, either because of neglect, or because it was thought that the enterprise was limited to the Mississippi, they failed to notify, as they should, the viceroy of New Spain, where everything the French were doing in its immediate vicinity was ignored for a long time, until an accident revealed the secret. In 1686 [1685] a French frigate, called *Nuestra Señora de Regla,* was captured in the gulf of Mexico, and it was from its crew that information concerning La Salle's settlement on the bay of Espíritu Santo was secured.[68] The declarations of the prisoners were transmitted to the viceroy, the marquis of Laguna,[69] who communicated the information to the court, and, while waiting for his instructions, dispatched Captain Juan Enrique Barroto to reconnoiter the location of the new establishment in a small vessel.[70] It was fortunate for Barroto that he did not discover the bay, and that the *Belle* was shipwrecked, for had he crossed the bar, he and the few men who accompanied him would have gone inevitably to increase the number of unfortunate wretches in Fort St. Louis, such was their lack of proper equipment for an encounter [with the enemy]. Nevertheless, his trip was not altogether fruitless, for he discovered the celebrated bay of Pensacola.[71]

149. The king, informed of the settlement of the French in a country so near to Veracruz, ordered the viceroy to continue, at all costs, the reconnaissance of the bay of Espíritu Santo.[72] Two other expeditions were undertaken, therefore, from Veracruz, by different cap-

tains,[73] with no greater success than the first. Without any further efforts, either by land or sea, to reach the colony planted by the French on the coast of the gulf of Mexico, the province of Texas and La Salle were forgotten in Mexico until the year 1688.

150. *1688.* During this year, a Frenchman by the name of Juan Enrique [Jean Géry],[74] who had succeeded in winning the favor of the Indians among whom he lived [as king], was captured on the frontiers of the province of Coahuila. He was taken to Mexico city, where he informed the viceroy of La Salle's undertaking, the establishment of the fort, and of its location. He offered to lead or guide such troops as his excellency should decide to send to dislodge the French. No doubt he was one of the deserters who fled before misfortune overtook the leader, for he was ignorant of the fate of his companions.[75]

151. The viceroy could no longer disregard so detailed a report, made in public, and in order to carry out the orders given him by the court, he issued instructions, availing himself of the offer of the Frenchman to the governor of the province of Coahuila, Alonso de León,[76] for him to explore the country and question La Salle if he found him.

152. *1688.* This expedition could have no other purpose, if it is considered that the viceroy knew the number of Frenchmen who had been left at the bay of San Bernardo, that a fort had been built there, that this was provided with artillery—though but a few pieces,—and that the garrison had a frigate to protect it. The small number of men taken by De León, fatigued by the long journey, without artillery, and with no hope of aid from the natives whom they did not know, could not expect to dislodge the French. Consequently, his intentions were

peaceful, and he hoped that when the new colonists were informed of our rights, they would leave. If they refused, this would justify the use of force in the future.

153. *1689, Discovery of La Salle's colony by De León.* On March 23, 1689, Alonso de León, with one hundred men and all the necessary supplies, left the villa of Santiago de la Monclova, taking as his guide the Frenchman Juan Enrique.[77] They proceeded on their journey without mishap and reached the coast of the bay of San Bernardo, now called Espíritu Santo [present Lavaca bay], by which name we shall refer to it in the future, on April 22. He found the fort destroyed, the houses in ruins, and the French either dead or dispersed. He rested there that night, and on the following day, the 23rd, he explored the bay, which he judged was capable of accommodating small vessels (though we have seen how Beaujeu's ships were able to anchor there). On the 26th, they examined and sounded the Guadalupe river,[78] which flows into the bay.

154. The first of May, the captain or chief of the Texas presented himself to De León, and brought with him two Frenchmen,[79] whose faces were marked with stripes as those of the natives. They told him of the tragic end of La Salle and the disastrous fate of his followers, but their account differs somewhat from that given by Prévost. They declared that more than one hundred had died of smallpox, and the rest had perished at the cruel hands of the barbarous Carancaguases. With regard to Joutel and those who accompanied him back to France, they knew nothing.

155. Alonso de León took the two Frenchmen with him, feasted and gave presents to the captain of the Texas, who bade him a grateful farewell and promised to visit him in Coahuila with some of his braves, and de-

parted, without any further investigations and leaving no one to occupy the bay to prevent a second landing. He proceeded to Monclova, whence he rendered an account to the viceroy of the expedition, and commended the great advantages the country offered for settlement. He sent the two Frenchmen to him, that they, having had experience, might acquaint him with the facts more in detail and with greater clearness.[80]

NOTES TO FRENCH INCURSIONS AND THE SPANISH EXPLORATION OF TEXAS

1. The river was known to the Spaniards before this date. Alonso de Pineda was the first to note it in his map of the exploration of the gulf coast from Florida to Tampico, in 1519, in which he calls it Espíritu Santo. (Cervantes de Salazar, *Crónica de la Nueva España,* opposite page 1.) Cabeza de Vaca also knew of the river, as shown by his *Relación.* Just why Morfi fixed upon the year 1543 is not clear, as De Soto first reached the river early in May, 1541, crossed it some time in June, and returned almost a year later to die on its banks (May 21 or June 24, 1542). The survivors of the expedition, under Moscoso, finally reached Pánuco, September 10, 1543, and a few went on to Mexico city. This is perhaps the reason for the date given by Morfi. Garcilaso de la Vega, *La Florida del Inca; Narrative of the Expedition of Hernando de Soto into Florida, by a Gentleman of Elvas,* in French, *Historical Collections of Louisiana,* II, pp. 114–123.

As to the logs and timber, the Gentleman of Elvas says: "There came down the river continually many trees and timber, which the force of the water and stream brought down." See also Francis Borgia Steck, *The Jolliet-Marquette Expedition,* pp. 7–21.

2. It was a Jesuit missionary, Claude Allouez, who first learned from the Indians that the "Great Water" was a river and that its Indian name was "Messipi." "Where it emptied the Indians could not tell him; but the missionary concluded that it flowed probably toward Virginia." Steck, *Jolliet-Marquette Expedition,* pp. 109–110. Between 1665 and 1667, Allouez learned further details concerning the river from the Hurons, Ottawas, Foxes, Illinois, Dakotas, and Sioux, and on his return from Chequamegon bay to the mission of Sault Sainte Marie, where Marquette was stationed, he confided this information to him. *Jesuit Relations,* vol. 51, pp. 47, 53. It was Claude Dablon, another Jesuit missionary, who first suggested the possibility of the river's flowing to the gulf of Mexico or the South sea. In a letter to the superior general at Quebec, he says: "A great river . . . coming from the region of the north, flows south . . . to such a distance that the savages who navigated it . . . after a good many days' journey have not found its mouth, which can be only toward the Sea of Florida [gulf of Mexico] or that of California [South sea]." *Ibid.,* vol. 54, pp. 137–139.

3. M. Jean Talon was appointed intendant for the first time on March 23, 1665. Brodhead, *Documents relative to the Colonial History of New York,* IX, pp. 22–23. He served from 1665 to 1668, returned to France, where he remained till 1670, when he was reappointed intendant of New France, in which capacity he served until 1672. He was very much interested in the discovery of the Mississippi.

4. Talon was deeply interested in the "Great River." Before the

Jolliet-Marquette expedition, he had dispatched Jean Péré and Louis Jolliet, two merchants, as early as 1668, to explore the country west and northwest of Canada. Many attempts to reach and explore the river followed, one of these having been undertaken by La Salle, all of which are ably discussed in the scholarly study of Rev. Francis Borgia Steck, O.F.M., in his *The Jolliet-Marquette Expedition,* pp. 101–140.

Morfi is correct in stating that Talon was no longer intendant when the expedition set out, though he was instrumental in organizing it and selecting the leader, Jolliet. "Talon was ill at ease," declares Steck. "Before long the vessels would arrive from France, bringing the new governor and his own discharge. Was he then to have no share in the project which he had hoped to make the crowning achievement of his career in the colony?" *Ibid.,* p. 146.

As to the qualifications of Jolliet for the expedition, he says: "In the summer of 1667, after leaving the seminary at Quebec where he had been studying for the priesthood, Jolliet accompanied Tracy to France. Here he took a special course in hydrography and the allied sciences; whereupon, probably the next summer, he returned to Canada. During the ensuing four years, as trader and trapper, he penetrated far into the western regions, traversed the Great Lakes route to Green Bay, learned several of the Indian languages, and manifested remarkable tact in his dealings with the natives." *Ibid.,* p. 146.

5. The expedition set out on May 15, and not the 13th or 17th, as has been asserted, from Mission St. Ignace. It followed a westward course along Lake Michigan. *Ibid.,* p. 151.

6. They reached this river on June 5, after having visited St. Michael mission on the Menominee river, and mission St. Francis Xavier on the present site of De Pere. *Ibid.,* p. 152.

7. There are two rivers of the same name. The one meant here is the Upper Fox, which empties into Lake Winnebago. *Ibid.,* p. 152.

8. They ascended the Upper Fox to the present town of Berlin, Green Lake county, Wisconsin, reaching an Indian village situated there, on June 7. A short distance above "a portage of 2700 paces brought them to the Wisconsin." *Ibid.,* pp. 152–153.

9. It is surprising that Morfi should have the facts of this expedition so accurately. Steck has quoted from a manuscript relation to prove this is the correct latitude and has pointed out that Jolliet's map places it at 41°. *Ibid.,* p. 153.

10. There is evidently an error here. Morfi meant *above* instead of *below* the Missouri. *Ibid.,* p. 159.

11. There were seven men in all. The reasons for the decision to return, as given by the explorers themselves, may be summarized as follows. They had reached a point 33° 40′ north latitude; they figured correctly that they were but a short distance from its mouth and that the river must enter the gulf, as they were below the latitude of Virginia;

the general southern course proved it could not empty into the South sea; and, lastly, to continue to the mouth meant to risk capture by the Spaniards or destruction by the Indians, who were more hostile as they proceeded down the river. *Ibid.,* pp. 151, 163.

12. On the return trip the expedition ascended with difficulty to the Illinois river, then up this stream to a point near the present site of Utica, up to its northern fork, the Des Plaines, which they followed for a short distance, then, crossing a short portage to the Chicago river, they followed this stream to Lake Michigan, arriving at the mission of St. Francis Xavier in September, 1673. *Ibid.,* p. 167.

13. Marquette had been in poor health for some time. He remained among the Miamis, after his return, in the neighborhood of Chicago. The following year he undertook a trip to the Illinois and on his return, on May 18, 1675, he and his two companions were forced to seek shelter, because of the weather, at a small stream that empties into the lake. Father Marquette was very low, and he died that night. The river bears his name to this day. French, *Hist. Col.,* II, p. 280, note; Steck, *Jolliet-Marquette Expedition,* pp. 190–191.

14. La Salle was born at Rouen, November 22, 1643. His connection with the Jesuits has been questioned, but the fact that he lost the right to the family estate is substantiated. "His connections with the Jesuits had deprived him, under the French Law, of the inheritance of his father. . . . An allowance was made to him of three or . . . four hundred livres a year, the capital of which was paid over to him; and with this pittance he sailed for Canada, to seek his fortune, in the spring of 1666." Parkman, *La Salle and the Discovery of the Great West,* pp. 3–4.

15. Jolliet made another visit to the Illinois before going to Montreal. He did not start back until May, 1674. On his way, he stopped at Fort Frontenac, about 150 miles from Montreal. This fort had been erected in the summer of 1673 by Frontenac, who placed La Salle in charge of it. According to Shea, it was here that Jolliet first met La Salle and told him of his explorations, showing him his diary and map. (Shea, *Discovery and Exploration,* p. xxxiv.) Steck says: "If that is correct, we can understand why La Salle, so soon after the meeting, took steps to have the fort granted him in seigniory. This fort, he figured, might well be made the center of his operations for the exploration of the Mississippi." Steck, *Jolliet-Marquette Expedition,* p. 169.

16. Jean Baptiste Colbert was the trusted and able minister of Louis XIV. He became minister of marine, commerce, the colonies, and the king's palace in 1669. His influence was all powerful until the rise of his rival Louvois. He did not die until September 6, 1683. Morfi is evidently in error here. Boulenger, *The Seventeenth Century,* pp. 333–345.

17. This was Jean Baptiste Colbert, jr., son of the great minister. He was born November 1, 1651, and died November 3, 1690. In 1669, he became *secrétaire d'Etat en servivance.* In 1683, he succeeded his father as

secretary of marine. As La Salle did not return to France until the fall of 1677, it was to Colbert's father that he presented his project. *La Grande Encyclopédie,* XI, p. 893; Parkman, *La Salle,* p. 110.

18. Fort Cataraqui, soon renamed Fort Frontenac.

19. The letters patent read: "To accomplish this [the discovery of the mouth of the Mississippi and a road to penetrate Mexico] . . . we give you full powers; on condition . . . the whole be done at your expense, and that of your company, to which we have granted the privilege of the trade in buffalo skins." French, *Hist. Col.,* I, pp. 35–36.

20. The prince of Conti was at this time (1677–78) about seventeen years of age, but very influential because he was a descendant of the house of Bourbon-Condé. *La Grande Encyclopédie,* XII, pp. 783–784.

21. This was Henri de Tonty, son of Lorenzo de Tonti, a Neapolitan banker who came to France in 1650 and originated a plan of group insurance known as Tontine. For details concerning his life, see "Chevalier de Tonty's Petition to the King," in French, *Hist. Col.,* I, pp. 79–82. This is also published in Margry, *Découvertes,* I, pp. 573–616.

22. Fort Crèvecour, from a careful examination of all information available, seems to have been on the upper Illinois and not on the Niagara. It was the third fort established by La Salle and not the second. Tonty says: "As it was necessary to fortify ourselves during the winter we made a fort which was called *Crevecoeur* [Jan. 3, 1680]. . . . He [La Salle] gave me the command of this place and left us on the 22d of March." French, *Hist. Col.,* I, pp. 54–55. Reynolds says, however: "About the last of December [1679] they reached the village of the Illinois. . . . This village is supposed to have been near Rock Fort, La Salle County, Illinois. The party entered Peoria Lake on the 4th January, 1680, and proceeded some distance down the river, where they were well received by the Indians. . . . About the middle of January, the news of the loss of the *Griffin* and cargo reached La Salle. Other disasters had visited him, so that he called the fort Creve Cour." John Reynolds, *The Pioneer History of Illinois,* p. 32.

As to the location and description of the fort, which is claimed to be "the first civilized occupation of the region which forms the State of Illinois," Parkman says: "It was half a league below the camp, on a low hill or knoll, two hundred yards from the southern bank. On either side was a deep ravine, and in front a marshy tract, overflowed at high water. . . . They dug a ditch behind the hill, connecting the two ravines, and thus completely isolating it. The hill was nearly square in form. An embankment of earth was thrown up on every side: . . . The lodgings of the men, built of musket-proof timber, were at two of the angles; the house of the friars at the third; the forge and magazine at the fourth; and the tents of La Salle and Tonty in the area within." Parkman, *La Salle,* pp. 167–168.

23. In contemporary documents it is written Ako, Accau, Acau, D'Ac-

cau, Dacau, Dacan, and D'Accault. Though Father Hennepin tries to make it appear that he was the leader, Morfi is correct in stating that the enterprise was entrusted to Dacan. Parkman, *La Salle,* p. 232; French, *Hist. Col.,* I, p. 205.

24. The expedition set out on February 29. Morfi has fallen into error because some of the accounts of Hennepin read, "the last day of February," but 1680 was leap year. The 1683 edition of Hennepin, which is the most reliable, entitled *Description de la Louisiana* . . . gives the date as February 29. Margry, *Découvertes,* I, p. 478; French, *Hist. Col.,* IV, p. 107.

25. Dacan [Accau] did not return from the falls of St. Anthony; rather all three, Hennepin, Picard du Gay, and Accau were captured by a group of Sioux Indians and taken to their country above the falls. The captives were not exactly well treated by the natives. It was on July 25, 1680, that they were found by Sieur Du Luth and four French traders, in whose company they later made their return, not to Crèvecour to render an account, but to Montreal. French, *Hist. Col.,* IV, pp. 139–145.

26. On the margin, Morfi observes, "Prévost does not make fun of these formalities which the French ridicule in us." He has reference to the *Histoire générale des voyages* . . . , edited by Antonie François Prévost in Paris between the years 1780–1786, the first volumes of which must have been known to him.

27. Here again Morfi has written on the margin of his manuscript: "Prévost remarks in a note, at this point, that although Hernando de Soto crossed the Mississippi more than once, he did not establish a settlement thereon. May I inquire, what establishments were made by La Salle up to this time to give validity to the rights of France?" The Act of Possession is given in full in French, *Hist. Col.,* I, pp. 45–50, from which we quote: "I, in virtue of the commission of his Majesty which I hold in my hand, and which may be seen by all whom it may concern, have taken, and do now take, in the name of his Majesty and of his successors to the crown, possession of this country of Louisiana . . . from the mouth of the great river St Louis, on the eastern side, otherwise called Ohio . . . as far as its mouth at the sea, or Gulf of Mexico, about the 27th degree of the elevation of the North Pole, and also to the mouth of the River of Palms." This last statement is the chief foundation for the claim to Texas as part of the Louisiana purchase and the extension of its boundary to the Rio Grande, or Rio de las Palmas, as it was originally called. For the French text, see Margry, *Découvertes,* I.

28. The king himself received him. "Le Roy l'a escouté, bien receu et contenté," declared l'abbé Tronson. Margry, *Ibid.,* II, p. 354. The agreement made with the king is given in full in Margry, II, pp. 378–380.

29. See "Commission pour le sieur de La Salle," and "La Salle a le commandement des Francais. Beaujeu dirigera la manouvre du vaisseau," and "Mémoire pour servir d'instruction au sieur de Beaujeu, Capitaine entretenu dans la Marine." *Ibid.,* IV, pp. 381–384.

30. The ships were fitted out at, and sailed from, La Rochelle. See Joutel, "Journal," in French, *Hist. Col.,* IV; also Le Clercq, "Account," in *ibid.,* I.

31. The summary given here is borne out by the account of Le Clercq, who says: "Those who were appointed, while M. de La Salle was at Paris, picked up a hundred and fifty soldiers, mere wretched beggars soliciting alms, many too deformed and unable to fire a musket. The Sieur de la Salle had also given orders at Rochelle to engage three or four mechanics in each trade; the selection was, however, so bad, that when they came to the destination . . . it was seen that they knew nothing at all." Le Clercq, "Account," French, *Hist. Col.,* IV, p. 188.

32. The three ecclesiastics were M. Cavelier, M. Chefdeville, and Maïulle, or Mazulle, also called Daimanville by Joutel. *Ibid.,* IV, p. 186.

33. Morfi has confused the names and identities of Father Marquette, the companion of Jolliet in his expedition, and Father Dennis Morguet, of whom Le Clercq says: "Father Dennis Morguet was added as a fourth priest; but that religious finding himself extremely sick on the third day after embarking, he was obliged to give up and return to his province." Le Clercq, "Account," in French, *Hist. Col.,* IV, p. 187.

34. Up to this point and throughout the account of La Salle's expedition of 1684, Morfi has ably summarized the most significant details as given by Joutel and Le Clercq in their respective "Accounts." See French, *Hist. Col.,* I, pp. 85–193; IV, pp. 185–196.

35. According to Le Clercq, the ketch was named *St. Francis.* French, *Hist. Col.,* IV, p. 188.

36. "The bowsprit of our ship, the Joly, on a sudden broke short, which obliged us to strike all our other sails, and cut all the rigging the broken bowsprit hung by." Joutel, "Account," in French, *Hist. Col.,* I, p. 86.

37. The *Joly* cast anchor at Petit Gouave, September 27, where it was joined by the two other vessels on October 2, after they had been separated by a storm. The three set sail from this port on November 25, 1684. *Ibid.,* I, pp. 90–91.

38. Evidently intended for December. According to Joutel, the expedition first touched the coast of Florida, near Apalachee bay, December 28. *Ibid.,* I, p. 94.

39. "We had been told the currents were strong, and sate [*sic*] swiftly to the eastward, it made us suspect that we were fallen off, and that the land we saw must be the Bay of Apalache." *Ibid.,* I, p. 94. Le Clercq adds: "He [La Salle] had been persuaded at St. Domingo, that the gulf stream ran with incredible rapidity toward the Bahama channel. This false advice set him entirely astray." *Ibid.,* IV, p. 190.

40. This bay was known to the Spaniards before as Espíritu Santo bay. (Hackett, *Pichardo,* I, pp. 423–427.) The first to call it San Bernardo

in Spanish was D. Carlos de Sigüenza y Góngora, according to Pichardo, influenced by the name given to it by La Salle. It is modern Lavaca bay.

41. For a long time it was thought the river on which La Salle made his settlement was the Lavaca, but it has been definitely established that it was Garcitas creek. Bolton, "Location of La Salle's Colony," in *Mississippi Valley Historical Review,* II, pp. 165–182.

42. Evidently an error. The order for the entrance of the *Amiable* to the bay was given on the 20th. Joutel, "Journal," in French, *Hist. Col.,* I, p. 104; Margry, *Découvertes,* III, p. 148; Parkman, *La Salle,* p. 358.

43. The wreck was first discovered by the Rivas-Iriarte expedition, which set out from Veracruz December 25, 1686. "On March 30 while they were exploring the mouth of a river, which was named Rio de las Flores, the wreckage of a vessel was seen which bore signs of French make." This was the second maritime expedition sent by the Spanish authorities in Mexico to search for the French settlement. Dunn, *Spanish and French Rivalry,* p. 77; Bolton, "Location of La Salle's Colony," II, p. 173.

44. Joutel says of this incident: "They found the Sieurs Oris and Desloges dead upon the spot, the Sieur Gayen much hurt, and the rest all safe and sound." Sieur Moranget was slightly wounded by an arrow. French, *Hist. Col.,* I, p. 109; Margry, *Découvertes,* III, p. 160.

45. Not only La Salle believed the commander of the *Amiable* was responsible for the shipwreck, but Joutel and others were of the same opinion. "Aigron, who commanded her, had disobeyed orders and disregarded signals." Parkman, *La Salle,* p. 360; Margry, *Découvertes,* II, p. 604.

46. The date of departure, according to Beaujeu himself, was March 12. "Le 12 mars, je partis pour aller à la baye du Saint Esprit." Letter of Beaujeu to Seignelay, in Margry, *Découvertes,* II, p. 580. Joutel in his journal says, "I cannot be positive as to the day of M. de Beaujeu's departure, but believe it was the 14th of March, 1685." French, *Hist. Col.,* I, p. 111. Parkman does not give any date. Perhaps the one given by Morfi is taken from Prévost, *Histoire Générale.*

47. I have been unable to discover the source of information used by Morfi for the figures given here. He seems to be somewhat confused with regard to the various short tours of inspection and the longer expeditions undertaken by La Salle. A careful examination of Joutel's "Journal," Le Clercq's "Account," Parkman's version of the ill-fated expedition, and other sources failed to confirm the figures given by Morfi. "About one hundred and eighty persons were thus left on the southwestern shore of Matagorda Bay," declares Bancroft. Joutel says: "When our fort was well advanced, M. de la Salle . . . ordered fifty men to attend him. . . . There remained in the fort about one hundred and thirty persons;" and Le Clercq says: "The sieur de la Salle having thrown up a house with planks and pieces of timber to put his men and goods in safety, left a

hundred men under the command of the sieur de Moranget, and set out with fifty others." Bancroft, *North Mexican States,* I, p. 396; French, *Hist. Col.,* I, p. 111; IV, p. 192.

48. "After a short time the temporary encampment of the colony on the shore of the bay was abandoned for a site about five miles up the course of one of the small streams in the vicinity—the present Garcitas Creek." Dunn, *op. cit.,* p. 34. Bolton, citing the diary of the Llanos-Cárdenas expedition, describes the river and the location of the fort as follows: "We continued up the river until we arrived at a little village of Indians whom we did not understand and who did not understand us. From here we continued up the river till we saw some houses, on the highest elevation. Proceeding toward them, we landed on the banks and discovered that they were the settlement and fort of M. de la Salle [Munsuir de Salas], from many signs which we found there, such as wheels of cannon carriages, musket breeches, and many burned planks and beams of the fort. . . . As to the site, it is on the highest point of the plain. It overlooks two-thirds of it in the direction of the river, and one-third is a level extending indefinitely northwest." Bolton, "Location of La Salle's Colony," II, pp. 174–175.

49. La Salle set out the last day of October. Margry, *Découvertes,* III, p. 192.

50. "About the middle of January, 1686, when, being all, one evening, in our mansion, the sentinel came to acquaint me that he heard a voice towards the river. Some men . . . found a man in a canoe, crying Dominick." Joutel, "Journal," in French, *Hist. Col.,* I, p. 119.

51. This river has been identified with the present Navidad, which is the east fork of present Lavaca. For a discussion of the identity of this river and its location, see Hackett, *Pichardo,* I, pp. 483, n. 3, 505–508.

52. In the English translation of Joutel's "Journal" it is stated that La Salle returned "about the middle of March, 1686." French, *Hist. Col.,* I, p. 123. But the French text of the "Relation" of Joutel, printed by Margry, says, "vers la fin du mois de Mars . . . j'aperceus de loin sept ou huit personnes venant du costé du nord-est." Margry, *Découvertes,* III, p. 218.

53. The "Journal" of Joutel says he returned in August, but the "Relation," published by Margry, leaves the impression that the return was in October. French, *Hist. Col.,* I, p. 128; Margry, *Découvertes,* III, p. 248.

54. Evidently an error. Both the "Journal" and the "Relation" of Joutel, which form the most reliable sources for this expedition, state clearly that the number was seventeen, including La Salle. As to the date of departure, Parkman declares it was January 7. *Hist. Col.,* I, p. 130; Margry, *Découvertes,* I, p. 394.

55. I have been unable to discover the source for the complete list as given by Morfi. Perhaps he compiled it from the several accounts used by

him and printed in the main in *Histoire Générale des Voyages,* of Prévost. I have verified the names given by Joutel and Douay, as well as those given by Parkman, but have not found all those cited by Morfi.

56. The date of the incident described here should be March 17. See Joutel, "Journal," in *Hist. Col.,* I, p. 142; "Relation," in Margry, III, p. 319; Parkman, *La Salle,* p. 401.

57. On the margin of the manuscript, Morfi has added a note which seems to be a quotation. It reads thus: "And it is said that in enterprises of this nature, in which the hardships predispose the spirit, treachery is not uncommon, etc." Evidently taken from Prévost, *Histoire Générale.*

58. It has been argued pro and con whether La Salle's settlement on the Texas coast was not premeditated with ulterior motives on the Spanish mines. Bolton, as late as 1915, contended that this charge was unfounded. "Some students have maintained that the passing of the Mississippi was not accidental, but designed by La Salle, in order better to attack the Spanish provinces of Mexico. This view, however, seems unwarranted." *Mississippi Valley Historical Review,* II, p. 166. But in view of the more recent investigations and the publication of new documents, the passing of the Mississippi was, to say the least, highly incriminating. See Hackett, *Historical Documents,* II, pp. 49, 234–289; and his *Pichardo,* I, p. 436.

59. This picturesque and extraordinary character was never a count. His full name is Diego Dionisio de Peñalosa Briceño. He served as governor of New Mexico from 1661 to 1664. He was delivered to the Inquisition in Mexico in May, 1665, accused of many crimes. After a long trial he was formally sentenced on February 3, 1668. "He was publicly humiliated, fined, deprived of his office, and exiled from New Spain and the Windward Islands forever." He seems to have wandered in Europe for a while, finally settling in Paris between the years 1678–84. It was during this time that he presented his three proposals to Louis XIV to attack New Spain in the name of France. See Hackett, "New Light on Don Diego de Peñalosa," in *Mississippi Valley Historical Review,* IV, pp. 313–335.

60. This work of Morfi has not been found. The reference is too definite to be doubted. Further proof that he must have written such a work is the inventory of his papers in which it is listed as one of the documents found in his cell after his death. Bolton, *Guide,* p. 207.

61. The party left the Asinais early in June, 1687, and reached the country of the Illinois and Fort St. Louis in October of that year. From here they set out the following spring and reached Montreal on July 17, 1688, embarked for France at the end of August, and arrived in La Rochelle in October. Marle was drowned while bathing in a stream before the party reached the Arkansas. Parkman, *La Salle,* pp. 426–436.

62. According to Parkman, after the destruction of Fort St. Louis, "the children of one Talon, together with an Italian and a young man

from Paris, named Breman, were saved by Indian women, who carried them off on their backs." Parkman, *La Salle*, p. 444.

63. The source of this interesting story has not been found. Probably Morfi has confused the Italian youth with Tonti, who made an effort to come to the rescue of La Salle on two different occasions, but failed to reach him.

64. Regarding the fate of the prisoners, Parkman says: "The Italian was imprisoned at Vera Cruz, Breman's fate is unknown. Pierre and Jean Baptiste Talon, who were now old enough to bear arms, were enrolled in the Spanish navy, and, being captured in 1696 by a French ship of war, regained their liberty; while their younger brothers and their sister were carried to Spain by the Viceroy." Parkman, *La Salle*, pp. 444–445.

65. See preceding note for the fate of some of the captives. Groslet and l'Archevêque were sent as prisoners to Spain, after they were examined in Mexico city by the viceroy. They were confined in prison at Cádiz until the summer of 1692, when they were permitted to return to New Spain, at their request. The later career of the two men in New Mexico has been told by Bandelier in his *Gilded Man*. Dunn, *Spanish and French Rivalry*, p. 108, and n. 45. See also the new material in Hackett, *Hist. Docs.*, II, pp. 470–481.

In support of Morfi's contention that no expeditions were undertaken from New Mexico is Dunn's study, just cited, which traces all attempts to locate the French colony, from Veracruz, Florida, Nueva Vizcaya, Nuevo León, and Coahuila, with no mention of New Mexico. The proposals of a certain Captain Juan Domingo de Mendoza from New Mexico went unheeded.

66. Juan Rodríguez de Albuerne, marqués de Altamira, was one of the ablest officials of New Spain. He was *fiscal*, member of the royal audiencia, and counselor to the viceroy in all matters pertaining to the northern frontier.

67. The reference is to two declarations made by Pierre and Jean Baptiste Talon, after they were rescued by a French war vessel (see note 64). The first of these, *Mémoire sur le quel on a interrogé les deux Canadiens*, is cited by Parkman, as well as the second, which is printed in Margry, *Découvertes*, III, p. 610, entitled *Interrogations faites à Pierre et Jean Talon*.

68. "On July 6 [1685] the corsairs, led by the notorious Grammont, entered Campeche, and sacked and burned the town. . . . On September 10 one of the pirate ships was captured by the windward squadron, . . . and taken to Vera Cruz, with one hundred and twenty prisoners on board. It was during the course of the examination of these prisoners that the Spanish officials received the first evidence that a French colony had been established on the coast of the Gulf of Mexico." Dunn, *Spanish and French Rivalry*, p. 36.

69. Don Antonio de la Cerda y Aragón, conde de Paredes y marqués de la Laguna, was the twenty-eighth viceroy of New Spain. He took possession of his office November 30, 1686. Rivera, *Gobernantes de México,* I, pp. 252–260.

70. The viceroy was notified by special courier on November 3, from Veracruz, and the gravity of the situation being fully realized, orders were issued for an immediate expedition. Barroto set out from Havana November 21. As to Barroto's qualifications, "He was an experienced draughtsman as well as a practical pilot, and a man of excellent ability. Antonio Romero, associate pilot of the flagship of the squadron, was appointed to accompany Barroto, as he had made many voyages from Havana to Apalache, and was personally familiar with that portion of the route to be followed." Dunn, *Spanish and French Rivalry,* pp. 39–40.

71. "On February 6 [1686] a bay was reached which was described by our diarist, Juan Jordan, as 'the best bay I have ever seen in my life.' This was the broad expanse of water known as Pensacola Bay. Its re-discovery by Barroto and Romero was to cause a revival of interest in this bay, which was eventually to result in its occupation by Spain." *Ibid.,* p. 61.

72. The news of the French settlement caused the greatest alarm in Spain. It was characterized as "a menace which threatened the safety of the Indies and of the whole Spanish empire." Consulta de la Junta de Guerra, A. G. I. . . . Audiencia de México, 61–6–20.

73. The first of these was the Rivas-Iriarte expedition, consisting of two well-equipped pirogues, propelled by sail and oars. It left Veracruz December 25, 1686, and succeeded in discovering the wreck of the *Belle.* It explored the coast to Mobile bay and returned to Veracruz on July 3, 1686.

The second (the third from Veracruz) was the Pez-Gamarra expedition, which set out July 1, 1686. It went over the same ground and returned early in September. For details, see Dunn, *Spanish and French Rivalry,* pp. 75–80.

74. This Frenchman was captured by Alonso de León at the end of May, 1688, sixty-three leagues northeast of Monclova or twenty leagues northeast of present Eagle Pass. He was demented, but ruled a tribe of Indians with a show of barbaric splendor. He was *diplomatically* kidnapped by De León, sent later to Mexico city, and returned to Monclova to act as guide the next year. He was about fifty years of age. *Ibid.,* pp. 85–92.

75. Morfi is mistaken in his deductions concerning Jean Géry. His declarations clearly showed he had never been with La Salle and that he had wandered from the French settlements on the Illinois to Texas. Hackett, *Historical Documents,* II, p. 50.

76. Alonso de León, jr., was born in Nuevo León, probably Cadereita, about 1640. His father was a trusted friend and adviser of Governor

Martín de Zavala, whom he represented legally in Spain before the court between 1650 and 1660. His son accompanied him, and, on the eve of his return to America, joined a Spanish armada, when sixteen years of age, "to serve His Majesty, as a volunteer, without salary." His service in the armada must have been short, for he was in Nuevo León at the time of his father's death in 1661. From that time on he was constantly engaged in the defense of the frontier, rising by his merit from a private soldier to the rank of general and becoming governor of Coahuila in 1689. He died in March, 1691, having been the leader of five expeditions to Texas between 1686–1691. These facts have been summarized from *Historia de Nuevo León,* vol. xxv, in Genaro García, *Documentos inéditos;* Dunn, *Spanish and French Rivalry;* Bolton, *Spanish Exploration in the Southwest.*

77. The complete list of the members of this expedition is given in the *Historia de Nuevo León,* the total number of men being 115, including the priests and servants. See García, *Documentos inéditos,* xxv, pp. 320–321.

78. This has been identified with the Lavaca. (Buckley, "The Aguayo Expedition.") The dates do not coincide exactly with the diary of the expedition. According to this, De León explored the bay on the 24th. The river, which he called the San Marcos instead of the Guadalupe, was explored on the 27th. The river was either the Lavaca or Navidad, which is the eastern branch of this stream. Hackett, *Pichardo,* I, p. 105.

79. These were l'Archevêque and Groslet.

80. On the margin, Morfi has added a brief note, taken from Solís' Diary, entry for April 23, which reads, "When he [Alonso de León] started back, he left on the banks of the river a bull, a stallion, a cow, and a mare."

Chapter IV

FIRST OCCUPANCY OF TEXAS, AND FRENCH ACTIVITIES TO 1715

155 [*sic*]. *1690, The establishment of missions.* The viceroy, count of Monclova, realized the error committed by De León in leaving the new country unprotected and his own blame for not having given him orders to establish a settlement. To repair this he issued new orders, to the same De León, to repeat the expedition.[1] This he undertook with one hundred and ten men and some religious of our holy father Saint Francis from the apostolic college of the Holy Cross of Querétaro, Father Hidalgo going along as their ecclesiastical commissary.[2]

While on this trip De León took away from the Indians two boys and a girl, survivors of La Salle's colony.[3] He reached Texas without mishap, but did not go near the bay.[4] The feast of Corpus Christi was celebrated on May 25, with the greatest solemnity, in the presence of the captain or chief of the Texas and a great number of Indians of that faithful nation. After the Mass was concluded, the ceremony of raising our standard and the act of taking possession of the country was held, a formality which Prévost does not record as having been performed by La Salle in the course of two years, as he declares was done at the Mississippi when La Salle temporarily stopped at its mouth before.[5] The missionaries then proceeded to found the mission of San Francisco de los Texas, where they remained when De León started back, leaving just a few soldiers, and these carefully chosen, that their conduct might not antagonize the natives.[6]

156. While De León was executing his second entrada [De León's fifth entrada], a report was made to the king of his former expedition and his new undertaking. The

account given by the governor, in which he praised the fertility and vastness of the new territory, the ardor with which the natives desired missionaries, and the number of inhabitants in the land, was further strengthened by an exposition of the ease with which other adjoining nations could be discovered and how they could be converted to our faith and reduced to vassalage. His majesty, moved by these pious motives, issued his royal cédula of May 27, 1690, instructing the count of Galve, viceroy of New Spain at that time,[7] to entrust this conversion to the Franciscan missionaries of the college of the Holy Cross, and recommended to him that, in order not to burden the royal treasury, means or ways of defraying the necessary expenses should be devised. In another royal cédula of September 1 of the same year, his majesty ordered that a new expedition by land and sea be undertaken.

157. *1691, The expedition of Domingo Terán.* The viceroy, in order to carry out the royal orders, commissioned D. Domingo Terán de los Ríos [8] to undertake the land expedition, appointing him, for the purpose, governor of the provinces of Coahuila and Texas, with a salary of 2500 pesos annually.[9] He was given fifty soldiers, each of whom was paid 400 pesos a year. Fourteen missionary fathers and seven lay brothers,[10] all Franciscans, accompanied him to found eight missions, three of them among the Texas, four in the country of the Cadodachos, and one on the Guadalupe.

158. On May 16, 1691, Terán and his men set out from the presidio of Coahuila and, following a northeasterly direction, reached the mission of San Francisco de los Texas on August 4. This was a poor beginning, requiring three months, with only fifty men, to travel a distance which De León, with one hundred and ten, covered in one month. On September 8, the expedition sent by sea, which had reached the bay of Espíritu Santo on

July 22 and had remained there until it learned the whereabouts of Terán, joined him.[11]

159. The founding of the missions, as ordered, was immediately begun. In the meantime Terán proceeded to reconnoiter the river of the Cadodachos [present Red river], which he found to be navigable. A few days later the soldiers began to annoy the Indians, and the missionaries asked Terán to stop such abuses, but he made light of their complaint. The outrages were repeated and fresh complaints were made, all of which displeased Terán, who, irritated by the check on his authority found in the missionaries, and disillusioned at not finding riches, decided to abandon the country. He left fifteen religious in the missions, with only ten soldiers and one corporal to protect them, and went to the bay of Espíritu Santo, where he embarked with the rest of his men and arrived in Veracruz the following year [1692].[12]

160. *1693.* I do not know what explanation he gave to the viceroy to justify his abandonment [of Texas]. The fact remains that this was the cause of the loss of the province at that time. The winter was so severe that the wheat crop was lost, and a large number of the cattle left at the mission died. A shortage of food naturally followed; the Indians became more disgruntled every day with the haughty bearing of the soldiers that had remained; and the latter, afflicted by hunger, and fearful of the Indians, suggested to the missionaries that they abandon the country and return to Coahuila. When the religious refused to listen to them, they threatened violence to their persons. The missionaries realized that, in their despair, the soldiers might be driven to extremes, relying on the possibility of laying the blame of the murders on the well-known cruelty of the natives. To avoid so terrible a disaster, they agreed to the proposal to return to Coahuila.[13] The fruits of all the previous en-

tradas that cost the royal treasury so much, as well as of the last one led by Terán, in which two hundred thousand pesos were spent, were lost through the greed and bad conduct of one man.[14]

160a. Nevertheless, malice did not fail to attribute the abandonment of the missions to the lack of fervor of the missionaries; they were charged with having been the cause of the expenditure of thousands of pesos by the king, and holding the college [of Querétaro] responsible for eighty thousand. This forced the *discretorio* [15] of the Franciscans to vindicate the honor of the missionaries, justifying the powerful motives that obliged them to abandon their post with reasons so obvious that they merited the approval of his majesty.

161. That same year [1693], the viceroy received a royal cédula dated December 30, 1692, in which his majesty, after approving the expedition undertaken by Terán, ordered that the conversion of the Indians be continued with all diligence.

162. When Barroto returned from the bay of Pensacola,[16] he communicated his information to his teacher and friend, the learned D. Carlos de Sigüenza y Góngora,[17] who wrote a very eloquent memorial to the king from it. Barroto, out of modesty, would not sign it; consequently, it was signed by Andrés de Pez, of the presidio of Veracruz, who delivered it to the viceroy, the count of Galve, and succeeded in being sent to Spain to present it to the council of the Indies. By this means he was promoted to the rank of general of the Windward squadron.[18] Such was the impression made by the memorial upon the council that the viceroy was urgently ordered to have a new exploration made of this bay with the greatest care, and if it was found to be as described in the memorial he was to establish a settlement there immediately and have it fortified.

163. *1693*. The viceroy appointed D. Carlos de Sigüenza to examine the bay, as the man best qualified to do so.[19] He left Veracruz [March 25], and reached Pensacola [April 8] the same year. He drew a plan of the bay; accompanied this with a very favorable description of the country, its natural advantages for colonization, and the kinds of wood suitable for shipbuilding in which it abounds; and pointed out with so much eloquence the evils that might befall the crown, should it allow a foreign power to occupy the site, that the viceroy decided to establish a settlement on this bay (called Santa María de Galve), out of regard for him. This, however, did not prevent the abandonment of Texas, though it, too, exposed the interests [of the king] to similar dangers. As soon as the viceroy learned that the missionaries had returned, he called a council of *guerra y real hacienda* on March 11, 1694, in which, disregarding the petitions of the missionaries and far from granting them the desired aid to return to their post, it was resolved to postpone further attempts in that direction until a more opportune time.[20] His majesty was accordingly informed that same month of the determination taken. Had M. Prévost known all these facts, he would have been less laudatory of the foresight and political sagacity which he attributes to us.

164. *1697*. The French had not entirely forgotten La Salle's enterprise. Chevalier de Tonty, faithful friend of La Salle, descended the Mississippi in quest of him, but, not finding him, returned to Canada [21] very sad. This expedition made the French hesitant for a time, but, in 1697, there appeared a Canadian nobleman, well known already for his undertakings, who called the attention of the [French] ministry to Louisiana. As a result of his interest, the construction of a fort was planned at the

mouth of the Mississippi, which this officer, whose name was Iberville,[22] flattered himself he would discover.

165. *1698.* The count of Pontchartrain, minister of marine in France at the time, had four war vessels armed at Rochefort, of which the principal ones were the *France* and the *Famous,* and gave the command of one to Iberville, and of the rest of the fleet to the marquis of Chateaumorant. The fleet set sail October 17, 1698, for the gulf of Mexico, in search of the already famous river of St. Louis.[23]

166. These preparations were not kept secret from the court of Spain, nor was the destination of the fleet concealed. Consequently, in a royal cédula dated April 19, 1698, his majesty warned the viceroy to exercise care and be particularly vigilant on the gulf coast region, since four ships were being made ready in France, which were to sail to the gulf of Mexico to carry out the enterprise begun by La Salle.[24] This news, it seems, should have aroused the viceroy to action, making him suspicious of the possibility of the expedition's going to the bay of Espíritu Santo, and moved him to occupy it in time, establishing there a post strong enough to resist the attack of a squadron and capable of compelling the troops to reëmbark in case they effected a landing. But nothing was done. The province of Texas has been most unfortunate, in spite of its natural charm. The viceroy decided to wait and see where the force would strike before he took measures against it.

167. *1699.* On January 27, 1699, the French squadron, consisting of four ships [25]—Prévost mentions only the *France* and the *Famous,*—appeared at the entrance of the bay of Pensacola. The commander sent ashore one of his officers to secure information. He returned after a short while and reported that there were three hundred

Spaniards who had recently come from Veracruz, established on the bay. The officer had entered the fort and presented himself to the governor, D. Andrés Arriola,[26] and asked him for permission to get water and wood for the squadron. The governor, after inquiring in whose name this petition was made, told him that he would reply to his commander, and immediately sent aboard, to accompany the officer, a major to welcome the two captains. He supplemented this courtesy with a letter in which he informed the French commander that his ships were at liberty to take water and wood, and even to anchor in the bay at the place that best suited him. He said that he had express instructions not to receive any foreign vessels, but that, considering that perhaps adverse weather conditions had forced the French vessels to enter the bay, he would send a pilot to bring them into port.[27]

168. The Frenchmen replied to the governor through the same officer that the sea was so rough they could not hope to find any other shelter, for which reason they would accept his offer. Next day in the morning they sent Lorenzo Graff to sound the entrance to the port. He was the notorious freebooter who sacked Veracruz and was well known in New Spain as Lorencillo.[28] The French had taken him on board as they passed Santo Domingo. Iberville and the chevalier de Surgere also went out in their skiff and found twenty-one or twenty-two feet of water at the shallowest point. There were not lacking those who noted how improper the conduct of the governor was, not only in inviting the French to come into port, but in having afforded them the chimerical excuse of bad weather, and all this while admitting to them he had strict orders not to allow foreigners to come in. Arriola was ashamed of his conduct and sent word to the French to look for another place of shelter, to which

they courteously agreed, after they were informed how they could reach Mobile river, to which they said they were going.[29]

169. *1699.* Arriola could have dispatched immediately a detachment by land to occupy the entrance to Mobile, in the hope that those who had retired once with such slight resistance might do so again, since it was not credible that they would want to provoke a war between the two crowns or to give their enterprise the hateful name of conquest against a nation with which they were sworn to observe peace. But Arriola was far from doing this. Hardly had the French squadron been lost from sight when he called a council of all the officers of the presidio and explained to them his need of reënforcements in case he were attacked. It was decided that the governor himself should go to Mexico to request aid from the viceroy.

170. Leaving the presidio in charge of a subaltern, he embarked immediately, taking with him a few of his most trusted officers, on whom he could rely, to support his declarations.[30] Shortly afterwards he arrived in Mexico to safeguard his military honor by being away from the seat of trouble in case the rights of the settlement had to be defended by force of arms. It was necessary, therefore, to persuade the viceroy of the uselessness of the establishment to induce him to order its abandonment. For this purpose he drew up a report in which, by misrepresenting the natural advantages of the bay, he made it appear as uninhabitable, impossible of defense, and useless.[31]

171. *1699.* He knew well that as long as D. Carlos de Sigüenza was alive, he could not expect these untruths to be accepted, and he tried by all means to obviate this difficulty. He was informed that this learned presbyter had, on various occasions, condemned his abandonment

of the presidio of Pensacola at the time when a foreign squadron, the aims of which were suspicious then, was still in sight. Claiming offense at these words, he presented himself to the viceroy and complained against the injury done to him by D. Carlos. He asked that, in order to vindicate his veracity in a matter of such grave importance to the king's service, the viceroy should order a new exploration of the bay by D. Carlos and himself, offering to pay out of his own pocket all expenses incurred. He won the ear of the *fiscal* and with a report from him succeeded in getting the viceroy to issue a decree ordering Sigüenza to undertake the trip. Arriola had insisted on his proposition with such firmness because he believed D. Carlos would refuse the challenge, which he could not accept without grave danger to his life, on account of his age and the many ailments that afflicted him.[32]

172. But he was deceived in his deductions. D. Carlos replied to the notification of the decree in a long document in which he pointed out the unfairness of the contentions of Arriola and the falsity of his statements, restated the exactness with which the previous examination of the bay had been made, admitted the challenge with new conditions, and eloquently proclaimed the necessity of maintaining the presidio. So forceful were the reasons with which he supported all his statements that he succeeded in unmasking Arriola, frustrated the purpose of the *fiscal,* and secured the maintenance of the presidio of Santa María de Galve.[33] Though he foretold [accurately] what could be expected from the French squadron, Texas remained forgotten, and the government to which Prévost attributes so much sagacity allowed the French the long space of fifteen years to establish themselves securely at Mobile and slowly to penetrate from there into our territory.

173. *1699.* So closely are the events of the history of Louisiana connected with those of Texas that it is not possible to describe with clearness what took place in the second without giving, at least, a brief summary of the first. A history of Louisiana was written by M. l'Page [du Pratz]. M. L. L. M. [M. Jean Baptiste le Mascrier] wrote a history based on the *Memoir* of Mr. Dumont [de Montigny], and Father Charlevoix has written on the same subject, while the Abbé Prévost has compiled all these works and supplemented them with many notes.[34] I will attempt a brief analysis of Prévost here, and try to vindicate the Spaniards from the covetousness which he attributes to them.

174. *1699.* After the French squadron left Pensacola, Iberville went ahead to reconnoiter the coast, and cast anchor to the southeast of the eastern extremity of Mobile bay. On July 2 of the same year, he landed on an island near by, four leagues in circumference, which he called Massacre island because he found there many human bones. It was later called Dauphin.[35] From thence he passed to the mainland and discovered the river of the Pascagoulas,[36] where he found some Indians. He entered this river with fifty men and a Franciscan missionary to search for the Mississippi.[37] He had the good fortune of finding it on August 2, and, seeing its mouth filled with the trunks of trees brought down by the floods, he realized why we call it Palisade.[38] After he had carefully examined some sites that he had long desired to see, he gave notice to Chateaumorant, who followed him with half sail. Since he had come to accompany Iberville until he discovered this river, he now returned to France in the ship under his command, considering his mission ended.[39]

175. *1699.* After the departure of the commander, Iberville entered the Mississippi for the purpose of as-

cending its stream. He soon reached an Indian village belonging to the Bayagulas [Bayogoula]. From there the French proceeded upstream to the Umas [Houma], who received them kindly.[40] Iberville was still in doubt as to whether the river was the Mississippi, but a letter given then to him by an Indian convinced him of its identity. It was from the chevalier de Tonty, addressed to M. de la Salle, governor of Louisiana, dated April 29, 1686,[41] in which Tonty informed the governor that, having found the pillar on which he had raised the king's arms knocked down by the waves, he had had another one erected about seven leagues from the coast, where he left a letter for him on a tree that stood by its side. Tonty declared that he had been well received by the Indians, who seemed to respect him highly, all of which he attributed to the respect with which La Salle had known how to inspire them; that he was deeply sorry to return without having found him, but that he had sent two canoes to explore the coast for thirty leagues in the direction of the gulf and for twenty-five in that of Florida.[42] This information induced Iberville to return to the bay of Biloxi, situated between Mobile and the Mississippi. He built a fort there, three leagues from the Pascagoulas, and left Sauvolé [43] as commander and Bienville as his lieutenant before he returned directly to France.

176. *1700.* He made the trip in such a short time that, by January 8, 1700, he was already back in Biloxi. Upon his arrival he was informed that at the end of September an English corvette, carrying twelve guns, had entered the Mississippi; that Bienville, who had gone there to make some soundings at the mouths of the river, found the English in the bend formed by the Mississippi, later known as English bend; that he had told them that if they did not leave he would have to use force to expel them; and that this threat had been effective. He was told,

however, that the English had declared that they would return presently with a stronger force, that they had discovered this country more than fifty years before, and, consequently, had more right to it than the French. Iberville learned also that Englishmen from Carolina were among the Chicachas [Chickasaw], where they carried on trade in furs and slaves.[44]

177. This information made him determine to renew the act of possession made by La Salle twenty years before. He then ordered a small fort built on the bank of the river [the Mississippi], which he called St. John the Baptist. He placed four guns there and gave the command to M. Louis de St. Denis, a Canadian of noble birth, whom we shall shortly see playing an important rôle in the history of Texas. This fort, which was situated almost at the mouth of the river, on the east bank, did not last long.[45]

178. *1700.* While engaged in this work, Iberville had the pleasure of seeing the chevalier de Tonty arrive, accompanied by some twenty Canadians of those settled in the country of the Illinois. He spoke with them at length and acquired much important information.[46] Prévost relates at this point the attempt of the English to occupy the Mississippi, and how, failing to find its mouth, one of their ships went as far as Pánuco in New Spain. He tells of the proposal made by the French refugees [in London] to Louis XIV to establish a flourishing colony in Louisiana under his protection and vassalage, a proposal which the great king refused, declaring that he was determined not to suffer in France, or in any of her dependencies, other religion than his own; and he declares that, after the death of the king, the same refugees renewed their petitions to the duke of Orleans, who became regent of the kingdom, but that these were not heard for the same reason.[47]

179. Prévost then continues: "We note with the historian (of New France) that the Spaniards did not protest as vigorously as the English against the establishment of a settlement [by the French], which they had viewed with grave suspicion, but adopted a more astute policy to hinder its progress. They succeeded, for a time, in keeping the French, through the lure of a relatively unimportant trade, between the river they disdained to settle, and Pensacola, on the sandy shore of Biloxi, on Dauphin island—not much better—and on Mobile river, which was not in truth unworthy of being occupied, but not at the sacrifice made by the French." [48]

180. It is evident that in order to add merit to the enterprise [of the French] Prévost has attributed to policy what was the result of nothing else than indolence. Little reflection is needed to realize this, even after reading the narrative of Prévost. We will not deny that the governor of Pensacola carried on trade with the French at Mobile, but no one will take this to be a crafty policy adopted to retard the progress of the French colony. In the first place, if true, the governor would have defrauded [by this policy] the royal revenues of the imposts and duties on the goods introduced clandestinely in Veracruz, and he would have injured [thereby] the interests of the merchants of the kingdom, who, having to pay these charges on their grains, could not sell them at a price as low as that of the governor's agents, a thing that would have diminished [the amount] and delayed the disposal of their goods.

181. *1700.* Furthermore, Prévost himself confesses (page 191) that all the silver that circulated in the [French] colony came from Pensacola, and, consequently, the colonists complained bitterly when this trade was prohibited. Who has ever claimed that to enrich a neighbor is to hinder the progress of his establishment?

What could the Spaniards hope for from so singular a policy? To arrest the progress of the French, or put a stop to their settlement, would it not have been easier to occupy the territory? The Spaniards had the facilities to put it into effect, as Prévost knew well, for he realized their strength in New Spain. He knew they had entered the province of Texas, that they had found out that the Cadodachos river was navigable, that this river led to the Mississippi, and that from the time the French reached Mobile, D. Carlos de Sigüenza had urged the occupation of the place. In spite of these facts the Spaniards did nothing, they offered no resistance, they allowed the French to go on undisturbed for fifteen years, and they even enriched them with their trade (page 131). Can this be called a sagacious policy adopted to arrest the development of the [French] colony? It is a pity that a man, as well informed as Prévost, should show such partiality. But let us return to the Mississippi.

182. After the fort of St. John the Baptist was finished, Iberville ascended the river to Natchez, where he planned to establish a settlement to be called Rosalie, in honor of the wife of the minister. He then returned to the bay of Biloxi, which he had made the headquarters of his new colony. In his instructions he had been expressly charged to investigate the trade in buffalo wool and the pearl fisheries as the two principal objects in the establishment of a flourishing settlement.[49] Iberville ordered that buffaloes be sent to France in order to experiment with raising them in that country, but these instructions were not observed.

183. *1700.* He commissioned his kinsman, Le Sueur,[50] and twenty men to establish a settlement in the country of the Sioux, in order to take possession of a copper mine discovered in that territory. This expedition ascended the Mississippi to the falls of St. Anthony, entered St. Peter's

river, and, traveling forty leagues up this stream, came to another river that joins it from the left. Le Sueur called it Green river because the soil seems to impart this color to the water. Though it was still September, the ice that covered the river allowed him to travel only one league up the stream, where he constructed a fort in which to spend the winter, which lasted until the beginning of April. During this month they visited the mine, which was only three-quarters of a league away. Various accidents prevented Le Sueur from carrying out his enterprise.[51]

184. *1701.* In 1701, Iberville made a third trip to Louisiana and began a settlement at Mobile. He laid the foundations for a fort to which a short while afterwards M. de Bienville, now commander in chief of the colony as a result of the death of Sauvolé, removed everything that was in Biloxi, and abandoned that bay.[52]

185. *1702.* In 1702, Iberville returned for the fourth time [53] and constructed warehouses and cellars on Massacre island, where there was a good port. It was much easier to discharge the goods that came from France there than to transfer them by means of flatboats from the vessels to the fort at Mobile. It was at this time [54] that it received the name of Dauphin island. It was settled gradually, and a few years later a new fort and larger warehouses were constructed. Imperceptibly, it grew in importance and became the general headquarters for the colony.

186. *1708.* But the settlement of Louisiana did not really begin to assume a formal aspect until the year 1708, when Diron de Artaguiette arrived as intendant commissary.[55] His first care was to set the settlers to cultivating the soil, which appeared to be of excellent quality along the banks of Mobile river. This was in order to save them from an evil that has frequently befallen the

colonists of the New World,—the need of penetrating the country in search of game or of joining the Indians when the ships fail to bring them supplies. Unfortunately, his efforts did not meet with the success he expected, because the good soil in the vicinity of Mobile forms only a thin layer. But this [failure] was compensated for a time by the plantations of tobacco, which proved more successful. D'Artaguiette considered the tobacco of Mobile superior to that of Virginia.

187. *1710.* The damage caused the settlement on Dauphin island by an English corsair, who burned the residences and warehouses, made [the French] think of adequately fortifying the island.[56] D'Artaguiette returned to France and gave a glowing account of the country he had just left. It was then that M. Crozat [57] solicited [of the king] the exclusive privilege of the trade of Louisiana. This was granted him for sixteen years, together with all rights over such mines or minerals as he might discover.[58] Among the conditions stipulated in the patent, the king required him to send on board each ship going to Louisiana six young men or young women.[59] M. de la Mothe Cadillac was appointed governor and M. Duclos intendant commissary. As there was no judicial officer in Louisiana and judges could not be appointed until its population increased, the court decided to create a superior council to try all civil and criminal cases. This council consisted of the governor, the intendant commissary, and an official secretary.

188. *1712, 1713.* M. de Crozat, who had entered into partnership with M. de la Mothe Cadillac,[60] recommended to him that posts be established in the direction of the country of the Illinois to discover mines, and toward Mexico and New Mexico to establish relations with the Spaniards of those provinces.[61] But very little was gained from the first of these projects and still less from

the second. After M. de la Mothe Cadillac landed on Dauphin island, he dispatched to Veracruz the vessel that had brought him. It proved a useless voyage. M. de la Jonquière, who was in command, was unable to secure permission from the viceroy to dispose of his cargo. The viceroy presented M. de Jonquière with some supplies he was in need of, and ordered him to sail out of the port. And this was the astute policy of the government of Mexico [!] to make presents to the French [62] and allow them to fortify themselves and extend their possessions in peace.

189. *1713.* This somewhat detailed summary of the history of Louisiana has gradually led us to the province of Texas. We are there now. M. de la Mothe Cadillac flattered himself he would be more successful if he undertook a land expedition, and it was this that opened the eyes of the viceroy and determined him to take opportune measures to prevent the French from becoming masters of the country [and take possession of] New Mexico, Vizcaya, and Coahuila, as far as Parral, to all of which they aspired, as we have seen Prévost himself previously admit.

190. *1713.* The new expedition was entrusted to M. de St. Denis—the same [officer] who was left by Iberville in charge of Fort St. John the Baptist [see paragraph 177]. He was a native of Canada, the son of a man who was ennobled in recognition of his courageous deeds.[63] La Mothe de Cadillac delivered merchandise to the value of ten thousand francs to him, and agreed that he should leave the merchandise deposited among the Natchitoches, who live on the banks of Red river. An alliance had been made with these Indians since 1701, a few years after which many of them established themselves on the Mississippi, in the vicinity of the Colapisas [Acolapissa].

191. *1713.* St. Denis thought it advisable to take along some of the Natchitoches Indians established on the Mississippi. He made the proposition to them through a Frenchman called Pénicault,[64] a ship carpenter who had accompanied Le Sueur to the copper mine, and who, having made other trips on the Mississippi, understood almost all the languages spoken by the Indians of Louisiana. It was easy for him to induce the Natchitoches to follow him [with St. Denis], having been the one who had influenced them to move before, and enjoying their confidence as he did. But the Colapisas, who had welcomed the Natchitoches, were much enraged because they left without notice. They set out in pursuit of the Natchitoches, overtook them, killed seventeen and captured many of their women, the rest of their group being forced to take refuge in the woods. Fortunately, the Natchitoches joined St. Denis at Biloxi.[65]

192. *1713.* St. Denis set out with them in September, 1713. He went by way of the village of the Tonicas and persuaded their chief to join him with fifteen of his most skillful hunters. The pueblo of the Natchitoches is situated on an island in Red river, forty leagues above its juncture with the Mississippi. St. Denis, having reached this village without mishap, had some of the French who were to remain there build some houses. Here he persuaded other Indians to join him and the Natchitoches, assuring them of his constant protection. He also distributed some tools suited to the cultivation of their lands, as well as some seed to plant. He then chose twelve Frenchmen from among those who had followed him, and a few Indians, and left Red river, taking up his march to the west.[66]

193. *1713.* From here, Prévost does not only depart from the truth, but, giving rein to his imagination, he fabricates a thousand tales and inadvertently falls into

contradictions. On page 126 he asserts that Jalot accompanied St. Denis to Mexico, and on page 127 he declares that upon his return to Coahuila St. Denis found him there in high esteem for his ability in surgery. It would take too long and would be foreign to my subject to stop to explain all this compiler says, or to point out the probable reasons for his silence on other points. The reader, knowing that everything I state herein is based on authentic documents in the office of the secretary of the government of Mexico, will readily see the insidious policy of this famous writer by comparing his account with mine.

194. *1714.* When St. Denis left Natchitoches, winter was over and 1714 well begun. A twenty-day march brought him to the Texas, who received him with much pleasure, and, learning from him his determination to visit our frontiers, Captain Bernardino and twenty-four Indians decided to accompany him in order to ask the Spaniards to send them missionaries. They were particularly interested in seeing Father Hidalgo and Captain Urrutia, native of Vizcaya,[67] whom they knew and esteemed from their acquaintance with them since the establishment of the old abandoned missions. By this time only seven Frenchmen were with St. Denis, five of them having abandoned him. He left four of his companions among the Texas and with only three others and Bernardino and his Indians he continued his march.

195. *1714.* Nothing occurred until he reached the banks of the San Marcos, where he met a group of two hundred Apaches, who unceremoniously received him by discharging a volley of arrows. He resisted the attack with courage and, in spite of the small number of his followers, obtained a complete victory, thanks to the effectiveness of his four rifles. A peace or truce was negotiated with the vanquished, and twenty-one Texas Indians, in-

cluding Bernardino, returned home. With the four remaining Indians and three Frenchmen—Medar Jalot, a surgeon, and Pénicault being included—St. Denis arrived safely at the presidio of San Juan Bautista, on the Rio Grande, in August, 1714.[68]

196. *1714.* The captain of the presidio received the French with great courtesy and entertained and lodged them as was becoming an officer of honor. St. Denis presented his passport [69] and declared, with respect to his commission, that he had set out from Louisiana with orders from the governor to purchase grain and cattle, of which they were in great need at Mobile, from the missions which it was thought still existed among the Texas; that having found the missions abandoned, and learning from the Indians that our settlements were not far away, he had continued his march [to the Rio Grande] for the same purpose.

197. *1715.* The captain replied that he could do nothing in the matter himself, but that he would communicate with the governor and await his decision. He did so, and the governor immediately dispatched a special messenger to the viceroy with the news. The viceroy was surprised when he read about the incident, and in order better to inform himself, ordered that St. Denis be sent to Mexico, but that he be treated always with the same attentions and courtesy shown him up to that time. Almost a year elapsed in the course of these deliberations and St. Denis did not enter Mexico city until June, 1715.[70]

198. *1715.* The viceroy received him with pleasure and obtained from him all the information he desired. On August 22, the viceroy called a *junta* of war and *real hacienda* to which he communicated everything St. Denis had told him of the fertility of the country, the docility of the numerous nations that lived there, and the insistence with which the Texas requested the return of the

missionaries. He concluded by presenting to the council the offer St. Denis had made of his personal services for any enterprise planned in that province. In view of this, the council was of the opinion that a new entrada ought to be undertaken and that the offer of St. Denis for that purpose should be accepted.[71]

199. *1715*. It is not strange that this young man should have forgotten the commission entrusted to him by the governor of Mobile, nor that he should have entered the service of Spain. During the time he was detained in Coahuila he had occasion to make the acquaintance of a niece [72] of the *alférez,* Domingo Ramón. He found in her all those virtues he had conceived in his imagination as requisite for happiness, and seeing no other means of making her his wife than by establishing himself among the Spaniards, he made this decision. It may be, also, that he thought it compatible with his honor to enjoy the confidence of the viceroy and attempt the establishment of the trade he intended at the same time. He may even have thought that the new settlement in Texas was the most feasible way in which to obtain his end. Be that as it may, the fact remains that during the time he was among us, he served with great honor, and the most scrupulous investigation failed to reveal in his conduct the least reprehensible act on his part, as we shall see later.[73]

NOTES TO FIRST OCCUPANCY OF TEXAS, AND FRENCH ACTIVITIES TO 1715

1. De León was to accomplish two objects: To stamp out the last vestige of French occupation, and to determine the possibility of establishing missions among the Texas Indians. Of the reasons for this new entrada, Dunn says that however one "may question the relative importance of religious zeal as a factor in the general determination of Spanish colonial policy, there can be little doubt that the first definite steps taken by the viceregal government for the occupation of Texas were inspired largely by genuinely pious considerations . . . while the renewed fears of foreign encroachment had served to transform the new expedition from a peaceful missionary *entrada* into an avowedly aggressive campaign." Dunn, *Spanish and French Rivalry,* pp. 111, 119, 120.

2. Morfi is evidently in error here as to Father Hidalgo. Dunn declares that, "Five priests had been secured from the College of Querétaro, in addition to Father Massanet, who served as ecclesiastical commissary." Two of them were assigned to the new mission of San Salvador, "an offshoot of Massanet's old mission of Caldera." Father Hidalgo and Father Perea stayed at San Salvador. Fathers Fontcuberta, Jesús María, Bordoy, and Massanet went on with De León. *Ibid.,* pp. 120–121.

3. "They were Pierre Talon and Pierre Meusnier, aged twelve and twenty years, respectively," declares Dunn, but he says nothing about the girl. *Ibid.,* p. 122, note.

4. "On April 25 Governor León took a force of twenty men, and descended to the ruined settlement. The fort was burned, and the surrounding country then reconnoitered as far as Espíritu Santo Bay. Two objects supposed to be buoys were observed in the bay near the mouth of the San Marcos (Lavaca) River, but the party had no means of reaching them, and they were not investigated." *Ibid.,* pp. 121–122.

5. See chapter III, paragraph 113, and note 27 of that chapter.

6. De León started back on June 2, 1690, leaving three soldiers with the missionaries. Father Massanet returned with De León to promote plans for the establishment of other missions. The reason for not leaving more soldiers was the objection of the chief of the Texas, who gave his assurance that the missionaries would be safe without them. This was prompted by the vicious conduct of some of the soldiers. *Ibid.,* p. 122. The complete diary has been published by Bolton, in *Spanish Exploration,* pp. 405–423.

7. Viceroy D. Gaspar de la Cerda Sandoval Silva y Mendoza, conde de Galve, was the thirtieth to hold the office. He took possession September 17, 1688, and governed New Spain till 1696. Rivera, *Gobernantes de Mexico,* I, pp. 265–278.

8. Domingo Terán de los Ríos had been in the royal service for thirty years, the first twenty of which were spent in Peru. In 1681 he went to Veracruz as deputy of the *consulado* of Seville. He was later made captain of a company of infantry in the castle of San Juan de Ulúa, and from 1686 to 1689 he was governor of the provinces of Sonora and Sinaloa. He won royal favor for having opened a valuable mine, and the king had instructed the viceroy to provide Terán with a suitable office. A. G. I., *Aud. de México,* 61–6–21.

9. His patent as governor was issued to him on January 23, 1691. This makes him the first official governor of Texas. Dunn, *Spanish and French Rivalry,* pp. 111, 130.

10. According to Dunn, there were only ten priests and three lay brothers. *Ibid.,* p. 132.

11. The maritime expedition consisted of two vessels, fitted out at Veracruz, which were to carry the supplies and fifty troops under command of Captain Gregorio Salinas. The ships were commanded by the experienced pilot, Juan Enríque Barroto. When Terán reached the present Colorado, he sent Captain Martínez, with twenty soldiers and two hundred horses and mules, to San Bernardo bay. He stayed on the coast for six days and returned without making contact with the ships. It seems that the day after Martínez left, Barroto arrived, this being July 2, 1691. *Ibid.,* pp. 132–133.

12. Unfortunately, a bitter misunderstanding had developed between Massanet and Terán. "Had it not been for Massanet, it is probable that the missions already established would have been abandoned. As it was, six of the priests decided to return with Terán. Massanet and two companions remained, and were given a guard of nine soldiers to protect them." Consequently, Morfi is in error as to the number of missionaries who remained in Texas. Dunn, *op. cit.,* pp. 136–137.

13. After the departure of Terán, the missionaries suffered untold hardships, but they stuck tenaciously to the missions. In May, 1693, Gregorio de Salinas Varona, governor of Coahuila, set out in search of them. The missionaries were glad to get the needed supplies, but refused to abandon their posts until ordered by the viceroy. It was in October of the same year that they were literally compelled to leave. "The flight was begun on October 25, the mission being burned to the ground as they left. The fugitives were pursued for several days, but were not molested. . . . For forty days the priests and their escort were completely lost, and wandered down to the Gulf coast before getting their bearings. After four months of almost incredible suffering, they arrived at the presidio of Monclova on February 17, 1694." Dunn, *op. cit.,* p. 143.

14. Morfi is somewhat severe on Terán, but the facts bear him out, and Dunn himself says: "The royal officials in Spain, however, were not entirely deceived as to the results of the expedition. A perusal of

Terán's diary showed a notable discrepancy in the description of the country given in it and that contained in his letter." *Ibid.*, p. 138.

15. The *discretorio* was the council of the senior members of the order, who acted as an advisory and administrative body in matters concerning the welfare of their order.

16. In the first maritime expedition undertaken from Veracruz in search of La Salle's colony, the bay of Pensacola was rediscovered. This expedition returned March 13, 1686. The diary of Juan Jordán de Reina of this expedition is in A. G. I., *Aud. de México,* 61–6–20. Cf. also ch. III, paragraph 148.

17. Sigüenza y Góngora was the outstanding scholar and scientist of Mexico in the seventeenth century. He was born in Mexico city in 1645 and died there in 1700. He was a historian, mathematician, man of letters, and royal cosmographer. During his time numerous titles and honors were bestowed upon him. The best study of his life and work is I. A. Leonard, *Don Carlos de Sigüenza y Góngora.* See also his *Mercurio Volante,* Quivira Society Publications, III, 1932.

18. Andrés de Pez is one of the most interesting characters of this period. At the time of his death, in 1724, he was one of the most highly honored and influential men in Spain. His father and brother were both captains in the royal navy. Andrés de Pez began as an ordinary sailor in 1673, serving in this capacity eight years. In 1681, he was transferred to the Windward squadron of New Spain where he distinguished himself for bravery in fighting the pirates in the Caribbean, and soon became captain. He was a member of the third, fourth, and fifth maritime expeditions that set out from Veracruz in search of La Salle. In 1689, he presented a memorial formally proposing the occupation of Pensacola bay. He was at that time captain of a presidial company at Veracruz. He was soon after made admiral; later he became general of the fleet to New Spain, governor of the council of the Indies, and finally one of the king's confidential ministers.

The memorial "presented by Pez in 1689, Sigüenza averred, had been the work of Juan Enríquez Barroto, one of Sigüenza's students. Barroto was of a retiring disposition, however, and had not pushed the matter, whereupon Pez stepped in, appropriated the report as his own, and obtained sole credit for the ideas it contained." Dunn, *op. cit.*, pp. 146–147, 177.

19. "Sigüenza's instructions were limited to the details of the work in which he was expected to engage. He was to draw maps of Pensacola Bay, the coast-line of the Gulf, and the Palizada River, and to write an accurate and scientific description of the regions visited." The real leader of the expedition was Andrés de Pez, who was now admiral. "Sigüenza kept a journal, which is a striking testimony to his reputation as a scholar, and constitutes the chief authority for the expedition." Dunn, *op. cit.*, p. 159.

20. Shortly before his return, Massanet made a detailed report in which he pointed out that, for the success of the missions in Texas, a presidio, a more suitable site, and the congregating of the Indians, were necessary. Massanet to the viceroy, June 14, 1693. Again, on February 17, 1694, Massanet, when asked to found new missions, replied that he was without supplies and "destitute" of everything.

A *fiscal,* Doctor Juan de Escalante y Mendoza, practically decided what Morfi attributes to the junta, which met the next day, March 12, and approved the *fiscal's* report. Briefly summarized, it declared that under the circumstances further attempts in Texas should be postponed, that the reports of Frenchmen in Texas were "chimeras," and that no missions should be attempted for the time being. Dunn, *op. cit.,* pp. 141, 144.

21. Tonty set out in search of La Salle on April 7, 1689, believing he was still alive. By July, 1690, he had visited the Cadodachos and learned of the fate of La Salle and his men at Fort St. Louis. He returned to the Illinois in September, 1690. French, *Hist. Col.,* I, pp. 71–80.

22. Le Moyne d'Iberville was born in Montreal in 1662. He distinguished himself for his service against the English before he explored the mouth of the Mississippi in 1698. He died in Havana July 9, 1706. *La Grande Encyclopédie,* XXXI, p. 1267. According to French, *Hist. Col.,* III, p. 10, note, he was the first royal governor of Louisiana.

23. According to Dunn, the expedition set sail from Brest on October 24, 1698; it consisted of four ships commanded by Iberville, which carried about two hundred men and all necessary supplies for the founding of a colony. A powerful frigate, under the command of the marquis of Chateaumorant, had been dispatched to Santo Domingo with orders to join the expedition there. Dunn, *Spanish and French Rivalry,* p. 190. These facts are further borne out by the documents published by Margry, *Découvertes,* IV.

24. The cédula summarized the whole course of events from the first attempt of La Salle to date, and urged very particularly the immediate occupation of the bay of Santa María de Galve. "Testimonio de autos . . . en virtud de real cédula. . . ."

25. The expedition actually arrived on January 26. It consisted of five vessels: three large frigates and two small ketches. The names of the three frigates were the *François,* the *Marin,* and the *Badine.* They carried fifty-eight, thirty-eight, and thirty-two guns respectively. Dunn, *Spanish and French Rivalry,* pp. 185–186.

26. Andrés de Arriola had been in the royal service for twenty-four years and had performed many important missions. In 1694, he made a record-breaking voyage to the Philippines, and in 1695 he had visited Pensacola bay while engaged in clearing the gulf of pirates. He was alcalde mayor of Guanajuato when he was appointed to lead the expedi-

tion to take possession of Pensacola. "Relacion de servicios," October 25, 1695. A. G. I., *Aud. de México,* 61-1-19.

27. Contrary to the account given by Morfi, Arriola acted with resolution and foresight. To the salute of five cannon shots of the French, he replied with three charged with ball. He immediately posted his men in the best order for defense and prepared to give the enemy a warm reception. Nothing happened on the 26th. The next day M. Escalette came ashore and was curtly told that they could not enter. He was offered a pilot "to assist in anchoring the vessels at a safer place along the coast where they would be able to secure the necessary wood and water." Perhaps the source used by him was biased. Dunn, *Spanish and French Rivalry,* pp. 185-186.

28. His name was Laurent de Graaf. He was acting as pilot and interpreter for the French. *Ibid.,* pp. 187, 188, 190.

29. The French squadron left Pensacola bay January 30, 1690, after "protesting against the unhospitality of the Spaniards." *Ibid.,* p. 189.

30. He sailed from Pensacola on February 2, leaving Francisco Martínez, an experienced pilot and officer, in command. *Ibid.,* p. 191.

31. There is some truth in what Morfi says, though in all justice it should be noted that Arriola vigorously demanded aid for Pensacola, while pointing out many disadvantages of the site. *Ibid.,* pp. 191-195.

32. The facts of this interesting episode in the life of the famous scholar are all borne out by evidence, Leonard, *D. Carlos de Sigüenza y Góngora,* pp. 159-181; Dunn, *Spanish and French Rivalry,* p. 195.

33. In the *junta* held on May 18, 1699, "In spite of the adverse reports of Arriola, Franck, and most of the officers of the garrison, it was decided that the only possible course to follow would be to hold the bay until the king should give orders for its abandonment. Arriola was continued in chief command of the presidio, much to his disappointment." Dunn, *op. cit.,* p. 196.

34. Four editions of this work are known, two published during the lifetime of Prévost and two abridged editions by Jean Baptiste de la Harpe, published after his death. The title of the first edition is, *Histoire générale des Voyages, ou nouvelle collection de toutes les relations de voyages par mer et par terre . . .* [By the Abbé Prévost, continued by A. G. Meusier de Querlon, A. de Leyne and J. P. Rousselot de Surgy]. Vols. 1-19, Paris, 1746-70, 4°.

The second edition was called *Nouvelle édition, revue sur l'original anglois . . .* [with subsequent additions by J. P. J. Dubois and others]. 25 vols. La Haye, 1747-80, 4°.

The third edition carried the original title, with the addition, *abregée et redigée sur un nouvelle plan . . . par M. de la Harpe.* 32 vols. Paris, 1780-86 [9?]. 8°.

The fourth edition was published in 1816, in Paris, under the same title as the third, but in 24 octavo volumes.

Morfi used the Paris edition of 1780–86, the first volumes of which he must have acquired before his death, for he distinctly declares that the volumes were octavo size [see chapter III, paragraph 144], which precludes the first two editions, while the fourth was too late for him to use it.

As to the other works cited, Le Page du Pratz published his *Histoire de la Louisiane, contenant la découverte de ce vast pays: sa description géographique; un voyage dans les terres; l'histoire naturelle, les moeurs, coûtumes et religion des naturels, avec leurs origines; deux voyages dans le nord du Nouveau Mexique, dont un jusqu'à la mer du sud,* Paris, 1758, 3 volumes. It was translated into English and published in London, in 1763, and again reëdited in 1774.

The M. L. L. M. referred to is M. Jean Baptiste le Mascrier, who published in Paris, in 1753, a work in two volumes, entitled: *Memoires historiques sur la Louisiane, contenant ce qui y est arrivé de plus mémorable depuis l'année 1687 jusqu'a présent; avec l'establissement de la colonie francois dans cette province de l'amérique septentrionale sous la direction de la compagnie des Indes . . . composés sur le mémoires de M. Dumont.*

Charlevoix, Pierre François Xavier de, *Histoire et description génerale de la Nouvelle France . . .* Paris, 1744. 6 vols. 8°. There are several French editions of this work of the same date, some in quarto. It was translated into English but not into Spanish, except such parts as were included in Prévost, whose works were translated into Spanish by Miguel Terracina.

35. The actual date of discovery of this island was February 4, 1699. French, *Hist. Col.,* 2ᵈ series, II, p. 42.

36. Referring to the river of the Pascagoulas, the official diarist says: "The River they visited is situated ten leagues east by northeast of the island where we were anchored [Dauphin]. . . . It divides into four branches which form two islets at the outlets." *Narrative of the expedition . . . ,* in French, *Hist. Col.,* 2ᵈ series, II, pp. 51–52.

Morfi is considerably confused as to the details of the early part of this expedition, but this is due to the sources used. The official diary, cited above, remained in manuscript until 1875, when it was published by French in *ibid.,* 2ᵈ series, II, pp. 32–116. The original is in the ministry of marine, Paris.

37. There were fifty-one men in this expedition, which set out on February 27, in two longboats. The Franciscan was the experienced missionary, Father Anastasius Douay, who had accompanied La Salle. Iberville did not ascend the river of the Pascagoulas, but followed the coast closely to the southwest in search of the Mississippi, keeping as near to the land as possible. *Ibid.,* II, p. 52.

38. The mouth of the river was discovered on March 2, 1699. "We perceived a pass between two banks which appeared like islands. We saw

that the water had changed; tasted and found it fresh. . . . As we advanced we saw the passes of the river, three in number. . . . The banks are also bordered by trees of prodigious height which the current of the river draws down to the sea, with their roots and branches." On the 3rd a *Te Deum* was sung in gratitude for having found the river. *Ibid.,* II, pp. 56–57.

39. On Saturday, February 21, the marquis of Chateaumorant set sail for Santo Domingo. *Ibid.,* II, p. 50.

40. As late as 1907 there were still between 800 and 900 so-called Houma, but these included the descendants of other remnant tribes of Louisiana. For valuable information, see Swanton, "Indian Tribes of the Lower Mississippi Valley."

41. This date is given in the report of Iberville, printed in Margry, *Découvertes,* IV, but does not agree with the facts given concerning Tonty's trip in note 21 of this chapter. Tonty made several attempts, however, and this may account for the discrepancy.

42. The letter was delivered by the chief of the Mogoulachas (Mugulasha). It was written from the nation of the Quinipissas and was dated in April, 1686. Tonty left another letter "eight leagues from the sea, suspended upon a tree." French, *op cit.,* 2[d] series, II, pp. 101–102.

43. It is said that M. de Sauvolé de la Villantray was one of the brothers of Iberville, though it does not appear to be true from his diary and letters, or from the references made by Iberville in his correspondence. He died in Biloxi August 21, 1701, before the third return of Iberville. His diary appears in *ibid.,* 1st series, III, pp. 223–240, in English; the original text is published by Margry, *Découvertes,* IV, pp. 447–462.

The fort was begun on April 8, 1699, and completed by May 1 of the same year. It was called Maurepas. "The fort was made with four bastions, two of them of square logs, from two to three feet thick. . . . The other two bastions were stockaded with heavy timbers, which took four men to lift one of them. Twelve guns were mounted." Iberville departed on May 3, 1699. French, *op. cit.,* 2[d] series, II, pp. 110–113.

44. The facts given here coincide with the letter written by Iberville to the minister of marine from the country of the Bayogoulas, dated February 26, 1700. For the full text, see Margry, *Découvertes,* IV, pp. 360–364.

45. According to Iberville, he left his brother Bienville in command of this fort, which was finished on February 10, 1700, and was provided with six guns, two capable of shooting four pounds apiece. Fifteen men were left there. Margry, *Découvertes,* IV, pp. 364, 404. Pénicault, in his "Relation," says that Iberville made Bienville and M. de Saint-Denis joint commanders and left twenty-five men at the fort. Margry, *op. cit.,* IV, p. 399. Nowhere does the name given by Morfi to the fort appear. For a biographical sketch of St. Denis, see note 63 of this chapter.

46. Tonty arrived on February 16, in a canoe with two men. Nineteen other Canadians came along in five canoes. All agreed to enter the service of Iberville, who declared to the minister of marine that Tonty would prove of great value to him, because he, as well as his companions whom he would use as interpreters, knew the language of the Illinois and other tribes. *Ibid.*, IV, pp. 364–365.

47. The facts in the case are stated in the various documents published by Margry. See vol. IV, pp. 397–398, 482–486, 550–552; V, pp. 369–371; also Bernard de la Harpe, "Journal," in French, *Hist. Col.*, III, pp. 16–17.

48. Quoted from Prévost, *Histoire Génèrale des Voyages*. See Terracina, *Historia general de los viages,* XXVI, p. 102. The French edition was not available to the editor.

49. The instructions given to Iberville for his second voyage are printed in Margry, *Découvertes,* IV, pp. 348–354. Though he was to study the possibilities of buffalo wool and the pearl fisheries, "the most important question," declare the instructions, "is the discovery of mines." *Ibid.*, IV, p. 351.

50. Le Sueur was a distinguished geologist sent especially to examine some mines on the Mississippi and St. Peters rivers, described by Dugay and Hennepin in 1680. There is no evidence to show he was related to Iberville. He set out on his expedition to visit the Sioux and examine the mines in June, 1700, reached St. Peter's river on September 19, wintered there, and returned the summer of the following year. *Ibid.*, IV, p. 352; French, *Hist. Col.*, III, pp. 18, 23–27.

51. The account as given here is taken mainly from Pénicault's "Relation." For the French text, which gives many details regarding the expedition, see Margry, *Découvertes,* V, pp. 400–421. Morfi must have used the summary given by Prévost. Terracina, *Historia General,* XXVI, p. 103.

52. Iberville set out from France for the third time in August, 1701; after a short stop in Santo Domingo, he arrived, on December 15, before Pensacola bay, from whence he went on to Mobile, arriving there December 17. He remained in Louisiana until April 27, 1702, when he sailed for France, where he arrived in June of that year. For details, see Margry, IV, pp. 501–523. Sauvolé died August 22, 1701. *Ibid.*, p. 504.

53. Morfi is in error. Iberville never returned to Louisiana after the third voyage. What he calls the fourth voyage here is the return of Iberville from the Mississippi to Mobile bay in April, where he stopped on his way to Pensacola. See Iberville's "Relation," in Margry, IV, pp. 506, 511, 515; also Nicolas, "La Salle's Recit." *Ibid.*, pp. 513–534.

54. According to Pénicault it was in 1707 that the island began to be settled and became known as Dauphin island. "This year," he says, "many families who lived in Mobile asked permission of M. de Bienville, who granted it, to settle Dauphin Island. . . . This proved of great

advantage to the vessels that came from France." Margry, IV, pp. 474–475.

55. M. Diron d'Artaguiette [spelled also Artaguette] was a counsellor of the king and a very efficient officer. "He was an accomplished gentleman, and soon made himself acquainted with what was necessary to make the colony flourish." *Hist. Col.*, III, p. 37; Margry, V, pp. 689–690. "Until he took charge of affairs and introduced order, the settlement could not be called a colony." After his return to France, in 1711, he became a director of the famous Mississippi company, due, no doubt, to the prestige gained in Louisiana. *Appletons' Cyclopaedia of American Biography*, I, p. 98.

56. According to La Harpe, an English corsair made a descent upon Dauphin island in September, 1710, and destroyed fifty thousand livres of property. French, *Hist. Col.*, III, p. 37.

57. Anthony Crozat, marquis de Chatel, was born in Toulouse in 1655 and died in Paris in 1738. He was a celebrated financier, who amassed an immense fortune from overseas trade. His Louisiana venture proved a financial failure and he gave it up five years after the monopoly was granted him. *La Grande Encyclopédie*, XIII, pp. 506–509.

58. The patent granted to Crozat by the king was dated at Fontainbleau September 12, 1712, and granted him many privileges for fifteen years, not sixteen, as Morfi states. For an English translation of the document, see French, *Hist. Col.*, III, pp. 38–42.

59. The number required was ten. See document cited in preceding note. *Ibid.*, III, p. 41.

60. Antoine de la Mothe, Sieur de Cadillac, was a native of Gascony (ca. 1656–1730). He was the founder of Detroit. Before coming to America he served in the army in France. He first lived at Port Royal (present Annapolis), in 1683, being made commander of Fort Mackinac (the most important post in the West) by Frontenac in 1694 (Margry, V, pp. 75–132). In 1712, he was appointed governor of Louisiana while in France. He arrived at his new post in 1713, but does not seem to have been able to get along with Bienville. "During the three years in Louisiana, Cadillac sought every means to enrich himself." He was recalled in 1716. "He seems to have been a typical Gascon, alternately buoyant and depressed, of inordinate pride and much self-esteem, but withal able and clever." *Dictionary of American Biography*, III, pp. 397–398.

61. "The object of M. Crozat," declared La Harpe, "was to open a trade with the Spaniards in Mexico, and to establish a commercial depot at the Dauphin Island, with brigantines to convey merchandise to Pensacola, Tampico, Vera Cruz, Tuspan, and the coast of Campeachy, in which he would have succeeded if the Spaniards had not refused since the peace [of Rastadt] to open their ports to the French." French, *Hist. Col.*, III, pp. 39–41; see also Pénicault, "Relation," in Margry, V, pp. 494–505.

62. La Harpe declares that on July 16, 1707, M. de Chateaugué, brother of Iberville, brought from Pensacola "a large quantity of bacon, presented to the colony by the Vice Roy of Mexico," French, *Hist. Col.*, III, p. 36.

63. The biography of Louis Juchereau de St. Denis has yet to be written. Considerable confusion exists in the data now available between Louis de St. Denis and Juchereau de St. Denis. Juchereau was the father of Louis. He was lieutenant general of Montreal, and in 1700, while in Paris, offered his services to the king to colonize the Mississippi, declaring that "after twenty-five years of experience I should be able to establish a flourishing colony." The king granted him a concession for the establishment of a tannery on the Mississippi, June 4, 1701. The *Compagnie de Canada* presented a long remonstrance against this grant and Juchereau de St. Denis ably defended himself. In a letter dated September 6, 1704, Bienville informs the minister that word has just reached him of the death of Juchereau de St. Denis, who died during the preceding autumn (1703) in the region of the Missouri. He never came to Louisiana.

It was his son, Louis de St. Denis, sometimes called Louis Juchereau de St. Denis, who came to Louisiana down the Mississippi from Canada, probably with Tonty, in 1700, and remained an active and important member of the colony from that time on. It was Louis whom Cadillac chose to lead the expedition, as stated by Morfi, who clearly points out that he was the son of a Canadian who had been made a nobleman by the king. This brief summary is based on the documents published by Margry in volumes IV and V, and on the declarations of Louis de St. Denis himself while in Mexico. A. G. I., *Aud. de México,* 61–6–35.

64. His full name was André Pénicault. There is very little known about him other than what is revealed by his "Relation." The account given here follows closely in the details that of Pénicault, who gives a whole chapter to the expedition of St. Denis up to the time of his departure from the Texas (Asinais). This account remained long in manuscript. It was dedicated to d'Artaguiette. The number of Frenchmen accompanying him was twenty-two. Margry, *Découvertes,* V, pp. 495–505. Morfi doubtless had access to the declarations made by St. Denis while in Mexico (see reference in note 63), but he must have read also Pénicault's account as summarized by Prévost in his *Histoire générale.*

65. See Margry, *Découvertes,* V, p. 496, for details.

66. Here it was that St. Denis was helped greatly by an Indian woman named Angelique, "who had been baptized by the Spanish priests, who had established a mission in her village," declares Pénicault, but other sources seem to indicate she was baptized in a mission on the Rio Grande. Through her, St. Denis was able to speak to the Asinais in Spanish. This is the same woman to whose name is attributed the name of Angelina river. *Ibid.,* V, p. 500. See also chapter I, note 75.

67. Father Francisco Hidalgo came with Terán and Massanet in 1691 and was one of the four missionaries who remained with Massanet among the Texas Indians after the withdrawal in 1693. When he finally reached the Spanish settlement in 1694 (see paragraph 160, note 13) he remained at San Juan Bautista on the Rio Grande from whence he wrote twice to the French in Louisiana to inquire about the Texas. It was his second letter that is said to have induced Cadillac to send St. Denis on his mission. Shelby, "St. Denis's Second Expedition," *op. cit.*, XXVII, p. 196.

Joseph Urrutia, who later played an important rôle in the history of San Antonio, was one of the four soldiers who deserted the little troop of nine guards and three missionaries, as they painfully made their way from East Texas to Coahuila in 1694. He lived among the Indians for several years and led them in many campaigns against their neighbors before he returned to civilization. Dunn, *Spanish and French Rivalry*, p. 143, note.

68. Both the marquis of Altamira in his "Informe" and Bonilla in his "Breve Compendio" merely declare that St. Denis arrived "a year and nine months after his departure from Mobile." But in the declarations made by St. Denis, the exact date is given, as Morfi has it here, August, 1714. *Historia*, MS., XXVII, ff. 121–126; Hackett, *Pichardo*, I, p. 222; West, "Bonilla's Brief Compendium," *Quarterly*, VIII, pp. 21, 24.

It is evident that Morfi used all the original documents available in Mexico city at the time he was writing this work, as he claims. See paragraph 193 of this chapter.

69. The passport or patent given St. Denis by Cadillac for this expedition, dated September 12, 1713, is translated into English in Hackett, *Pichardo*, I, p. 219.

70. St. Denis must have arrived in Mexico city early in June, for the declaration is dated June 22, 1715 (*Historia*, MS., ff. 121–126). La Harpe and Pénicault make the date of his arrival June 25, while Le Page du Pratz says it was June 5. "The latter is no doubt correct," declares Clark in "Louis Juchereau de St. Denis," VI, p. 14, note 2.

71. At this point Morfi has added a note on the margin as follows. "When his excellency had concluded all the necessary arrangements, he called a *junta*, on September 15, to which he manifested the reasons proposed by St. Denis to persuade him how convenient it would be for the security of these dominions that the Mississippi be declared the boundary between the two crowns, and that the western bank be settled by us to avoid all disputes and [future] contentions. These recommendations were approved by the council and the king was informed on the same date of the action taken. How can this be reconciled with what Prévost declares?"

It was the *fiscal*, Espinosa, who presented the considerations attributed to St. Denis by Morfi, to the *junta*. He made a vigorous plea for immediate action, and with unusual foresight pointed out the true significance of the activities of St. Denis. Cf. Clark, *op. cit.*, pp. 16–19.

72. This was Doña María Ramón, granddaughter of Diego Ramón, commander of the presidio of San Juan Bautista, and niece of Captain Domingo Ramón. Shelby, "St. Denis's Second Expedition," XXVII, p. 197; Clark, "Louis Juchereau," VI, p. 20.

73. Clark observes shrewdly, it is of interest to note, that while St. Denis accepted a year's pay in advance to serve the Spanish government, "at the same time, under date of September 7, he wrote to the governor of Louisiana advising him that the viceroy was about to send a party to establish a mission among the Texas, and asked that a brigantine be sent to Espíritu Santo Bay, and declared that it would be necessary for the king of France to demand that the boundary of Louisiana be fixed at the Rio Grande." Compare these proposals with those which Morfi claims he made to the viceroy concerning the boundary between the two crowns (note 71 of this chapter). If he was not found out, it shows his ability as a diplomat. Clark, "Louis Juchereau," VI, p. 19.

Chapter V

FORMAL OCCUPANCY OF TEXAS, 1716–1722

200. *1716, The Ramón expedition.* The new expedition to the province of Texas having been approved, Domingo Ramón was appointed leader [1] with a salary of five hundred pesos a year, while Louis de St. Denis was to serve as conductor of supplies (*cabo comboyador*) for the expedition with the same salary. They were given twenty-five soldiers, each of whom was to receive four hundred pesos. The expedition was accompanied by five missionaries from the college of the Holy Cross of Querétaro, four from Our Lady of Guadalupe of Zacatecas, and three lay brothers.[2] By a decree of the viceroy the venerable Father Antonio Margil de Jesús [3] was ordered to accompany the expedition.

201. This little group set out from the presidio of San Juan Bautista on the Rio Grande, April 24, 1716,[4] and on June 18 following reached a river, not far from the Texas, which they called Corpus Christi.[5] They were met by four Indians who received them with the greatest demonstrations of joy. These were joined by others, to the number of twelve, and all manifested the joy and satisfaction they felt by insisting on not being separated from the Spaniards until the heart of the Indian country was reached. Thus they continued the march in company with the Spaniards.

202. *1716.* St. Denis now went in advance of the company to inform the chief of the Texas of the approach of the Spaniards and arrange for their reception. He sent back word by a son of Captain Ramón, who had gone with him, that he had executed his mission. The 26th of the said month of June, St. Denis arrived with five chiefs

and twenty-nine Indians. They came mounted on horseback, some of them armed with French guns, and all following St. Denis in single file. When they reached the camp of Ramón, they dismounted, left their horses and arms in the care of other Indians who had followed them on foot, and came before our men in the same order. Our troops were drawn up in two lines, in the center of which stood Captain Ramón and the missionaries.

203. They all embraced one another in testimony of their undoubted and sincere affection, our soldiers fired a salvo, and, this ceremony being over, they all went to a cool and curiously constructed bower made for the purpose by the Spaniards out of green branches, where everyone sat down according to rank. The Indians presented the calumet of peace to Ramón. This consists of a pipe, highly decorated with white feathers and filled with tobacco. The chief of the Texas lighted it, puffed for a moment, and gave it to our captain. It was then passed alternately from the mouth of one to that of the other. When this ceremony was over, during which everybody kept profound silence, the most distinguished chief [of the Indians] stood up and delivered a very eloquent address in his own language to express the joy of the Indians in seeing the Spaniards come back to settle in their country. St. Denis replied to them as interpreter for Ramón. Various chiefs then joined different members of their [respective] tribes [families], and with singular joy offered to take the oath of allegiance to our Catholic monarch.

204. *1716, Missions founded by Ramón.* Ramón distributed to the Indians the presents brought for them. He appointed the son of Bernardino as chief of the Texas and governor of the Indians, and established alcaldes and fiscales [justices and magistrates] in each pueblo.[6] He founded six missions, not four as Bonilla

states:[7] San Francisco de los Neches, Purísima Concepción, Nuestra Señora de Guadalupe de los Nacogdoches, San José de los Nasones, Nuestra Señora de los Dolores de los Ais, and San Miguel de los Adaes, the last being only seven leagues from Natchitoches.[8] Over five thousand Indians, all of the same language, were gathered in these missions and great hopes of their conversion were entertained.[9]

205. *1717, Ramón visits Natchitoches.* When Captain Domingo Ramón concluded the principal matters entrusted to him, he went with St. Denis to the French post of Natchitoches. He saw that, on the island, which we have pointed out is formed by Red river in its center, the French had erected a fairly good fort, garrisoned by thirty men. He learned that they had established another on the Cadodachos river, and that they expected fifty men to reënforce the garrisons of the two [forts]. Blue cloth, rifles, glass beads, and other French trinkets were found among the Texas, a proof that the Frenchmen left there by St. Denis with merchandise had not been idle.[10]

206. *St. Denis' second expedition.* Upon his return [from Mexico] St. Denis had married the niece of Captain Ramón.[11] His presence not being so necessary in Texas [after the establishment of the missions], he asked for permission to return to Mobile to gather his belongings [property]. This petition was freely granted. A few days later he returned to Texas with fourteen bundles [bales] which contained all his worldly possessions.[12] The envy which his talent and the favor he enjoyed aroused in others was irritating and contributed to St. Denis' ruin. He was denounced to the viceroy and charged with having introduced a large quantity of illicit merchandise from Natchitoches, in fact the equivalent of the cargo of four vessels. He was accused of being on very intimate terms with the Texas Indians, among whom [it

was said] he had lived for short periods of time, sometimes continuously as long as four months; and it was claimed that he knew their language and was held in high esteem. A report from the governor of Pensacola, D. Gregorio Salinas, contributed to make him suspected. It came at this time and declared that the Frenchmen who had set out from Mobile in 1713 for our frontier [settlements] had returned with much stock, proclaiming they had penetrated to Coahuila.[13]

207. *1717.* As a result of these suspicions, his excellency the viceroy, marquis of Valero,[14] who had just taken charge of the viceroyalty, ordered that St. Denis be conducted to Mexico with the greatest speed and vigilance and that a detailed investigation of his conduct be made.[15] These orders were carried out, and in the investigation [that followed] he was found innocent. There was nothing but the fourteen bundles of merchandise, constituting his personal property, as declared by him from the beginning. The missionaries pleaded his innocence and the need of his presence in the missions, but their petitions went unheeded and he continued in prison.

208. *1717.* The king was informed of this incident, and his majesty, by a royal cédula dated January 30, 1719, ordered that the goods be returned to St. Denis; that he and his wife be compelled to live in Guatemala; and that his uncle [Domingo] Ramón be removed from his post at the presidio of San Juan Bautista on the Rio Grande and assigned to another place where he would be unable to communicate with the French.[16] But Ramón died a natural death in 1724 [in the presidio of San Juan Bautista]. It is not known why the royal order was not executed. St. Denis succeeded in escaping, and he returned to Louisiana with his wife,[17] where he was able to say what he pleased and make of his desertion so singular a merit that his most Christian majesty honored him with

a commission as captain of the presidio of Natchitoches and conferred the cross of St. Louis upon him through the good offices of the count of Champmelin, chief of the fleet, who made a very flattering report of his prudence and courage to the council of marine.[18] I have anticipated the facts in order not to interrupt the course of the narrative and because it still remains for us to see St. Denis in Texas. "In this manner was thwarted," declares the marquis of Altamira, "the permanent residence [among us] of a man so well versed in all that pertains to that country [Texas] and its natives; who was loved and esteemed by the Indians, and who would have facilitated greatly their conversion and reduction, as the missionaries declared in requesting that he be sent to them." [19]

209. *1718, Alarcón and the founding of the presidio of San Antonio de Béxar.* The commander, Ramón, and the missionaries did not cease asking for aid, recounting the needs they endured and the [danger] to which their establishments were exposed if they were not given relief quickly. Forced by necessity, they had appealed to Natchitoches and the commander there had generously helped them.[20] The marquis of Valero acceded to their demands and, having confidence in the character of D. Martín de Alarcón, knight of Santiago, who he thought would be able to place the province in a flourishing condition, appointed him governor of Coahuila and Texas with a salary of twenty-five hundred pesos a year.[21] Since the beginning of the century Alarcón had been a soldier of fortune in the royal navy, a distinguished soldier in Orán, captain of infantry in the kingdom of Valencia, alcalde mayor of Tacona and Zamora by appointment of the viceroy [conde de Galve], and, lastly, sergeant major of militia in Guadalajara.

210. The new governor was to take fifty married soldiers, three master carpenters, a blacksmith, and a stone

mason to teach the Indians and put the settlement on a firm basis, each of the latter to receive four hundred pesos a year, as the soldiers. The governor was given a year's salary in advance to enable him the better to make all preparations. These measures were approved by his majesty in the royal cédula of June 11, 1718.[22]

211. *San Antonio de Béxar and San Antonio de Valero.* Early in 1718, Alarcón entered the province of Texas, founded the presidio of San Antonio de Béxar, and attended to other matters concerning the government of the province. This same year, by order of his excellency, the marquis of Valero, the mission of San Antonio de Valero was [officially] established.[23] It was situated on the banks of the San Antonio river, very near to the presidio of Béxar, and scarcely more than two gunshots from the [site of the] villa of San Fernando, founded later. The mission was established by the religious of the Holy Cross [of Querétaro] with Jaranames, Payayas, Zanas, Ipandis, Cocos, Tops, and Carancaguas Indians.

The missionaries, who entertained the hope of seeing the orders of the viceroy carried out by Alarcón, were disappointed in their expectations. Without losing time, impelled by the obligation their conscience imposed upon them, they complained to his excellency that the new governor had not brought the master mechanics as ordered; that the number of soldiers was incomplete; that those who came were not only worthless fellows but injurious to the new settlement because of their vices and because they were all [recruited] from the lowest class; and that [such] measures as the governor had adopted were directly opposed to the progress desired. Alarcón, at the same time, appealed to the viceroy for more money, supplies, and one hundred and seventy-five additional soldiers.[24] This request was refused and Alarcón, disgusted, presented his resignation, which was accepted.

He managed his affairs with so much art after his resignation, however, that the king ordered, in his cédula of October 31, 1719, that he be thanked for his zeal and efficiency.[25]

212. *1719, French hostilities in East Texas.* War having broken out between Spain and France during the regency of the duke of Orleans,[26] the French from Mobile surprised the fort of Pensacola on May 19, 1719; and on the same day in the month of June following, St. Denis entered the province of Texas and expelled the Spanish missionaries, without failing to observe the most scrupulous courtesy. Thus he made himself master of the entire province, with the exception of the presidio of San Antonio de Béxar, where the missionaries took refuge.[27] All this he was able to execute with only six soldiers, because there were no other troops in the province, other than the twenty-five unarmed Spaniards who were with the missionaries and retired with them, except those at the presidio, which St. Denis did not dare approach. The French surprised [first] the mission of Los Adaes, which had only one soldier as guard. They took him prisoner together with the missionary,[28] but the latter escaped and notified the captain [of the Spanish guard] who, without notifying the other missions, decided to retire [to San Antonio].

Though the viceroy did not know it, the French attempted to take possession of Espíritu Santo bay at this time also. But they found such determined opposition in the Carancaguases that they were forced to desist.[29] Once more the [old] calumny was repeated. The cowardly abandonment of the missions was attributed to Reverend Father Margil, when, in fact, the military were the ones who determined the retreat from the presidio and missions [of East Texas], the efforts of Margil and Espinosa to restrain them having been of no avail. When these [two missionaries] and the other religious saw themselves alone in those solitudes [*páramos*], they retired as far as a post which they called Santiago,[30] whence they later retreated to San Antonio. Espinosa presented himself to the marquis of Aguayo, there to vindicate the honor of the missionaries. The fugitive soldiers themselves testified [as to the facts] and the religious were exonerated. The marquis then wrote to the viceroy concerning the matter.

213. *1719, The Aguayo expedition.* Informed of these hostilities, the viceroy, marquis of Valero, immediately took measures for the defense of the province, ordering that a company [of soldiers] be recruited with the greatest speed possible in Nuevo León and the villas of Saltillo and Parras. He appointed the marquis of San Miguel de Aguayo, who was at that time in his country estate to take charge [of the preparations], and ordered twelve thousand pesos paid to him for the necessary expenses. Aguayo immediately recruited a company of eighty-four men, equipped them with uniforms, arms, saddles, horses, and with supplies for a year, consisting of flour, corn, and meat. In this he spent the twelve thousand pesos paid him and nine thousand more which he made up out of his own pocket.

214. He notified the viceroy of what he had done and offered him, at the same time, his sword and his fortune for the service of his majesty. His excellency accepted the offer and in reply sent him his appointment as governor of the two provinces of Coahuila and Texas. As soon as the marquis received these dispatches, he set out with the new troops for Coahuila and arrived at its capital, the villa of Monclova, October 21 of the same year [1719].[31]

215. *1720, Preparations for the expedition.* Having been informed of the condition of the frontier, he re-

ported to his excellency the small number of the force there and the exposed state of the provinces [Coahuila and Texas] because of their extended confines. In view of this report his excellency decided that five hundred men be enlisted in the cities of Querétaro, Zacatecas, and San Luís and in the villas of Zelaya and Aguascalientes. He ordered the amount corresponding to the total expense for a year, at the rate of four hundred and fifty pesos per soldier, paid over to the agent of the marquis [of Aguayo], and an additional twenty-five thousand for other expenses [*gastos de paz y guerra*]. I cannot tell, therefore, on what they base their claim, those who say that he made this entrada at his own expense.[32]

1720, The founding of San José. In the meanwhile the zeal of the marquis was not idle. In order that the religious, who had retired to the presidio of Béxar, should persevere in their labors, he authorized the founding of the mission of San José y San Miguel de Aguayo, a short distance from the said presidio, with three nations of Indians gathered [*reducidos*] by the venerable Father Fray Antonio Margil de Jesús. This was approved by the viceroy, who ordered that the aid generally allowed for such foundations be supplied.[33]

216. *1720.* On April 1, 1720, the five hundred recruits, equipped by the agents of the marquis, started on their march from their respective places, thirty-six hundred horses having been bought for their use and transportation. As this is the driest season of the year in that country, they suffered much while on the march. They reached the villa de Monclova on June 23 with only five hundred and sixty horses, having left the rest on the road either dead or fatigued, while those that reached [Monclova] were so exhausted that they needed a long rest to start anew. The marquis wrote immediately to all the neighboring places where horses are raised to so-

licit remounts. Thirty-four hundred were bought and, the drought continuing, they were taken to Coahuila [Monclova] by such slow stages that they did not arrive there until the end of September. During the middle of October there arrived six hundred mules, which had set out from Mexico on April 24 with clothes, arms, munitions, and six field pieces ordered by the marquis.

217. Upon receipt of news of the approach of the mules and remounts, Aguayo organized a regiment of dragoons, which he called San Miguel de Aragón, dividing the five hundred men into eight companies. In accord with the authority given him by the viceroy, he appointed Don Fernando Pérez de Almazán as his lieutenant governor and captain general [34] and issued commissions as captains to Tomás Zubiría, Miguel Colón, Gabriel Costales, Manuel de Herrera, Francisco Becerra Luque, José Arroyo, Pedro Uribe, and Juan Cantú, appointing at the same time their respective subalterns.

218. On October 5, the marquis received a communication from the viceroy in which he was instructed to proceed to the reoccupation of the province of Texas and New Philippines, and to restore the religious to their missions; but not to use force of arms, unless the province were occupied [*invadida*] by the enemy, as a vessel sent for the purpose had just brought the news of the truce negotiated between the two crowns.[35] The viceroy also sent him private instructions in which, citing the royal dispatch just received, he told him how to conduct himself in regard to the French. He was to invite and to accept the services of all those who desired to serve in our forces or to live in our settlements.

219. *1720, The expedition sets out.* On November 16, the expedition set out from Monclova, under the command of Lieutenant general Almazán, the marquis of Aguayo being obliged to remain in Monclova to dis-

patch various matters. A picket of veterans from the presidio [of Monclova] was placed in the vanguard to act as guides; there followed the equipment of the companies; then the companies in order of seniority, each one protecting its own horses; then came the pack droves, consisting of four hundred mules laden with supplies and munitions; then the stock and sheep; and in the rear guard one of the companies. A soldier was drowned in crossing the Sabinas river,[36] and much difficulty was experienced in crossing the stock and baggage because of the high water.

220. On December 20, they reached the Rio Grande del Norte,[37] which they were unable to cross because it carried so much water that it was more than one and a half rods in depth and more than a gunshot in width. They camped on its bank and proceeded to construct rafts to facilitate its crossing. In this manner they were delayed here until December 29.[38]

221. *1721, Rumors of St. Denis.* In the meantime the marquis, accompanied by Fray Isidro Felix de Espinosa, arrived in camp [shortly after Christmas], and a few days later Doctor José Codallos y Rabal, who had been appointed chaplain and vicar general of the expedition by his excellency the bishop of Guadalajara, joined them. On February 2, 1721, a message from the captain of San Antonio was received in which he notified the marquis that word had reached him, through some Indians of the Sanas nation, that Captain Louis de St. Denis and other Frenchmen had convoked many Indian nations [to a council] and together had proceeded to within thirty leagues of the said presidio, without their intention being ascertained.

222. The marquis called a council of war, to which he read the letters of García,[39] and after hearing its deliberations it was decided to send a party of one hundred

recruits and sixteen presidial troops to aid San Antonio in case of attack, and if necessary to go out to meet the enemy to restrain them. The necessary orders were immediately issued and the party left camp at once in two companies, commanded by captains Tomás Zubiría and Miguel Colón, under the direction of Lieutenant general Almazán. The marquis also sent Diego Ramón with forty men to go and occupy the bay of Espíritu Santo.[40]

223. When Almazán arrived in San Antonio, Captain García informed him that, as soon as he sent word to the marquis, he had dispatched Juan Rodríguez (who was one of the Indian chiefs of Ranchería Grande of the Sanas nation, who had come to San Antonio with fifty families to solicit a mission for his people) to go out with other friendly Indians to explore and reconnoiter the locality held by the enemy. They [the Indians] returned on February 25 and said they had traversed the country to the banks of the Brazos and that in all that distance they had not found a single person, not even of those who reside at Ranchería Grande, situated far on this side [of the Brazos], for which reason they concluded all were gone to the great council, but they had not dared to go beyond the Brazos. [They further declared] that, after their return to the presidio, Rodríguez was informed by his own people that they had met a Sana Indian from whom they had learned that [the members of] Ranchería Grande were at the French council; that the French had many horses; and that they had armed the Indians with guns; and, lastly, that all [the Indians] were between the two branches of the Brazos, to the left [north] of the road that led to the [country of the] Texas.

224. Almazán, on hearing the news, sent a party of thirty men and sixteen presidial troops, under command of Captain García, to reconnoiter [the location of] the enemy. This officer went as far as the Brazos river, but

was unable to proceed farther on account of a lake formed by the flood waters of the river. He discovered only some smoke [columns] on the opposite bank of the river, which made him conclude that the consultation was being held there, a deduction which was confirmed by his not having found a single Indian along his route, either on the way to or from the river.

225. *1721, Arrival of Aguayo in San Antonio.* Captains Alonso de Cárdenas and Juan Cortina joined Aguayo while on the Rio Grande, bringing with them their respective companies. Here came also Fray Benito Sánchez,[41] of the college of Querétaro. The expedition [finally] set out from the eastern bank of the Rio Grande March 24, and traveled without any mishap the seventy leagues of uninhabited country to San Antonio de Béxar, where it entered the presidio April 4, the day on which the feast of Our Lady of Sorrows was being celebrated. The marquis and his men passed on to the mission of San Antonio de Valero, where he was awaited by the reverend fathers Fray Antonio Margil, Fray José Rodríguez, Fray José Albadadejo, and Fray José Pita,[42] who were to accompany him and to be restored to the missions which St. Denis had caused to be abandoned.

226. The expedition remained at this mission until May 13 to spend holy week there and allow the horses and mules to rest. In the meantime the marquis sent forty men and an officer to look for some salines said to be a few leagues from the presidio of Béxar. They explored fifty leagues without finding anything, and, on the return trip, four days' journey from the presidio, they discovered other salines of which they brought samples.[43]

227. *1721, Ramón takes possession of Espíritu Santo.* The marquis [of Aguayo] felt uneasy because no news had been received from Captain Ramón.[44] He knew he had arrived safely in San Antonio and departed from

there for his destination on March 10, but ignored what success he had met with. In order to find out, he sent four trusty Indians on holy Friday [April 4] to take a letter to him. On April 18 a lieutenant and four men sent by Ramón presented themselves to the marquis. Through this officer he learned that possession of the bay had been taken in the name of the king on the 4th of the month; that a cross was erected and the royal standards set up; and that the delay was occasioned by their having spent twenty-five days [45] on the road as a result of an error of the guide and the difficulty encountered in crossing two rivers; that the lieutenant had taken only six days [46] for the return trip; and that La Bahía was about sixty leagues from the mission of San Antonio. Rámon sent word that the bay was very roomy and capable of giving shelter to many ships. He had not taken soundings because there was no timber to build a canoe.

228. The marquis celebrated the news with much joy and sent a special messenger to the viceroy on April 26 to acquaint him with the facts. At the same time he sent a memorial to his excellency stating that the four hundred and fifty pesos allowed each soldier were not sufficient to defray the necessary expenses to keep the men in fit condition for service because of the long distances that had to be traversed by the supply trains that brought the clothes, munitions, and supplies. For this reason he asked to be allowed to buy a vessel in Veracruz in which he could transport from that city [to Texas] whatever he was in need of. He declared that, not anticipating any objections to the request made, he was writing also to his agent, ordering him to buy and equip and load with supplies a vessel to be sent to him at the bay [of Espíritu Santo] as soon as possible.

Condition of San Antonio Valero and San José. Having dispatched this important matter, he visited the two missions [of San Antonio Valero and San José]. He found there were two hundred and forty persons in the old one of San Antonio,[47] and in the one recently founded [1720] of San José [48] two hundred and twenty-seven, including all ages and both sexes. He distributed among them [the Indians] some clothes, not forgetting to make presents to chief Juan Rodríguez and his fifty families, with whom he was equally generous.

229. Two days before the marquis' arrival in San Antonio, the Apaches [49] attacked a pack train and after a lively fight killed a driver and wounded a soldier. This incident moved the marquis to divide his force into several detachments which he sent to patrol the vicinity of the presidio and missions, with instructions to the officers that if they met with any Apaches they should try to capture them alive in order to see if by kind treatment their wild nature could be modified and a lasting peace established by these means. But these measures proved worthless, because the Indians took good care to avoid all encounters.

230. *1721, Choosing a route.* The date of departure being set for May 13, the selection of the route [to be followed] was discussed. The Indian Juan Rodríguez argued that the old road [lower] would be impracticable, because, being nearer to the coast, the creeks joined the rivers above and made them impassable; the woods were thicker; the ground marshy; and the mountains that crossed the province longer. He admitted that by following the route which he would show them farther to the north, more rivers would be crossed, and they would come closer [to the country of] the Apaches, but he pointed out that these Indians were not to be feared by this route because the country was more open and level, and the enemy would not dare attack them face to face.

231. These reasons made the council choose the upper road which Juan Rodríguez offered to show them. To guard against surprise the marquis ordered that in the march the various companies should act alternately as vanguard, the rear being similarly protected by one of the companies. In other respects the order of march was the same as that observed on the departure from Coahuila. The expedition set out from San Antonio and followed more or less consistently a northeasterly course with slight variations. Nothing worth noting occurred until they reached the first branch of the Brazos,[50] where the expedition halted for three days during the feast of Pentecost. During these days, June 1, 2 and 3, a council of war was held and it was determined to send a party to explore the country in search of Ranchería Grande and gain information concerning the designs of the French, not having found a single Indian on the way from whom to inquire.

232. On the 4th, the expedition set out again and continued its march until the 6th, when it halted on San Norberto creek,[51] the point where the officer in charge of the exploring party was told to rejoin it. The detachment returned on the 12th, without having found a single Indian in the entire thirty leagues it had traveled. Such huts as were seen gave sign of having been long abandoned. While encamped here the marquis was overtaken by a train of supplies, consisting of one hundred and twenty-eight mules laden with provisions. With these and the buffalo meat prepared by the soldiers, the expedition had nothing to fear from hunger for many days to come. Up to now they had experienced no want.

233. The march was resumed[52] and continued in the same direction, veering south, until the creek of San Buenaventura was reached, after crossing which the old road to Texas was reëntered.[53] This was followed to a

point six leagues beyond Santa Clara, where the marquis ordered a halt, upon having been informed by his scouts that there were Texas Indians in the neighborhood.[54] On July 8 a party went out in search of the ranchería of the Texas, Father Espinosa and two other religious going along with the soldiers. They followed a path that led south, off the main road. Three leagues beyond, they came upon some cultivated fields which they recognized as belonging to Texas Indians, but they saw no huts. They called out in the language of the Texas and reply was made from the woods. The missionaries went in advance, and crossing a small stream found some Indians from Ranchería Grande. Juan Rodríguez, their chief, was with the scouting party. The Spaniards were welcomed with great joy and taken to their humble huts a short distance away. Various families of the Bidais and Agdocas [Deadose] had gathered there with the Sanas of Ranchería Grande.

234. *1721.* About this time the vanguard of the main body [which had continued its march] came upon fresh Indian tracks, and, hearing the Indians shout, the captain sent the ensign to notify the marquis, who was with the center. As soon as he heard the news, he took one of the companies and hurried to the front, leaving orders for the entire expedition to follow. On reaching the vanguard a halt was called, and, following a well-beaten track [with a few men] for about a league, he discovered the scouting party and the missionaries holding a conference with the Indians. He ordered the royal standard unfurled and the bugles sounded. The Indians immediately came forth, on hearing the martial strains, and saluted our soldiers by firing their rifles and waving a white taffeta flag with blue ribbons which they had secured from the French. They all came up to the marquis with signs of reverence and submission.[55]

235. *1721.* He then ordered them to lower their flag before the royal standard in proof of their vassalage to the king [of Spain]. They complied gladly, and all were so anxious to prove their attachment that, though the marquis was on horseback, even the women and children came to him and begged that he place his hands over their heads as a sign of his overlordship. During this ceremony more than two hundred persons were counted, including all ages and both sexes. Aguayo then dismounted and entered the hut of one of the chiefs. Through an interpreter he informed them that he came not only on a peaceful mission, but with instructions to defend them against all their enemies and show them the power of the king's protection. He declared that he knew their reception was sincere and wished to make his appreciation manifest with some presents. While waiting for the rest of the Indians who were out hunting, the marquis went out and circled the ranchería, which was [about] a league around. The hunters arrived that evening and came to the camp on horseback, firing repeated salutes. The marquis received them with much pleasure and sent them away happy, with presents of tobacco, which he gave them that they might distribute among their people.

236. *1721.* The next day, July 9, the chiefs paid a visit to Aguayo, who, after receiving them kindly, ordered a beef killed for them and their followers. He advised them to keep peace and live in harmony with the Spaniards, whose trade was so useful to them; to return to their former home south of the Brazos and wait for him there until he came back from the country of the Texas, when he would conduct them to the vicinity of the presidio of San Antonio, where they could live together in a mission under the protection of the troops. He asked them, however, to go to the Trinity river and wait for him there at this time. Having concluded his speech, he

gave orders for the troops to form, and, taking a horse, he skillfully put him through his paces, much to the admiration of the Indians. He then had the troops pass in review before him to awe them, and the march was continued to the said river [Trinity].

237. It took sixteen days for them to cross the river because of the high waters. But the crossing was made possible [finally] by a canoe which the missionaries had constructed in the last retreat [1719] and hidden in a creek nearby. A diligent search was made, and, having found it, it was brought to the river with much difficulty.[56] In the meantime the chiefs of Ranchería Grande arrived and Aguayo gave them some supplies, many trinkets, and abundant food. In addition to this he presented them with two mules laden with clothes, knives, and other things to be given to those who did not come, and dispatched a soldier, named Nicolás de los Santos, a great interpreter, to make the distribution. Upon his return, de los Santos declared the Indians were all highly pleased. There came also four Texas Indians who were liberally feasted by Aguayo to win, by these means, [the goodwill] of this nation. He sent them back at once to their country.[57]

238. *1721.* The river having been crossed and the canoe safely put away, the 25th there arrived in camp the chief of the Asinai nation, recognized by all the Texas tribes as their superior. He was accompanied by eight of the most important Indians [of his tribe] and four Indian women. Among the latter was one named Angelina [58] who had been raised on the Rio Grande in Coahuila and consequently spoke our language very well. The chief came before the marquis and for a long time was unable to pronounce a word, being overcome by the sighs that prevented him from speaking. At last, weeping with joy, he said that for fifteen days he had known of the

arrival of the Spaniards at the Trinity and, fearing ill had befallen them in view of their delay, he had grown impatient to see them and had decided to go out and meet them. [He declared] that when the missionaries and Captain Ramón departed from the province, he had been left in great sadness; that trusting in their promise of an early return he had waited for them each day; and that if they had delayed longer he would have gone to San Antonio in search of them. The governor treated him with the kindness and gratitude that were fitting. He assured the chief that the Spaniards had come this time to settle among his people permanently; that each one of our men would treat his people as brethren and the missionaries would regard his people as their children. Aguayo then gave him a complete suit: coat, vest, and trousers, all of woolen cloth, and a silver-mounted cane. He appointed the chief as governor and captain general of all the Texas Indians, and dressed the eight warriors and four women with equal generosity.

239. *Aguayo among the Texas.* These Indians accompanied our forces until the 27th [of July], when Father Espinosa went ahead with the new captain general of the Texas to arrange for the reception of Aguayo by the Indians at the site where the first mission had been founded.[59] The expedition arrived on the 28th, at the site called San Pedro, where the presidio and mission erected in the first entrada were situated. A great number of Indians, of all ages and of both sexes, came from the surrounding country to greet the Spaniards, all bringing some gifts, such as flowers, wild fruit, watermelons, *pinole,*[60] or beans, in proof of their love. Aguayo received them kindly and dressed every one of them, and they all went away very happy and grateful.

240. *1721.* There came also one of the chiefs of the Neches with sixty[61] men and women of his tribe. They

entered the encampment and fired several salutes with their guns, whereupon they were welcomed with pleasure. After the ceremony of the peace pipe,[62] the chief made an address in which he expressed their joy at seeing the return of the Spaniards and the fear their stay would be temporary. He offered, in his name and that of his followers, to coöperate with Aguayo to enable him and his men to establish a settlement. Thanks were extended to him, as were due, but the distribution of clothes was postponed until the site of the mission of San Francisco [63] was reached, which was near to their pueblo. They were given food supplies to last them until that time.

St. Denis asks for interview. At dusk that same day, a Frenchman arrived in camp, sent by St. Denis, commander of the French on that frontier,[64] who declared that his superior officer was at the site on which Concepción mission and the capital of the province [of the Texas] had been. He solicited a passport for St. Denis, who, if granted permission, was ready to call on the marquis of Aguayo to acquaint him with the instructions he had received from the governor of Mobile. Aguayo replied that he [St. Denis] was free to come whenever he pleased, and gave his [Aguayo's] word of honor to assure his personal safety. The messenger left the next morning.

141 [241]. *1721, Visit of the Nacono tribe.* The expedition continued its march and, after crossing the plain on which the presidio was established in 1716,[65] set up its camp, July 29, on the bank of the Neches. The following day about one hundred Indians came, of both sexes and all ages, all of the Nacono tribe,[66] who lived five leagues away from where our camp was situated and belonged to the mission of San Francisco de los Neches. They were led by a chief who was also their high priest and of whom it was said he had put his eyes out in his

old age in order to obtain this dignity, there being the custom among them that the high priest be blind.[67] He made a long speech and accompanied his words with the most pathetic gestures to express his joy and that of his people for the return of the Spaniards. Aguayo replied through the interpreter,[68] and his words so pleased the chief that he addressed his followers and pointed out the blessings that would accrue to them from living together [with the Spaniards] and winning their friendship. [He urged them] to look upon us as brothers who were the friends of their friends and the enemies of their enemies, and he entreated them to prove their love by going immediately in search of game to present to their new neighbors.

142 [242]. The next day they brought tamales, fresh ears of corn, pinole, beans, and watermelons, which, though in a moderate amount, made a bountiful present considering their poverty. Aguayo was deeply impressed by their action and dressed all of them, distributing many pocket- and butcher-knives, scissors, combs, and sundry trinkets, all of which are highly prized by them. To the chief he gave a silver-mounted cane and a complete suit of Spanish clothes, and to his wife twice the number of presents given the others. This pleased and overjoyed all the Indians, who were delighted to see their chief in his new attire.

This same day Captain Louis de St. Denis arrived on the opposite bank of the Neches, and, plunging his horse into the stream, swam across and presented himself to Aguayo. After the customary salutation, he begged to be allowed to retire to take a much-needed rest after his long journey in the hot sun, asking to be permitted to spend the night with the missionaries.[69] This was granted him.

143 [243]. *1721, The interview with St. Denis.* On August 1, after hearing Mass, all the captains and the lieutenant general met in council in the tent of Aguayo, who sent for St. Denis, and on his arrival commanded him to declare frankly the purpose of his visit. St. Denis replied that he was now in command of the French on the frontier; that, having heard of the entry of his lordship into the province with an armed force, he desired to know if Aguayo was determined to observe the truce negotiated in Europe between the two nations; that, if such were the case, he was disposed to do likewise, observing the most friendly relations, particularly since he was led to believe by some letters recently received from France that a definitive peace had now been signed. The marquis of Aguayo in answer said that, in accordance with the instructions given him by his excellency, the viceroy of New Spain, he was resolved to observe the truce faithfully, on condition that St. Denis and his men evacuate immediately the entire province of Texas and retire to Natchitoches, without impeding or trying to impede directly or indirectly the reoccupation which he was determined to carry out for the king's arms of all that which had been previously possessed by the crown up to and including Los Adaes. St. Denis easily agreed to everything, though he tried to persuade our men of the unhealthfulness of Los Adaes and the impracticability of raising crops there. But we did not need his advice, being well acquainted with the place as a result of our long occupation of the site. His remonstrances were, therefore, interpreted as an expression of his regret at losing a point that was so advantageous to the French for their communication with the Cadodachos and which offered them an accessible route to New Mexico, the ambition of the government of Louisiana. Its possession,

however, was not of such great positive value to us.[70] He took immediate leave and promised to retire with all his men to Natchitoches.

In relating the capture of Pensacola and the efforts to occupy the bay of San Bernardo [Lavaca bay], M. Prévost says nothing concerning this incident. Perhaps it was not recorded in the memoirs of St. Denis which he saw.[71]

144 [244]. *1721.* The following day, August 2, Aguayo sent two detachments, which swam [on their horses] across the river, one with Father José Guerra [which was] to go to mission San Francisco, and the other with Father Gabriel Vergara and Benito Sánchez [which was] to go to Concepción, in order to rebuild the churches and missions formerly occupied by the missionaries that they might be ready for use when the marquis of Aguayo came.[72] On the third, the expedition crossed the river over a bridge constructed for the purpose and encamped near San Francisco mission, on the site where the presidio[73] was first established in 1716. Aguayo sent reënforcements to the mission to speed up the work of reconstruction, in order that Mass could be said in the church on the 5th when the mission was to be officially reëstablished.

145 [245]. *1721, Reëstablishment of San Francisco de los Texas.* The church having been made ready, the marquis of Aguayo marshaled the entire regiment and proceeded on the 5th to the mission of San Francisco de los Neches, commonly called *de los Texas.* The troops were drawn up before the church to observe the customary ceremonies during Mass. This was sung by the venerable Father Margil with the greatest solemnity. The Indians attended, filled with joy and admiration, and all knelt devoutly at a slight sign from Father Espinosa. After the celebration of the Mass, the Indians all gathered in the quarters of the missionary and, in the presence

of all the captains of the expedition and the missionaries, Aguayo appointed, in the name of the king, the one acclaimed, by the Indians themselves, governor of the Neches, to whom he gave a cane and a complete suit of Spanish clothes. He [likewise] dressed one hundred and fifty-eight Indians of both sexes and all ages, which pleased them exceedingly, never before having received so splendid and generous a gift. Through the reverend Father Espinosa, who was skilled in their language, he said to them that the zeal of his majesty for the salvation of their souls was the only motive that had induced his pious heart to send the Spaniards to their land to impart to them his royal protection and defend them against their enemies. [He asked them] to reflect and compare the presents previously made to them and those just now received with what had been given them by the French and they would see that the gifts [of the French] had for their object the trade of deer and buffalo skins, horses, and particularly women and children, whom they wanted to take into Louisiana as slaves. On the other hand the Spaniards asked nothing in return, their only desire being to incline them to that which would lead them to embrace Christianity, wherein they would find true happiness. For this purpose it was that they were entreated to abandon their wild and anti-social lives, and to desire to live in society in the future, congregated like the Spaniards in a town; but not as they had done in the past, a few of them and only for a short time, but all and forever. The Indians expressed their thanks for the solicitude shown by the Spaniards for their welfare and promised to come together after they gathered their crops which they had planted in different places. Father Espinosa, president of the Queretaran friars, then requested the governor [Aguayo] to assign and give possession to the Indians of the land necessary for the establishment of a pueblo and the corresponding farms and pastures. Aguayo complied with the request with all the formalities prescribed by law and ordered that the pueblo be named San Francisco de Valero.[74] The expedition continued its march to the neighboring mission, Father José Guerra, of the college of Querétaro,[75] having been left in charge of this mission.

146 [246]. *1721, Reëstablishment of Concepción mission.* On August 6, the expedition reached the mission of La Purísima Concepción, but in order that the men and horses should not cause the least damage to some fields which the Indians had thereabouts, it encamped one league beyond on the same site on which the presidio of Domingo Ramón was situated until, as a result of the invasion of St. Denis, the missions were abandoned.[76] Aguayo immediately dispatched some men to hasten the reconditioning of the church, which was the one that suffered the least during the abandonment.[77] That night [August 6, 1721] the Indian Juan Rodríguez told Aguayo that after St. Denis left the Neches, he stopped for three days at a place seven leagues from this mission, where the Cadodachos were waiting for him together with other nations of the province whom he had convoked to go with him to occupy the bay of Espíritu Santo, whence they were to march on the presidio of San Antonio to destroy it, or, if they captured it, to strengthen its defenses so as to resist all our efforts to recover the post; but that the entrada of his lordship had dissipated all these projects.[78]

147 [247]. On the 8th [of August] the marquis of Aguayo went to the mission with the eight companies of dragoons and the two of cavalry commanded by Captains Alonso de Cárdenas and Juan Cortina. As soon as he arrived there he presented the governor of the Texas with the best suit of his personal wardrobe, all of blue cloth, embroidered with gold lace, the vest of the same cloth,

and similarly adorned with all the corresponding trimmings. The reëstablishment of the mission was celebrated with even greater pomp than the preceding one. Mass was sung by the venerable Margil, and Father Espinosa preached. Numerous Indians of different nations attended, among them eighty Cadodachos, of those subject to the French, who had attended the convocation of St. Denis. Their chief resided a short distance from this settlement. The ringing of the bells, the concerted salvos of the artillery and rifles, and the great number of Spaniards, filled the Indians with awe, not having seen before, or even having conceived, that there were so many [Spaniards]. After the ceremony the chiefs of the various nations, together with many other Indians, met in the quarters of the missionaries, the women of the Texas being distinguishable because each brought a little present for the marquis in proof of her gratitude. He treated all of them kindly and, noting that the Texas, disappointed by previous entradas, doubted our permanence in the land, assured them that this time it would not be as in the past, that many Spaniards would be left in their country, and that these would never again forsake them. Knowing that Cheocas, chief of the Texas, enjoyed great prestige and had a large following, even outside of his own nation, Aguayo asked him to gather all his people, men, women, and children, because he wanted to give them presents to prove the preëminence of his love for them. The chief promised to do so shortly, but explained he could not bring them all together because it was necessary to leave a few in the ranchos [79] to guard them. The marquis entertained all the officers and missionaries with a great feast and gave possession of the necessary lands to the Indians. Father Espinosa, president of the missionaries from the college of Querétaro, and Father Gabriel de Vergara [80] remained at this mission as ministers, and that evening Aguayo returned with all his men to the camp. This was greatly appreciated by the Indians, knowing that it was done in order not to harm their cornfields.

148 [248]. *1721.* On August 10, the marquis of Aguayo sent a party with Father Margil to the mission of Our Lady of Guadalupe of Albuquerque of the Nacogdoches, which was eight leagues distant.[81] This mission was situated in a not very spacious plain, surrounded by heavy woods, with a permanent stream that carried abundant water, but the bed of which was so deep that it precluded the possibility of irrigation. No sign of the church they were going to rebuild had been left. The following day, August 11, Cheocas, who had gathered all the Asinais Indians, came to see Aguayo, together with the eighty Cadodachos. After repeating to them the speech previously made to the Neches in which they were entreated to form a pueblo, which they promised to do when their crops were gathered, the marquis ordered the entire group of four hundred to be dressed, and distributed among them, besides, many pocket- and butcher-knives, scissors, combs, mirrors, awls, steel for use with flint in striking fire, ribbons, belts, and other ornaments for women, with many trinkets. He gave complete suits of clothing to two Cadodacho chiefs and presented to them a bale of clothes and trinkets to be distributed among their people. They were struck by this generous gift, but more surprised still by the disinterestedness of the Spaniards, who knew the Cadodachos were the friends of the French. The Texas Indians were grateful too for the gifts made to the Cadodachos, because they were their friends and considered that the gift had been made as a courtesy to them.

149 [249]. *1721, Mission San José de los Nasonis.* In order not to tire the troops and horses with unneces-

sary marches, the marquis left the main force at the site of Ramón's fort,[82] and with only one company went to the mission of San José de los Nasonis, which was eight leagues away.[83] The Indians received him with great joy, and the reëstablishment was solemnized on the 13th [August] with the same ceremonies as the preceding ones. Lands were officially given to the Indians and the usual speech made to them, appointing as their captain the one chosen by themselves, to whom a complete Spanish suit of blue cloth and a cane were given. Father Benito Sánchez [84] was placed in charge of the mission and given presents for the Visanis [*sic*] Indians, congregated in this mission. All were so pleased that, the entire day, they kept bringing gifts such as pumpkins, watermelons, beans, and pinole, to the members of the company that accompanied Aguayo. Three hundred Indians were dressed at this mission. The marquis returned to his camp on the 14th.[85]

150 [250]. *1721, Reëstablishment of the presidio de los Texas.* On the 15th [August], after solemnly celebrating the feast of the Assumption of Our Lady, Aguayo officially reëstablished the presidio of [Nuestra Señora de los Dolores of] the Texas, in its former location, one league from the mission of Purísima Concepción de María, leaving there, as a guard for all the missions, captain Juan Cortina with his company of cavalry, consisting of twenty-five men.[86] That same day the expedition moved forward to a beautiful and abundant stream which was named Assumption.

151 [251]. *Refounding of Guadalupe mission.* The entire expedition reached the mission of Nuestra Señora de Guadalupe of the Nacogdoches, belonging to the college of Zacatecas, August 16. More men were put to work, and during the 17th the church and priest's house were put in condition. The 18th, the reëstablishment of

the mission and the blessing of the church were solemnized with the same ceremonies previously observed, and Father Espinosa preached [the sermon]. The Indians were given legal possession of the lands; they were entreated [to form pueblos] as on previous occasions; the chief elected by his people as captain was presented with a complete Spanish suit of English cloth,[87] together with the usual silver-handled cane and a written commission; and three hundred and ninety Indians were clothed. Father José Rodríguez was left as minister, and the ceremony was concluded with a great banquet offered by Aguayo to the missionaries and officers.[88]

152 [252]. *Refounding of Dolores mission.* From the lake of San Bernardo,[89] where the expedition halted on the 19th, the venerable Father Margil went in advance with a detachment to recondition the nearby mission of Nuestra Señora de los Dolores. The marquis of Aguayo arrived on the 21st and camped a quarter of a league beyond the site of the former mission of Los Adaes, of which he found no trace. Father Margil, seeing that a more advantageous location could be found, moved it to a new site not far away and rebuilt the mission beside a stream, near a spring, on higher and clear ground, where it was surrounded by a great plain suited for planting.[90] The mission was situated on a small plain, surrounded by a thicket; the earth, being of a deep reddish color, similar to red ochre, soils the clothing of those who live there, with this color. It resembles gold ore and, as a matter of fact, a gold mine was found near the mission, from which a quantity of ore of this precious metal was extracted but it assayed very low.[91] There was abundant and permanent water, but the bed of the stream was so deep that it could not be used for irrigation.

153 [253]. With the work done by Father Margil and the help given him by the troops on the 22nd, it was pos-

sible to dedicate the church and officially reëstablish the mission on the 23rd [August]. Possession of the land was given to the Indians, and a governor appointed, who was clothed, together with all his people, as had been done up to this time [with the others]. Father José Albadadejo was left in charge of the mission, after one hundred and eighty Indians had been dressed. The marquis of Aguayo left a detachment of soldiers to finish the construction of the church and the priest's house, renewing the march on the 24th.

154 [254]. This same day, after camp was pitched by the side of the lake of San Bartolomé,[92] Aguayo dispatched a messenger to the presidio of San Antonio with various letters, urging particularly that the train of supplies be hurried. A great salvo was fired at prayer time that evening to commemorate the birthday of the prince [of Asturias].[93] This same day also came a courier from San Antonio, who brought the reply of the viceroy to the letters written to him from that city. In this he thanked the marquis for the offer he had made to establish communication by water, at his own cost, from Veracruz to the bay of Espíritu Santo to assist the province by this means, informing him that the authorization for the sailing of the vessel had been issued already. The same messenger brought a letter from Aguayo's agent notifying him that the cost of the cargo and the charting of the ship had amounted to thirty-five hundred pesos and that the ship would sail from that port [Veracruz] in July, as his lordship had ordered.

155 [255]. Encouraged by this news, the expedition continued its march, crossing the river of San Francisco de Sabinas.[94] On the 29th it was necessary to reënforce the vanguard to enable it to cut a road through the woods, which were so thick that they blocked the way. In this manner the former site of the mission of San

Miguel de los Adaes was reached. Camp was not made because there was no running water in the creek [at the time] and the ground, being low, was subject to overflow in case it rained. Aguayo ordered the vicinity reconnoitered, and, on learning that there was a beautiful spring the water of which flowed through a great plain half a league beyond, he immediately proceeded to pitch camp there. No Indians were discovered on this day or the following, for which reason several detachments were organized to search for them in all directions. On the 31st [August] these returned and declared that the nearest rancherías were from ten to twelve leagues away; that the Indians had welcomed them with joy; and that when their chief heard of the arrival of the marquis, he promised he would gather his people and come to see him as soon as possible.

156 [256]. *1721, French attempt to halt the Spaniards.* A Frenchman arrived in camp on September 1, bearing letters from M. Rerenor, French commandant at Natchitoches, in which he congratulated Aguayo on his successful arrival at Los Adaes and informed him that, immediately upon returning to Natchitoches in the middle of August, St. Denis had embarked on Red river to proceed to Mobile to give an account to the governor [of Louisiana] of the arrival of the Spaniards in Texas and of what had transpired in the province. He further stated that St. Denis had left him no instructions to allow Aguayo to settle at Los Adaes; consequently, he requested the marquis to abstain from his purpose until the return of St. Denis with the decision of the governor of Louisiana. This letter was taken into consideration by a council of war, in which it was decided that on the following day Lieutenant general Fernando Pérez de Almazán and Captain Gabriel Costales should go to Natchitoches to carry a verbal reply and to remove all misunderstand-

ings. The marquis of Aguayo instructed them to observe with all care the location and state of the fort and the number of its garrison, for it was only fair that, since the French had examined our camp, their strength should be known to our forces.

157 [257]. Almazán and Costales arrived in Natchitoches and were courteously received by the commandant, who opened the conference by stating that he had no instructions either to allow Los Adaes to be settled or to oppose it; that, knowing of the truce signed in Europe between the two crowns, he was disposed to observe it faithfully, if the marquis did not break it in America. Almazán replied that Aguayo was of the opinion that to recover territory that had been usurped and later abandoned by the usurpers was not a violation of the good faith of the truce; that, based on this opinion, he had come determined not only to reoccupy Los Adaes by reëstablishing the injured mission of San Miguel, but to construct a fort at such a location as suited him best, outside the limits of France, to protect the province from new insults. Finally, after some discussion, the French commandant and the Spanish representatives agreed that the marquis should restore to the dominion of his Catholic majesty, faithfully observing the stipulations of the truce, everything that had been under the jurisdiction of his arms in the province before the invasion; and that he should fortify as he chose whatever site he thought best on the frontier.

158 [258]. *1721, Establishment of presidio of Nuestra Señora del Pilar.* The envoys returned with this agreement and the marquis, without losing time, looked for a suitable place for the erection of a presidio. The ground in the neighborhood was carefully explored, and, after many considerations, there was no place found more suited [for the purpose] than the one where the camp

had been established, on the road to Natchitoches itself, seven leagues distant from that place, and one league from the lake through which the Cadodachos river flows before entering Red river. The rest of the country was found to be too thickly covered by heavy woods. Furthermore, in the location chosen there were good plains or valleys on which to establish the mission near the fort, with abundant land for both the Indians and the Spanish soldiers to have their separate fields, and an abundant supply of water suitable for irrigation. Here, then, the marquis established the presidio, the foundations of which gave considerable trouble, it being necessary to dig them with bars in the solid rock.[95] Taking into account the character of the ground, the number of the garrison that was to be left, and the scant artillery at his disposal for its defense, Aguayo constructed a hexagonal fort with three bastions. Each of these was provided with two small cannon mounted in such a manner as to protect two curtains of fifty-five [96] varas each. He left a garrison of one hundred men in order that thirty could always watch the horses of the fort and seventy be left free at all times for its defense. Of these, thirty-one had families. It was the intention that these, and such others as might come later, should gradually form a settlement, without causing new expense to the royal treasury. The water supply was protected by the artillery, being only a gunshot's distance, but, to prevent contingencies, orders were issued for the excavation of wells within the fort, which was enclosed by a stockade, the bastions being protected by earthworks, until they could be replaced by stone defenses. To the fatigue of this work was added that of cutting down many thick trees that covered the ground in order to clear the approaches,—this to keep the enemy from approaching under cover and surprising the fort.

159 [259]. *1721.* On the first of September also there came to the camp the chief of the Adaes Indians, accompanied by many Indians of his nation, all of whom showed by their actions their joy at the arrival of the Spaniards. The chief related how, when the French invaded the mission of San Miguel, they [the Adaes] had been treated with the utmost cruelty, particularly by the Natchitoches Indians who accompanied the French; and how, when the invaders retired, many of their people, of both sexes and all ages, had been carried away as captives. He told how the Adaes had been obliged to move to a more distant site because of the repeated hostilities of the French and their allies, and in order to find shelter in the thickness of the woods from so many insults. The marquis welcomed them all—they exceeded four hundred in number—clothed and made liberal gifts to them, giving assurance that the king would protect them; that, for this purpose and in order that they should not be exposed to the caprice of their neighbors, he would leave a large number of Spaniards among them to defend them at all costs; that for this purpose they should gather in the mission of San Miguel which was going to be established and was to be located in the vicinity of the presidio in order that they might have help at hand, and, consequently, on time. The Indians informed him of a saline located fifteen leagues from the fort. A lieutenant was sent with twenty men to reconnoiter it, who brought back twenty-five mules laden with salt ore, of such high grade that it yielded fifty per cent; that is, one arroba [97] of salt ore yields half an arroba of excellent salt.

160 [260]. The day of the feast of Saint Michael the Archangel [September 29], the reëstablishment of the mission of his name, San Miguel de Cuellar de los Adaes, was celebrated in the chapel of the presidio. The [build-

ings] of the mission were to be constructed a quarter of a league from the fort.[98] On October 12, the dedication of the church of the presidio was solemnized, it being consecrated to Our Lady of Pilar (the church celebrates her apparition on this day), who was the patron saint of the expedition and in whose honor the presidio was named. The temple was blessed, Mass was sung by Dr. [José] Codallos [y Rabal], and the venerable Margil preached the sermon. A devout procession was held in which a beautiful and blessed image of the [virgin] venerated in Saragossa was carried. The celebration was closed with an abundant banquet of which all the troops partook. The soldiers, seeing the successful accomplishment that [crowned] their fatigue, manifested their joy with dances, masquerades, and the representation of several comedies.[99]

161 [261]. *1721.* The marquis of Aguayo was fearful that, having only sufficient corn for the Indians congregated in the new missions of the Texas and Los Adaes, the supply for the troops might run low. But his fears were dissipated by the news received[100] [while in camp] that the vessel chartered to bring supplies had happily cast anchor in the bay of Espíritu Santo on September 8. The cargo consisted of three hundred and fifty loads[101] of flour, one hundred and fifty of corn, and other provisions. [The messenger] brought word at the same time that two hundred loads of flour were already on the way, being transported on the mules that were left in San Antonio for that purpose. Of these, forty arrived in Los Adaes October 20, and the remainder during the beginning of November, together with two droves of four hundred sheep and three hundred head of cattle that were brought from the frontier of New León, about three hundred and forty leagues distant from Los Adaes.[102]

162 [262]. The fort and the bastions were finished in the best form possible, considering the limited time, and a dispatch was sent to his excellency, the viceroy, on All Saints' day to acquaint him with the facts. He was notified that one hundred men had been left in the fort with six pieces of field artillery and sufficient ammunition for its defense. Though only ninety loads of flour were actually left, it was the intention to give one hundred more [to the garrison] out of the supplies that were still on the way. Having made all arrangements, the marquis set the date of departure for the 12th, but it was not possible to start on the appointed day because the day before, the 11th, a snow and sleet storm broke out which was followed by a severe frost. This caused ice to form so thickly and heavily on the branches of the trees that many were broken and others uprooted as they tumbled down under the unusual weight of the ice. In twenty-four hours more than two hundred trees fell down within the camp and more than a thousand in the surrounding country, killing many mules and horses as they fell. Fortunately, no man was hurt, excepting an officer who was surprised, while he slept, by a falling tree that hurt his shoulder, from which he suffered considerably, but soon recovered.

163 [263]. *1721, Return of Aguayo from East Texas.* The weather moderated and the [return] march started on [November] 17, with much difficulty, as many horses died because of the severe cold. After reaching the mission of Los Dolores, thirty leagues distant from Los Adaes, it became necessary for many of the soldiers to travel on foot. In the nearby mission of Guadalupe, the marquis met a messenger who brought the reply to the letters that had been sent from there to the viceroy. He brought a copy of the royal cédula dated at Aranjuez,

May [2]6 of this year [1721], in which his majesty approved all the measures adopted by the viceroy for the expedition and the placing of it in charge of the marquis. It again ordered that once the province was reoccupied without the clash of arms, the French were to be left in peace and that no aggressions were to be made against their possessions. His majesty likewise ordered that the province be fortified with as many forts as were deemed necessary, locating these in the most suitable places for its defense and the growth of the settlements. He particularly commended the fortification of La Bahía del Espíritu Santo, already occupied by forty men. The viceroy ordered that this garrison be increased by fifty more [soldiers] of the best troops Aguayo had under his command. The information was received [103] with joy and the march continued.

164 [264]. The marquis reached the presidio [Nuestra Señora de los Dolores] of the Texas on the 29th. He outlined the fort, which consisted of a square sixty varas on each side, with two bastions on the two diagonal corners, each covering two curtains. The fort could not be made larger because of the small number of men, twenty-five, assigned to the garrison. He placed it on a pleasant site which dominates the whole country round about because of its elevation, and has an abundance of water in the stream, called Assumption, that flows nearby.[104] Thus he was delayed three days, after which, leaving the execution of the plan to the experienced captain in command of the presidio, he continued his march, fearful that the floods might retard his progress.

165 [265]. *1721.* On December 9, while on the creek of Santa Efigenia,[105] he met the second train which he was expecting with provisions from La Bahía. That same day one hundred loads of flour, together with other provisions, were sent from these supplies to the presidio of

Los Adaes. The remainder was used to supply his own troops. The routes were studied and parties were sent out to reconnoiter the [two] roads. In view of the obstacles encountered, it was decided to follow the old road. The horses continued to die [in large numbers] as a result of the severe cold and the lack of fodder so that, from the presidio of the Texas on, most of the soldiers were obliged to walk. It became necessary to leave eighty loads [of provisions] on San Juan Evangelista creek with twenty soldiers to watch them because there were not enough mules to transport them. This contingency made the marquis fear his supplies would run low before he reached San Antonio, for which reason he sent ten men to this presidio with orders for them to bring provisions from there and return to meet him with all speed.

166 [266]. In truth, they carried out his orders so well that they met him at the place called El Encadenado, four leagues from the San Marcos, where he received his second relief. At the same time he received the sad news of the burning of sixteen of the small houses built for the troops in San Antonio, together with the storehouse where there were seven hundred loads of corn and a goodly amount of flour of which not one grain was saved.[106] This misfortune was much regretted by Aguayo, who, in order to repair the damage, sent urgent instructions to Saltillo that mules be brought to transport with the greatest speed the supplies stored at San Juan Bautista on the Rio Grande, where, for fear of some disaster to the vessel, he had ordered two hundred loads of flour and one thousand *anegas* [107] of corn to be gathered. These were transported to San Antonio and proved sufficient for the requirements of the presidio and for the needs of the troops [of the expedition] which were relieved on their march by the eight hundred remounts sent from Guadiana and other places.

1722. In the meanwhile, before this relief arrived, the expedition continued its march with greater hardships every day, the captains and officers finding themselves obliged to walk and the marquis keeping them company in this difficulty. It was a notable good fortune that the mortality having been so high among the beasts of burden—there remaining only fifty horses out of five thousand, and one hundred mules out of eight hundred that entered Texas—it did not extend to the men. Not only were no soldiers lost, but those that took sick at Los Adaes recovered while on the road in spite of so many misfortunes, and all entered the presidio of San Antonio in robust health on January 23, 1722. A special messenger bearing this news was sent to the viceroy.

167 [267]. *The new presidio of San Antonio.* The marquis, seeing that the remounts would be more than a month and a half in coming, and, taking into consideration, on the other hand, the bad condition of the existing presidio because of its poor location, lack of adequate defenses, and danger of fire, decided not to wait idly or keep the men idle. He chose a site in the angle formed by the juncture of the San Pedro and the San Antonio rivers for the location of the new presidio. This was a beautiful piece of ground, thirty varas from the first and two hundred from the second. The ground being thickly covered by trees, he had it cleared and the necessary timber for the church, storehouse, and soldiers' quarters fashioned. After a considerable number of mud bricks [adobes] had been made, he outlined a square seventy-three varas on each side, and had four bastions built, one on each corner, putting all the men to work. He arranged, at the same time that he was having the fort built, for a goodly crop of corn to be raised with which to supply the garrison and feed the friendly Indians that frequently

came to visit. At his own cost he ordered an irrigation ditch built, capable of irrigating the two leagues of fertile land found within the angle formed by the San Pedro and the San Antonio, taking the water from the former for the benefit of the presidial troops and the settlers that might join them. Today [1778] [108] nothing is left of the fort, not even a sign.

168 [268]. On March 8, the messenger sent to Mexico from Los Adaes the 4th of November [1721] returned, bringing letters from the viceroy in which he thanked the marquis in the most enthusiastic phrases, approving everything he had done in recovering the province and the measures taken for its defense.

169 [269]. *Founding of San Francisco Xavier de Nájera.* March 10, having previously chosen a suitable site between the missions of San Antonio and San José, the marquis proceeded to the erection of the mission which the Indian chief Juan Rodríguez had petitioned for his people of Ranchería Grande. Though they were only fifty families, the chief declared that when the rest [of the Indians] heard of this establishment all would, no doubt, come. The marquis gave possession of the mission, in due legal form, to Father José González [Rodríguez?] of the college of the Holy Cross of Querétaro, naming it San Francisco Xavier de Nájera.[109] All the officers attended the ceremony, during which Juan Rodríguez was presented with a complete suit of blue English cloth.

170 [270]. *1722, Reënforcement of La Bahía.* As soon as the first drove of horses arrived fifty men were immediately sent to Bahía del Espíritu Santo.[110] These were all picked men, selected from volunteers of the companies of the battalion, and they formed a splendid company of the best men, under the command of Captain

Gabriel Costales. On March 16, the marquis set out with an escort of forty men, accompanied by Dr. Codallos, and Captains Zubiría, Zilón y Portugal, Herrera, and Uribe, for La Bahía, where he arrived without mishap on the 24th. During the first eight days nothing could be done because Aguayo was ill and obliged to keep to his bed. He desired, furthermore, that Holy Week be observed with all solemnity and that an altar and cross be erected, all of which afforded great consolation to the men.

171 [271]. *1722.* The second day after Easter, April 6, the lines for the fort were laid down on the same spot where La Salle had constructed his. While excavating the foundations, nails, firelocks, and fragments of guns were found, and the place where the artillery had been buried and the powder burned was discovered. The foundations for the new structure were dug in fifteen days. These formed an octagon, with a moat all around and four bastions, to which was added a tower. Each curtain was forty-five varas in length.

172 [272]. When everything was finished, he proceeded to found the mission of Espíritu Santo de Zúñiga, near the presidio, with three Indian nations that voluntarily asked for a mission, and, because of their poverty and the manner in which they offered the marquis three children to be baptized, high hopes of them were entertained.[111] The marquis stood as godfather to one of the children. Gifts were distributed among the Indians as in the other missions and Father Agustín Patrón, of the college of Guadalupe of Zacatecas, was left in charge. All around the presidio there are beautiful fields of clear land which, judging from sight and the brief experience of one year, appear to be very fertile. Places suited to the raising of cattle, covered with good pastures, are not

lacking; the number of wild turkeys and deer is unusually great in all the surrounding country.

173 [273]. The completion of the fort of Nuestra Señora de Loreto de la Bahía, as planned, was left in the care of the captain in charge,[112] while the marquis returned to the presidio of San Antonio with those who had accompanied him, where he arrived, still sick, April 26. Much could have been done in the interim toward finishing the last-mentioned presidio, but the rains prevented all work, except for three weeks, and ruined thirty thousand mud bricks [adobes] already made by the marquis. He immediately ordered twenty-five thousand more made, got together the materials, and, with forty laborers paid by him out of his own pocket, added much to the projected structure.

174 [274]. *1722, The return to Coahuila.* On April 30, the last drove of horses of those sent from Durango arrived, and on May 5 the marquis departed with all his men from the presidio of San Antonio for Coahuila, having fulfilled successfully his commission in Texas. Soon after he started he lost eighty horses in a stampede, and forty more in another a few days later. He entered Monclova on May 25. The 31st of the same month, in obedience to orders from the viceroy, he disbanded the troops, paying them their salaries for the last two months of the second year [of the expedition], and giving them supplies for the return to their respective homes, for which they all set out on June 12, [1722].

175 [275]. *1722.* The marquis submitted a report to the government on the fertility and beauty of the province, [pointing out] the advantages that would result from establishing a [civil] settlement in the neighborhood of the presidio of San Antonio de Béxar with farmers, and [advising] that these [settlers] be sent from

the province of Galicia or the Canary islands. The king approved the plan in his royal cédula of May 10, 1723, by which he ordered that four hundred families from the Canary islands be transported for the purpose.[113] After his return to Saltillo, Aguayo organized a special guard of twelve men under a leader, generally called captain, to act as an escort as far as the Rio Grande to supply trains going to Texas.[114]

NOTES TO FORMAL OCCUPANCY OF TEXAS, 1716–1722

1. On September 30, 1715, the Duque de Linares appointed Domingo Ramón captain of the soldiers and leader of the expedition. Clark, "Louis Juchereau," Texas State Hist. Assn., *The Quarterly*, VI, p. 19.

2. The numbers given here agree with Bonilla's. (West, "Bonilla's Brief Compendium," in *ibid.*, VIII, p. 25.) The "Derrotero" mentions nine religious without distinction of college, but, if Margil is included, there were ten. The names listed by Ramón while at the Rio Grande are Benito Sánchez, Manuel Castellanos, Pedro de Mendoza, Gabriel de Vergara, Matías Saenz de San Antonio, Gabriel Cubillo, and Domingo (the last two lay brothers). To these should be added Francisco Hidalgo, Isidro de Espinosa, and Margil de Jesús. Clark, "Louis Juchereau," VI, p. 21, note.

3. The expedition was delayed at the Rio Grande from April 20 to the 27th, because of the illness of Father Margil de Jesús, chief of the Zacatecan friars. They set out without him on this date, but he overtook them soon afterward. Father Isidro Espinosa joined the expedition as head of the Queretaran friars and Hidalgo went along too. It seems that Olivares wished to go, but for some reason was not included. See "Derrotero," in *Historia*, XXVIII, MS., ff. 135–159; Clark, *op. cit.*, p. 21; West, *loc. cit.*

4. The expedition set out from the Rio Grande on April 27 (see note above). The total number of persons that went on the expedition was sixty-five. "Derrotero," in *Historia*, MS., XXVIII, f. 139.

5. This creek was named by Ramón. It was eight leagues northeast of present-day Brazos river. Hackett, *Pichardo*, I, p. 530.

6. With regard to the selection of a captain general, Clark says: "He instructed them . . . to select from their number one who should be their captain general. The Indians thereupon withdrew to confer together, and in a short time sent forward the youngest of their great chiefs, as the one whose rule they could the most easily endure. To him were given the baston and Captain Ramón's own jacket as insignia of his rank and office." Clark, *op. cit.*, VI, p. 23.

7. Bonilla says: "Finally, there were founded the four missions of San Francisco, la Purisima Concepcion, San Josef, and Nuestra Señora de Guadalupe." West, "Bonilla's Compendium," VIII, p. 27.

8. With regard to the location and order of founding, West says, quoting from *Historia* (Talamantes ?): "The first mission was that of San Francisco with the same persons who had founded it in [16]90. Twenty leagues farther on in the Asinais nation Concepcion Mission was founded. Fray Isidro Espinosa took charge of it on the 7th of the same month [July, 1716]. Ten leagues farther on, among the Nacogdoches nation, a place was selected for the mission of Nuestra Señora de Guada-

lupe. This belonged to the Zacatecan fathers, who took possession on the 9th. On the 10th, among a portion of the Nasones nations, ten leagues to the north of Concepcion, the fourth mission, called San José, was founded. . . . In 1717 Father Margil came to Texas and founded the Mission of Nuestra Señora de los Dolores among the Ais, and the Mission of San Miguel, in the Adaes country, fifty leagues east of los Dolores, both under the charge of Zacatecan religious." San Miguel is spoken of as being only ten leagues from the French fort of Natchitoches, nearer the French than any of the other Spanish settlements. The distance is given as seven leagues by Bonilla, the same as by Morfi. West, *op. cit.*, VIII, pp. 27–28, note. But, contrary to the general belief, Morfi is correct in the statement that six missions were founded in 1716. Cf. Castañeda, *Winning of Texas,* ch. 2.

9. Here Morfi added as a note to his original manuscript a page of interesting data concerning the missions. "The mission of Nuestra Señora de Guadalupe de Albuquerque [was founded] for the Nacogdoche Indians," he says, "who are divided into twenty-two rancherías, in which there were one hundred and twenty warriors. It was established in the center of these rancherías, which spread for a distance of ten leagues from south to north. Since the Indians were not gathered about the mission [*congregados*], the missionary had to travel frequently over the entire distance to visit and instruct them, and to administer baptism to those who requested it. Shortly after [the founding of the mission] they all moved to the northern extremity, because of the damages they claimed the Bidais, who were their southern neighbors, caused to their crops. This left the mission on the southern extremity of their new location, three leagues from the nearest ranchería, the others extending northward for a distance of forty leagues.

"The mission of Nuestra Señora de los Dolores de Benavente de los Ais [was founded] for the Indians of this nation, consisting of seventy families settled in eight rancherías, occupying a distance of two leagues, in the center of which was situated the mission.

"The mission of San Miguel de Cuellar de los Adaes is more or less similarly situated."

10. These facts are all found in the "Testimonio," used by West in her annotations on "Bonilla's Brief Compendium," and in the repeatedly cited "Informe" of Altamira, to which Morfi had free access. "A comparison with other documents will show that it [the "Informe"] is in the main accurate." West, *op. cit.*, VIII, p. 6.

11. "As soon, therefore, as he could come to an understanding with the high officers of the government, he returned to the *presidio* to celebrate his marriage with Doña María [Manuela]. . . . He had time to enjoy but a few weeks of conjugal felicity." Clark, "Louis Juchereau," VI, p. 20. There is a question as to whether they married on the Rio

Grande or in Natchitoches. See Castañeda, "Silent Years in Texas History," *Southwestern Historical Quarterly,* XXXVIII, pp. 122–134.

12. He must have left Ramón early in August, 1716, for he was in Mobile by August 25 (Margry, VI, p. 146). He did not return in a few days, as stated by Morfi, for he was in Mobile until October 1 (Shelby, "St. Denis's Declaration," Texas State Hist. Assn., *The Quarterly,* XXVI, p. 167) and he did not reach the Texas till December, where he remained until March, 1717, from whence he set out for the Rio Grande, arriving there on April 27 [1717].

13. For details and substantiation of the facts given here, see West, *op. cit.,* VI, p. 29; "St. Denis's Declaration," XXVI, pp. 168–183.

14. Baltazar de Zúñiga, marquis of Valero and duke of Arión, became viceroy of Mexico August 16, 1716, and held this office till the end of 1721, when he resigned because of illness. Rivera, *Gobernantes de Mexico,* I, p. 316.

15. Both Morfi and Bonilla are in error here. St. Denis proceeded to Mexico city of his own free will after the seizure of his goods at San Juan Bautista, and it was not until after his arrival there that the viceroy ordered his arrest. West, *op. cit.,* VIII, p. 29; "St. Denis's Declaration," XXVI, pp. 167–168; and Shelby, "St. Denis's Second Expedition," XXVII, pp. 197–216.

16. The facts in this interesting case have been recently established. St. Denis was tried in Mexico city, and was released under bond on November 22, 1717, but he was confined to the city. In December, he was allowed to return to the Rio Grande to recover and dispose of his goods, which he did, returning soon after to Mexico city as agreed. Becoming impatient, he indiscreetly threatened to provoke an uprising among the Texas Indians, and his immediate arrest was ordered. He succeeded in escaping, however, from Mexico city on September 5, 1718, and was safe in Natchitoches by February 24, 1719, so that the royal decree did not affect him. Shelby, "St. Denis's Second Expedition," XXVII, pp. 213–214.

17. See the preceding note for the time and details of his escape. St. Denis' wife did not accompany him to Louisiana at this time. In 1721, both Espinosa and Margil, while Aguayo was in Texas, petitioned the viceroy that permission be granted St. Denis' wife to join him. Aguayo addressed a similar petition to the viceroy on August 19 of the same year. Shelby, *loc. cit.*

18. He was made commander of the fort of St. Jean Bautiste aux Nachitos in 1721 (Margry, VI, p. 224); in 1735, he was still commander of this post (*ibid.,* VI, p. 238); and the "Testimonio," written in 1744, declares he was still at that fort that year (West, *op. cit.,* VIII, p. 30, note). In 1717, he declared he was thirty-eight years old (Shelby, "St. Denis's Declaration," XXVI, p. 169). This would make him sixty-five in 1744. He must have been made a chevalier of the order of St. Louis before 1735, because on that date St. Denis declared in a letter to González,

Spanish commander on the frontier, that he was a "chevalier de l'ordre militaire de Saint Louis." Margry, VI, p. 238.

19. This quotation is from the "Parecer" of Altamira, which was used freely by Morfi, as well as by Bonilla, in compiling their works.

20. The reference here is probably to the visit which four Franciscan fathers made to Natchitoches, who went there by order of the Spanish captain, accompanied by six cavalrymen, to say Mass among the Indians. Tissenet, the French commander, treated them kindly, gave them presents, and invited them to come back, according to Pénicault (Margry, V).

21. Alarcón was appointed governor of Texas on December 9, 1716. On August 5, he had also been appointed lieutenant governor of Coahuila, Bolton, *Guide*, p. 478. He did not set out on his expedition until 1718, however.

22. Alarcón was further instructed to establish settlements on the San Antonio, the Guadalupe, and in the intervening country from there to the Texas. (West, *op. cit.*, VIII, p. 30, note 4.) The policy of paying the salaries in advance proved a failure, because many men deserted before they reached the Rio Grande.

23. The mission seems to have been established *de facto* long before. There is some evidence that this mission was established earlier and that in 1718 it was simply given official sanction. Talamantes says: "The only thing he [Alarcón] accomplished was to bring a company of soldiers with their families to the banks of the San Antonio River, where the Mission of San Antonio de Valero had already been founded." Cited by West, *op. cit.*, VIII, p. 31, note 1. Cf. also the following documents in the archive of San Francisco el Grande: "José Dies to the viceroy, February 1, 1717," VIII, p. 765; "Nota de la gente que está en el parage de San Antonio," VIII, p. 786; "Dictamen del Virrey, November 7, 1718," IX, p. 800; and "Informe del Padre Olivares, October 6, 1716," VIII, p. 761. More recent investigation, however, has definitely established its founding in 1718. Castañeda, *The Winning of Texas*, chapter III; Hoffmann, *Diary of the Alarcón Expedition*, pp. 23, 40, 49.

24. Bonilla does not state the number of troops requested, but the "Testimonio" says, "Alarcón asked for money, supplies, and a hundred and fifty other soldiers." Morfi used the "Informe" of Altamira, where the number cited is given. "Bonilla's Compendium," *op. cit.*, VIII, p. 31, note 2.

25. There is a report of the services rendered by Alarcón in Texas, sent by him to the king on November 3, 1721, from Mexico city in the archive of San Francisco el Grande, IX, pp. 820–824.

26. France declared war against Spain on January 9, 1719. It was Spain's occupation of Sardinia and her invasion of Sicily that brought about the declaration. Hassall, *The Balance of Power, 1715–1789*, ch. 2.

27. The incident connected with the attack of the French is humorously recorded by Arricivita, one of the missionaries in East Texas. He

says in his *Chrónica Seráfica:* "So excessively thorough was he that not even the chickens escaped imprisonment. But these, on the move, and disgusted with [the show] of force, flapped their wings lustily in order to escape; the horses, terrified by the noise, knocked the commandant to the ground. . . . The lay brother seized the opportunity" and escaped. The friar then observes, "Doubtless the chief, in order to conserve his own life, did not spare, according to civilized rules, the lives of the chickens." Quoted from Hackett, *Pichardo,* I, p. 217.

Arricivita does not record any particular courtesies observed by the French during these hostilities. Morfi is in error as to the commander who led the attack. It was not St. Denis.

28. It was a lay brother that was captured and succeeded in escaping, thanks to the chickens. See preceding note.

29. Pichardo declares that St. Denis gathered the Cadodachos and other nations to go and take possession of the bay of Espíritu Santo, basing his statement on Aguayo's diary. Hackett, *Pichardo,* I, p. 219. See also Margry, VI, pp. 241–243, for the La Harpe expedition, 1720–21. The activities of St. Denis are also described in detail in the same volume and bear out the assertion of Morfi, who gathered his information from Aguayo's diary, Altamira's "Informe," and other documents pertaining to the investigation held by Aguayo in San Antonio. These will be found in volumes I and X of the archive of San Francisco el Grande.

30. "The two remained at Concepción mission, one hundred leagues from the French, to observe their movements through the Indians. . . . The captain continued his retreat. Seeing this they overtook him a short distance beyond and succeeded in inducing him to pitch camp there for a few days to await reënforcements [from San Antonio] . . . but, despairing of receiving aid, the camp was abandoned and the march to San Antonio renewed." This camp, which must have been a short distance from mission Concepción, is the one called Santiago by Morfi, though Arricivita gives it no name. Arricivita, *Chrónica Seráfica,* p. 100.

31. Aguayo raised a force of eighty-four men in Saltillo, as stated in the preceding paragraph, and from there proceeded to Monclova. From this point in the narrative Morfi seems to follow very closely the official diary of the expedition. The original copy of Peña's "Derrotero," duly signed and witnessed before a notary public at Monclova upon the return of the expedition, was found in the archive of San Francisco el Grande. The "Derrotero" was published by Juan Antonio de la Peña in 1722 and this edition is extremely rare. Sr. Federico Gómez de Orozco, of Mexico city, graciously allowed the author to make a photostat copy and it is to this that all references will be made. There are minor variances between the printed copy and the original certified manuscript described. These will be noted in subsequent citations.

32. These facts are sustained by the "Derrotero," where it is stated that the greater part of the expense was borne by the government. It

is true that Aguayo offered to pay all expenses, but the viceroy, while accepting his services, insisted upon paying the expenses. Peña, "Derrotero," f. 1.

33. The "Derrotero" reads, "which his excellency approved, ordering that the customary allowance be furnished for its founding." *Loc cit.*

34. Attention is called by West (*op. cit.*, VIII, p. 32) to the fact that though Bonilla states that Aguayo was appointed governor and captain general, neither the "Testimonio" nor the "Diario del viaje" that appears in *Memorias*, XXVIII, pp. 81–161, give him the second title. Both the printed "Derrotero," and its certified original refer to him as governor and captain general (see title page of "Derrotero," also first page of certified original, archive of San Francisco el Grande, I, p. 215) proving Bonilla and Morfi are correct.

35. Hostilities ceased in 1721 as a result of a convention signed in Madrid, June 23, 1721. Rivera, *Gobernantes de Mexico*, I, p. 324.

36. This river was crossed on the 25th, at a point twenty-five leagues distant from Monclova. Three weeks were required for the crossing of all the men, equipment, and stock. "Derrotero," f. 2.

37. According to the official diary, this was twenty-five leagues from the crossing of the Sabine, and must have been in the neighborhood of present Eagle Pass. Buckley is of the opinion that it was at the mission of San Juan Bautista. Buckley, "The Aguayo Expedition," XV, p. 30, note 3.

38. It took the expedition until March 23, 1721, to cross the river. "Derrotero," f. 3.

39. This was Captain Matías García, the commander of the presidio of San Antonio.

40. Domingo Ramón, not Diego. His men seem to have set out with the troops commanded by Almazán, and marched together as far as San Antonio, from whence they continued their journey to Espíritu Santo on March 10, 1721. "Derrotero," f. 6.

41. Fray Benito Sánchez had accompanied the Ramón expedition (see paragraph 200, note 2, of this chapter). He had been in charge of mission San José de los Nasonis. When Espinosa set out for Mexico in 1719, Fray Sánchez probably accompanied him as far as the Rio Grande, where he remained at the mission of San Juan Bautista. Buckley, "Aguayo Expedition," XV, p. 31, and note 3.

42. The last two mentioned were lay brothers. There were besides those mentioned by Morfi two other missionaries: Fathers José Guerra and Gabriel Vergara. These two names do not appear in the *Memorias* copy of the Aguayo expedition, but, as Morfi has been using the official diary of Peña, it is strange he should have overlooked them. Father Vergara had been with the Ramón expedition (*Memorias*, p. 165); "Derrotero," f. 5.

On the margin Morfi has added the following note: "Father [Brother] Pita was killed this year by the Apaches at a place called Carnizería [place of slaughter], about twenty leagues distant from where the San Xavier missions were founded later." For details and confirmation of this fact, see "Autos sobre diferentes puntos . . . por el governador . . . de Texas. Año 1724."

43. The party took twenty-two days for this reconnaissance, and, though they located some salines forty leagues away, they declared these were useless because of the warlike nature of the Indians. "Derrotero," ff. 5–6.

44. He set out from the Rio Grande with the forces sent to San Antonio with instructions to occupy Espíritu Santo. See paragraph 222, and note 40 of this chapter. At this point the original "Derrotero" refers to Ramón as Joseph.

45. The original diary says, "having spent thirty-two days on this trip." "Derrotero," f. 6.

46. Consequently, he must have left La Bahía on the 12th, where Ramón had been since the 4th.

47. It is to be noted that Morfi refers to this mission as "the old one," though Aguayo does not emphasize this distinction. This reënforces the statement made in note 23 of this chapter as to the time of its establishment.

48. The original diary says, with regard to the location of San José, "It is about one and a half leagues from the presidio, down the river." With regard to the presents, the diary says, "He gave clothes to all the Indians and distributed other trinkets which they esteemed highly." "Derrotero," f. 6.

49. The Apache Indians played a very important rôle in determining the policy of Spanish officials with regard to Texas and the success of Spanish efforts to settle the province. Until the publication of the interesting article, "Apache Relations in Texas, 1718–1750," by W. E. Dunn, little or nothing concerning these Indians was known. They were chiefly the Lipan and Natages in Texas. Unfortunately, the Spaniards befriended the Texas against the Apaches in East Texas in the beginning. "Had the Spaniards refused to give aid to the Texas, they might have been spared, possibly, a great deal of trouble." Texas State Hist. Assn., *The Quarterly,* XIV, p. 204.

50. This was not a branch of the Brazos but Little river, which was crossed "at a point about three-fourths the distance from Cameron to Belton." Buckley, "Aguayo Expedition," XV, p. 39.

51. This was one of many small creeks crossed by Aguayo. The diary declared that "not having been named before" they called it San Norberto. It was three-quarters of a league from Little river. See note 47, chapter I, for details.

52. This was on June 14. Though the scouting party had come back on the 12th, "the march was suspended Friday [June 13] to dry the buffalo meat with which every man was supplied." "Derrotero," f. 10.

53. The San Buenaventura has been identified with Navasoto river. The upper and lower roads to East Texas came together at this point. See paragraph 37 and note 61, chapter I, for details.

54. The expedition halted about ten or fifteen miles from the Trinity. Buckley, "Aguayo Expedition," XV, p. 41.

55. Here Morfi has followed very closely the account given in the "Derrotero," f. 13.

56. First Aguayo asked the Indians to construct a raft after their own fashion of dry wood and canes, but this proved useless. Another much heavier was built by the soldiers out of tree-trunks and barrels, but it was too awkward to manage and was given up. It was then that the old canoe was thought of. Two days were spent in hunting for it. When found, several teams of oxen, a carpenter, and a group of men went to fetch it and it took four days to get it to the river. But it proved well worth the trouble. "Instantly three companies crossed the river. Later all the baggage, stock, and horses were crossed, the remainder of the troops following." *Ibid.*, f. 14.

57. "He dressed them with care that they might spread the news of the liberality of the Spaniards," declares Peña in the "Derrotero." It is well known that the Indians were extremely proud of European articles of clothing and the impression these would produce on the Texas was well calculated to cause a favorable reaction.

58. See note 75, chapter I.

59. The reference here is to the first mission founded by De León in 1690, San Francisco de los Texas, "from one and a half to three leagues . . . from the Neches River at its nearest point, a league or more farther from the crossing, and still another league—in all some ten miles—from the Neches village on the other side of the river." (Bolton, "The Native Tribes," XI, p. 265.) This conclusion was later verified by Bolton personally, declares Buckley, and the distances were found to be about four and a half miles from the mouth of the San Pedro and seven or eight from the crossing. Buckley, "Aguayo Expedition," XV, p. 43, note.

60. *Pinole* is parched corn, ground and mixed with brown sugar, usually taken dry or mixed with water.

61. In the account by Buckley it is stated that the number was seventy, but a careful comparison of the original draft of the "Derrotero" and the printed copy reveals that Morfi is correct and the number was sixty. Buckley, "Aguayo Expedition," XV, p. 43; "Derrotero," f. 15.

62. The ceremony of smoking the peace pipe among the Texas Indians was a formal one. In order to indicate their desire for complete peace, the chief would take the highly decorated pipe and, lighting it, puff deeply and blow the smoke first toward heaven, then toward the north, the east,

the south, and the west; and, lastly, toward the ground. This operation was repeated by each Indian.

63. Reference is made here to the second founding of San Francisco mission by Ramón in 1716. The location of the second establishment was "at the Neche village, . . . and from two to four miles from the crossing." Bolton, "Native Tribes," XI, p. 262. Dr. Bolton subsequently identified the location personally as being on Bowles creek, not far from the crossing of this stream by the old San Antonio road. Buckley, *op. cit.,* XV, p. 45, note 3.

64. The appointment of St. Denis as commander of Natchitoches is dated July 1, 1720 (Margry, VI, pp. 220–221), but he did not take possession of the fort until 1721. *Ibid.,* VI, p. 224.

65. This was not the permanent location of the presidio, which was founded by Ramón in 1716 near Concepción mission, across the Neches, about one and a half leagues from the river, where the present town of Douglas, on Thomas creek, is today, according to Bolton. Morfi refers here to a temporary camp established by Ramón before crossing the Neches, from whence he set out in company with the missionaries to decide on the location of the mission. Ramón, "Derrotero," entry for June 30, 1716; Peña, "Derrotero," f. 15; Buckley, "Aguayo Expedition," XV, p. 43, note 4; also p. 47.

66. This tribe had its ranchería five leagues below the crossing on the Neches. Bolton, "The Native Tribes," XI, p. 267.

67. Buckley, in a note (XV, p. 44, note 2), points out that the chief had been blinded by the Indians, but she evidently misread the "Derrotero" of Peña, which she cites as authority, for it plainly states that the chief blinded himself, as Morfi says. "After having led them as chief for many years, he put his eyes out, as is customary among these Indians, in order to be their high priest." "Derrotero," f. 15.

68. The interpreter was Nicolás de los Santos, of whom Peña says: "He was one of the soldiers of Domingo Ramón, and was much skilled in the language [of the natives] and their signs." *Ibid.,* f. 15.

69. "This seems to suggest that St. Denis did not feel exactly safe among the Spaniards," declares Buckley, with some reason. (Buckley, *op. cit.,* XV, p. 44, note 3.) It is to be remembered that St. Denis had fled from Mexico city; that orders had come from the king for his deportation, with his wife, to Guatemala; and that he was suspected of the attack on Los Adaes (this was made by Blondel, not St. Denis). On the other hand the missionaries, with the exception of Olivares, had always befriended him. It was natural he should feel safer, or more at ease, among them. See paragraphs 206–208, 212.

70. St. Denis reluctantly agreed to abandon Los Adaes, though the imposing force of the Spaniards and the firm determination of Aguayo left him no other course. Contrary to the insinuation of Cox that, "Saint Denis on the frontier and the Western Company at home were equally concerned to re-establish the Spaniards in their vicinity," the fact re-

mains that St. Denis tarried for three days among the Indians, seven leagues from Concepción mission, after he had promised Aguayo to retire immediately to Natchitoches. He had with him a considerable number of Cadodachos, "Whom, since winter, he had gathered to go to take possession of La Bahía del Espíritu Santo." Peña, "Derrotero," f. 17; I. J. Cox, "Louisiana-Texas Frontier," x, p. 14; Buckley, "Aguayo Expedition," xv, p. 45.

71. Morfi is not as belligerent here against Prévost. It is questionable whether he is sincerely generous or whether he is ironic. The man who used St. Denis' *Memoirs* was Le Page du Pratz, in his *Histoire de la Louisiane,* I, pp. 10–24.

72. In the "Derrotero," Peña observes that up to this day seven Masses were celebrated daily and eight on feast days; that on Sunday sermons were preached by Fathers Espinosa and Margil alternately; and that crosses were erected everywhere camp was pitched from the time the expedition left San Antonio. "Derrotero," f. 16.

73. For the exact location of this mission and presidio, see note 65 of this chapter.

74. This pueblo was never officially founded but remained a cherished desire of Espinosa.

75. Father Guerra joined the expedition at San Antonio. He had been in East Texas and was one of those who took refuge in San Antonio after the retreat in 1719. See paragraph 225, note 42 of this chapter.

76. For the actual location of this presidio which was temporarily established west of the Neches and moved after the mission of Concepción was founded to the spot where Aguayo reëstablished it, see notes 59 and 63 of this chapter.

77. This mission was the only one that had not been entirely destroyed. It was less than half a league beyond the Angelina river. Buckley, "Aguayo Expedition," xv, p. 47.

78. See paragraph 243, note 70, of this chapter.

79. Indian villages.

80. Father Vergara first came to Texas in 1716, with Ramón, and was, at that time, left in charge of this same mission, which he was forced to abandon in 1719, when he retired to San Antonio. He waited there until Aguayo's arrival to return to East Texas.

81. According to Peña's diary, two other religious accompanied Margil. This mission was situated at modern Nacogdoches and was east-southeast from Concepción. "Derrotero," f. 18; Bolton, "Native Tribes," XI, p. 258.

82. This was the presidio of Dolores, situated one league from the mission of Dolores, or about one and a half leagues from the Angelina. See paragraph 241, note 65, of this chapter.

83. This mission has been located "some fifteen or more miles northeast of the Hainai [i.e., Purísima Concepción] . . . by one of the southern

tributaries of Shawnee Creek, near the north line of Nacogdoches County." (Bolton, "Native Tribes," XI, p. 268.) Bolton later confirmed this deduction personally and located the site of the mission on Bill's creek.

84. Father Sánchez came with Ramón in 1716 and was left in charge of this mission that year, when first founded, where he remained till 1719, when he accompanied Father Espinosa as far as the Rio Grande. He there joined Aguayo in 1720, when the expedition passed through San Juan Bautista. Espinosa, "Diario," entry for July 9, in archives of San Francisco el Grande, VIII, p. 672; Peña, "Derrotero," f. 3; see also note 42 of this chapter.

85. The date given here is correct. Buckley says Aguayo returned the 15th, but this is evidently an error, for the official diary kept by Peña clearly states: "On Thursday, the 14th [of August] the governor returned to the encampment to join the battalion." That he reached the camp that day is evident from the entry of the following day in which it is stated that on the 15th, "very early in the morning" the feast of the Assumption was celebrated, a thing that was not likely for Aguayo to do had he left San José that day. Peña, "Derrotero," f. 10; Buckley, "Aguayo Expedition," XV, p. 48.

86. For the location of this presidio, see notes 65 and 82 of this chapter. "It occupied an advantageous position on a hill, overlooking the country, with the arroyo of Nuestra Señora de la Asumpción (evidently the first eastern branch of the Angelina) running at its base." Buckley, "Aguayo Expedition," p. 48. The ground plan of this presidio, showing its location and giving some interesting details as to its surroundings, is printed in Peña, "Derrotero," opposite page 27.

87. It is interesting to note the irony of Morfi here. The original account says that a suit of English cloth was given the chief, but Morfi adds that it was a Spanish suit of English cloth.

88. The mission of Guadalupe was located on the site of modern Nacogdoches. (Bolton, "Native Tribes," XI, p. 258.) The mission was originally founded in 1716 by Father Antonio Margil. At this time, he was given official possession of it as representative of the college of Zacatecas. It was the capital of the missions in Texas belonging to this college. Peña, "Derrotero," f. 18.

89. This lake is referred to in chapter I as Laguna del Presidio. See paragraph 49, note 70.

90. The site of this mission has been identified with that of modern San Augustine (Texas); the stream by the side of which it stood corresponds to Ayish Bayou; and there are many springs in the neighborhood. Buckley, "Aguayo Expedition," XV, pp. 49–50.

91. *The Telegraph and Texas Register,* September, 1837, states that "gold has been found near the Old mission south of the city [of San Augustine]." Quoted by Buckley ("Aguayo Expedition," XV, p. 50), who

further states that the mission is half a mile south of the city on the old king's highway, on a little conical rise at the edge of the bottom of Ayish Bayou.

The data given here by Morfi regarding the location of the mission was obtained from *Solís' Diary,* entry for June 1, 1767. Forrestal, *The Solís Diary.*

92. This is the lake referred to as Laguna de los Adaes in chapter I. It has been identified with Spanish lake. See paragraph 59, note 79.

93. This was Luis Fernando, the son of Philip V of Spain and María Luisa of Savoy, later destined to reign for a few months, from January to August, 1724. He was born August 25, 1707, and died August 31, 1724. Altamira, *Historia de España.*

94. This is modern Sabinas river.

95. The presidio of Nuestra Señora del Pilar, as this fort was called, was located "one-half league beyond where the mission had formerly stood, by a spring or brook of water, on the side of a hill, where it could command the surrounding country." Buckley, "Aguayo Expedition," xv, p. 52. The ground plan, showing the exact location and the surrounding country, is printed in Peña's "Derrotero," opposite page 21. The relative position of the mission and presidio is shown by Le Page du Pratz, in *Histoire de la Louisiane,* I, p. 1.

96. Buckley says fifty, but the official "Derrotero" kept by Peña clearly says fifty-five. Evidently the copy used was defective, for she declares that the distance given in the "Derrotero" used by her from the fort to Natchitoches was seventy leagues and should be seven, as it is in the printed copy used by the editor. Cf. Buckley, "Aguayo Expedition," xv, p. 52, note 5; "Derrotero," f. 20.

97. A Spanish weight of twenty-five pounds.

98. It is to be noted that the mission was not actually built until later. The celebration held on this day was to observe the feast day of the titular saint and officially declare the determination to build a permanent mission at this site.

Buckley, in the "Aguayo Expedition" (xv, pp. 52–53), fails to note this incident, but she identified the location of the mission as being about two miles west of the town of Robeline, Louisiana.

99. This is the first record of a dramatic representation within the boundaries of Texas. See Castañeda, "The First American Play," in *The Catholic World,* January, 1932.

100. The news was received by Aguayo at Los Adaes, about the middle of October, and a few days later part of the supplies arrived. Peña, "Derrotero," f. 22.

101. The word used in the original is *carga,* which means *load,* literally, but which is the approximate equivalent of the one hundred and fifty pounds that make the average load of a pack animal.

102. Both De León and Terán brought some cattle along, but this is the first recorded herd of cattle ever driven across Texas, and should be regarded as the forerunner of the cattle droves that were to play so important a rôle in the later history of the state.

103. No date is given, but, judging by the distance from Los Adaes to the mission of Guadalupe and the slow rate of travel on the return march, it is safe to assume that the news was received by Aguayo either the 24th or 25th of November.

104. The ground plan and the principal features of the surrounding country are shown in the map published in Peña's "Derrotero." See note 90 of this chapter.

105. This small stream is in the immediate vicinity of Trinity river. Buckley, "Aguayo Expedition," xv, p. 54.

106. This incident and the return of the detachment sent to San Antonio by Aguayo are not mentioned in Buckley's "Aguayo Expedition," although they were given in great detail in Peña's "Derrotero," from which Morfi obtained his information. Peña, "Derrotero," f. 24.

107. An *anega* or *fanega* is a Spanish measure of grain or seed equivalent to about a hundredweight. It corresponds roughly to an English bushel.

108. Morfi visited San Antonio at the close of 1777 and refers here to conditions as they were at that time.

109. The mission was short-lived and its history was partially ignored until Bolton traced its outlines in "The Mission Records at San Antonio," from which the main facts are here set down. The site of the mission was identical with that of present Concepción. It was founded for the Hyerbipiames. Rodríguez was made governor of the district (*barrio*) of these Indians. They were kept separate from the other missions, though they had no building. The baptisms were performed at San Antonio de Valero, but were recorded in a separate book while waiting for their mission to be built. The idea of a separate building was given up in 1726, when the keeping of separate records was abandoned and the records of these Indians merged with those of Valero. Bolton, "The Spanish Mission Records at San Antonio," x, pp. 297–308.

110. The date is not given, but, from the context, it must have been a day or two before March 16.

111. Remarking on this observation found in Peña's diary, from which Morfi copied it, Bolton says, "By this utterance Peña proved himself either ignorant or defiant of history, a bad sociologist, and worse prophet." Bolton, "The Founding of Mission Rosario," x, pp. 116–117.

112. This was Domingo Ramón, not José, who remained there with ninety men until the time of his death in 1723. Peña consistently refers to him as José. It is possible that his full name was Domingo José Ramón. "Derrotero," f. 27; Bolton, "Mission Rosario," x, p. 116.

113. The royal decree ordered that 200 families be transported from the Canary islands to Campeche, from there to Veracruz, and thence to Espíritu Santo, but nothing was done until a new decree was issued February 14, 1729, which ordered that four hundred families, including the first two hundred, be sent. *Reales Cédulas.*

114. "The Aguayo expedition, the last of its kind into Texas, exceeded all others in size and results. It was perhaps the most ably executed of all the expeditions that entered Texas, and in results it was doubtless the most important." To summarize briefly its accomplishments it need only be stated that it left ten missions where there had been seven, four presidios where there had been two, and two hundred and sixty-eight soldiers where there had been some sixty or seventy before. For its significance see Buckley, "Aguayo Expedition," xv, pp. 60–62.